YOU'RE DOING REALLY WELL
GIVEN THE CIRCUMSTANCES

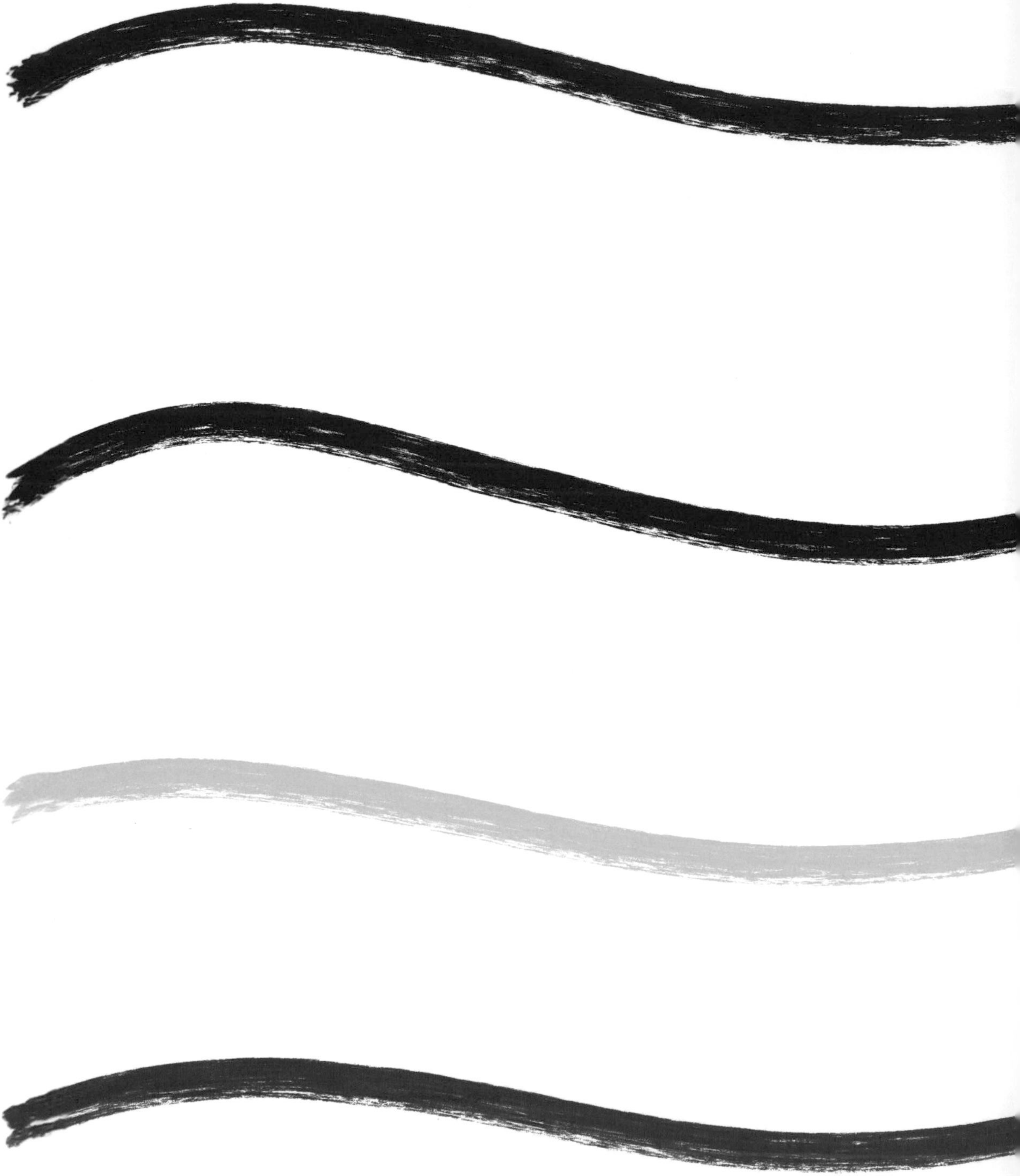

WORRY LINES

YOU'RE DOING REALLY WELL
GIVEN THE CIRCUMSTANCES

Andrews McMeel
PUBLISHING®

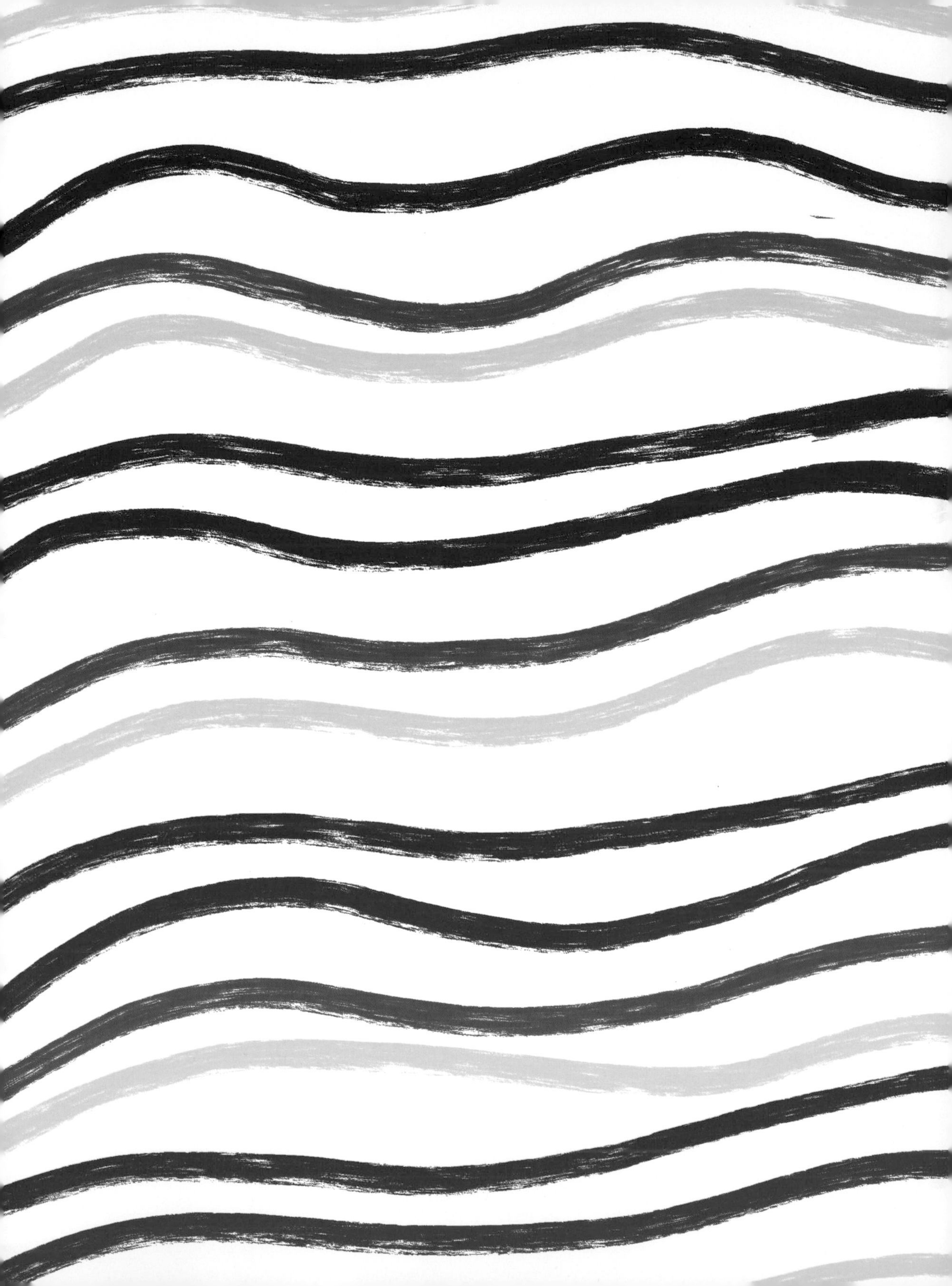

CONTENTS

WE ALL HAVE THOSE DAYS.

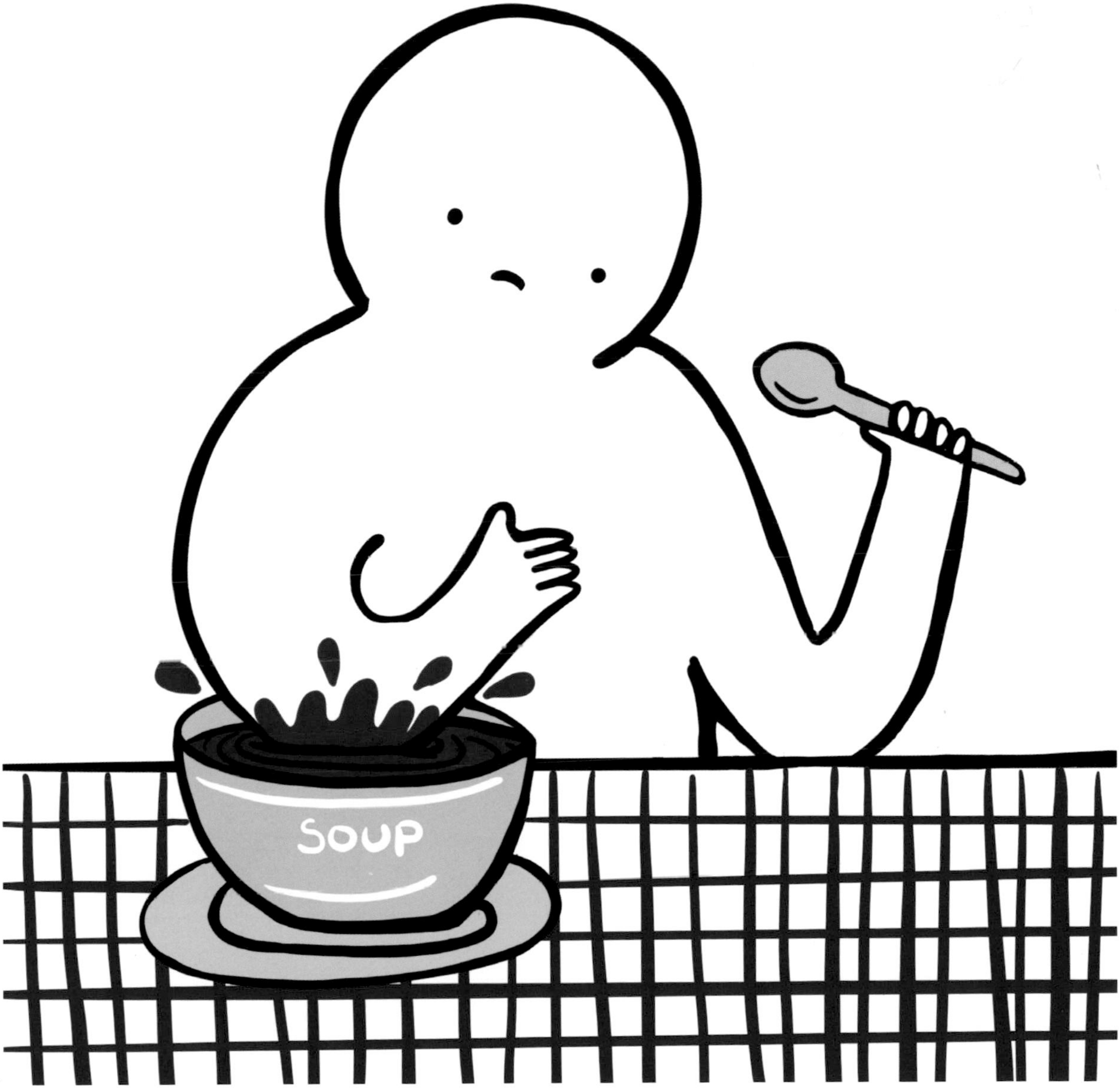
SOUP

THOSE
WRONG-SIDE-OF-THE-BED
DAYS.

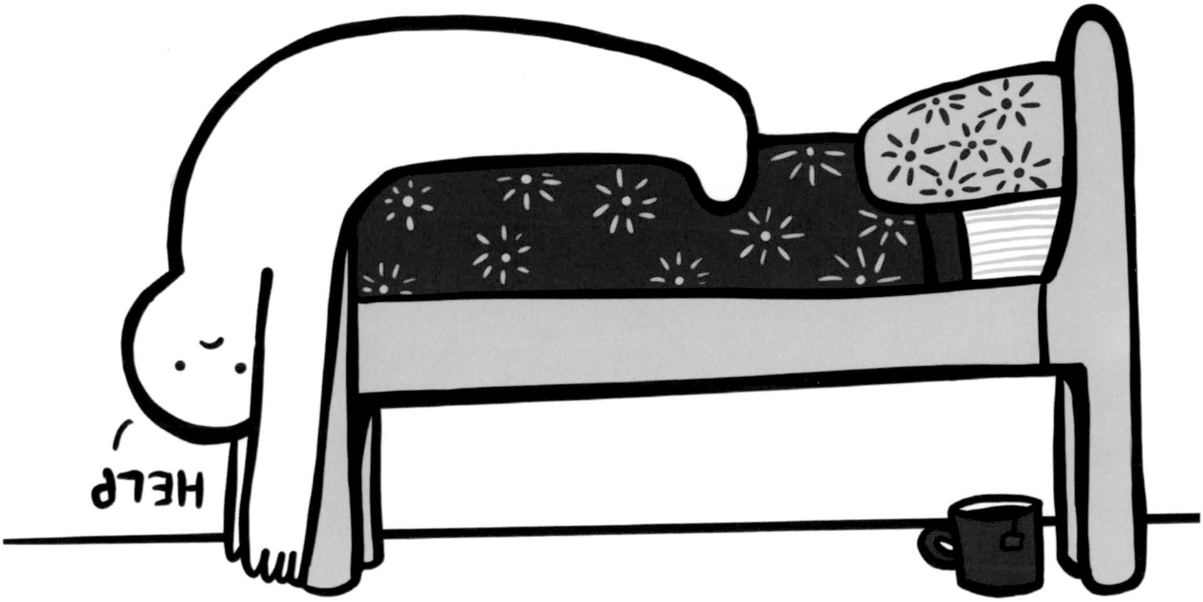
HELP

THOSE
COFFEE-ON-THE-CARPET DAYS.

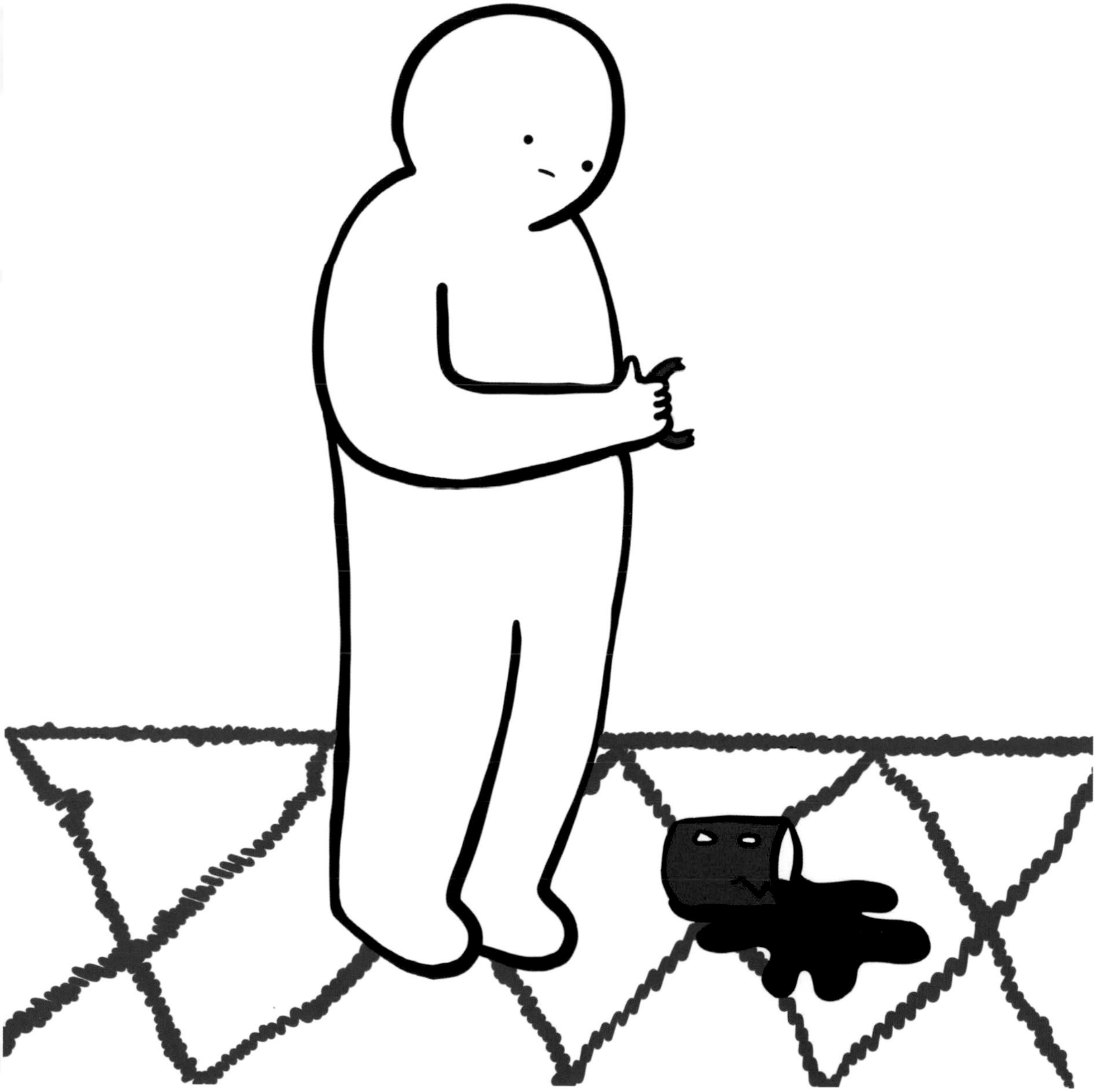

THOSE   MISS-THE-BUSSING,

COMPUTER-CRASHING,

TOE-STUBBING DAYS.

x

THOSE
PAPER-CUTTING,

BATTERY-
DYING,

FORGOT-
YOUR-KEYSING,

TRAFFIC-JAMMING,

OUT-OF-
MILKING,

LATE-FOR-
WORKING,

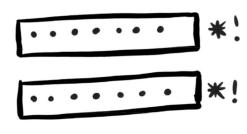

BROKEN-WEBFORM
DAYS.

SOMETIMES THE DAYS TURN INTO WEEKS

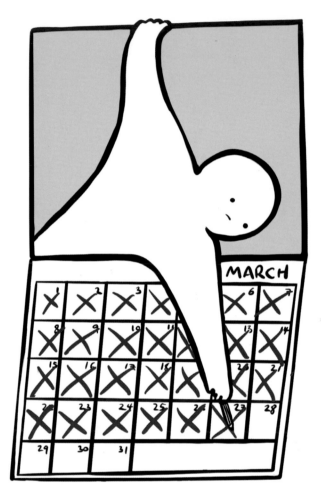

AND THE WEEKS TURN INTO MONTHS...

AND IT CAN START TO FEEL LIKE THE WHOLE WORLD IS OUT TO GET YOU.

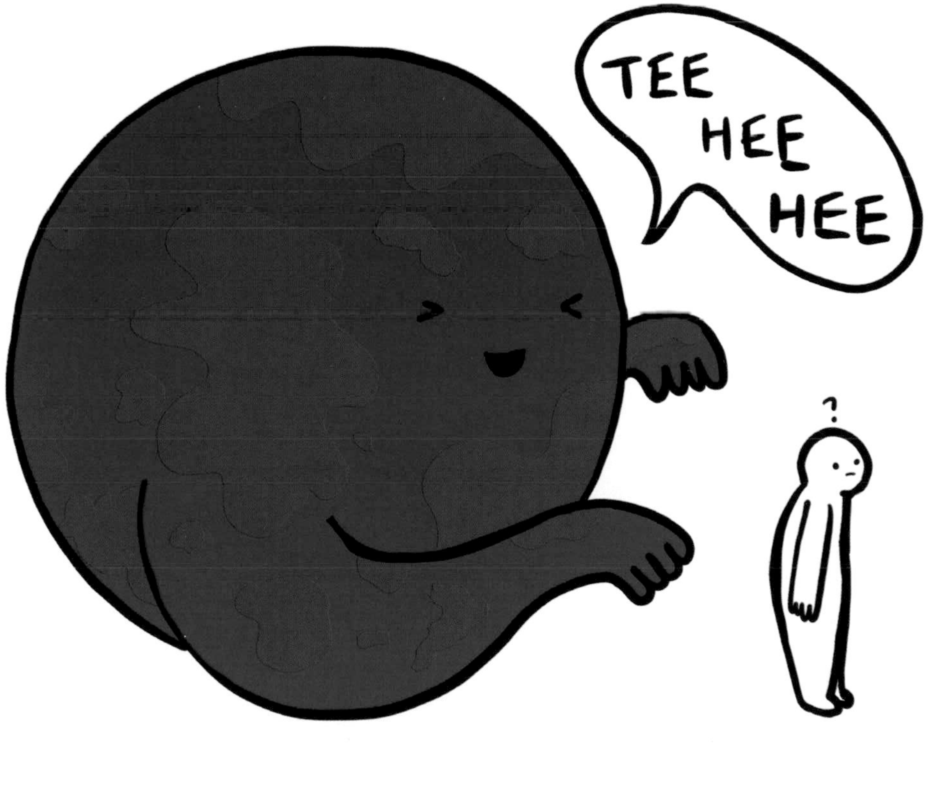
TEE HEE HEE
?

BUT I WANT YOU TO KNOW THAT I SEE YOU.

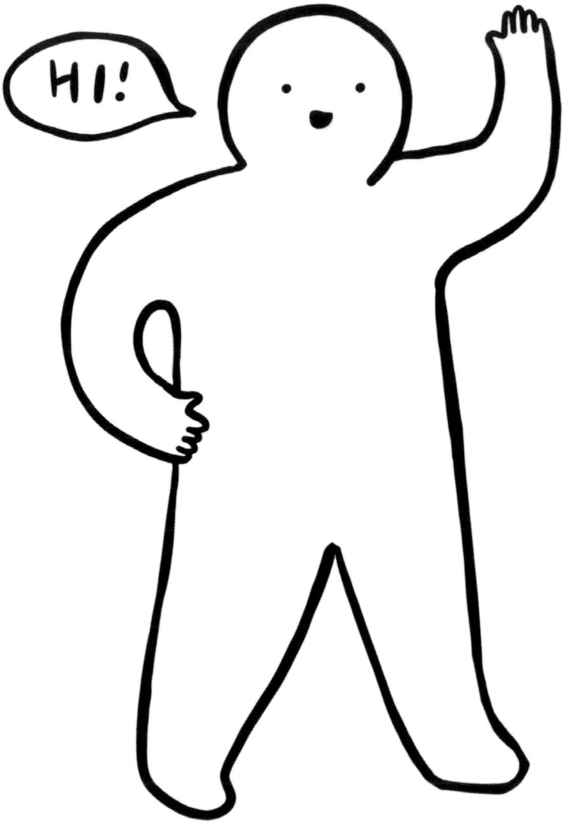
HI!

FROM MY PERSPECTIVE,
GAZING UP AT YOU FROM THIS PAGE,
I'M SO IMPRESSED BY HOW BRAVELY YOU NAVIGATE YOUR COMPLICATED 3D LIFE.

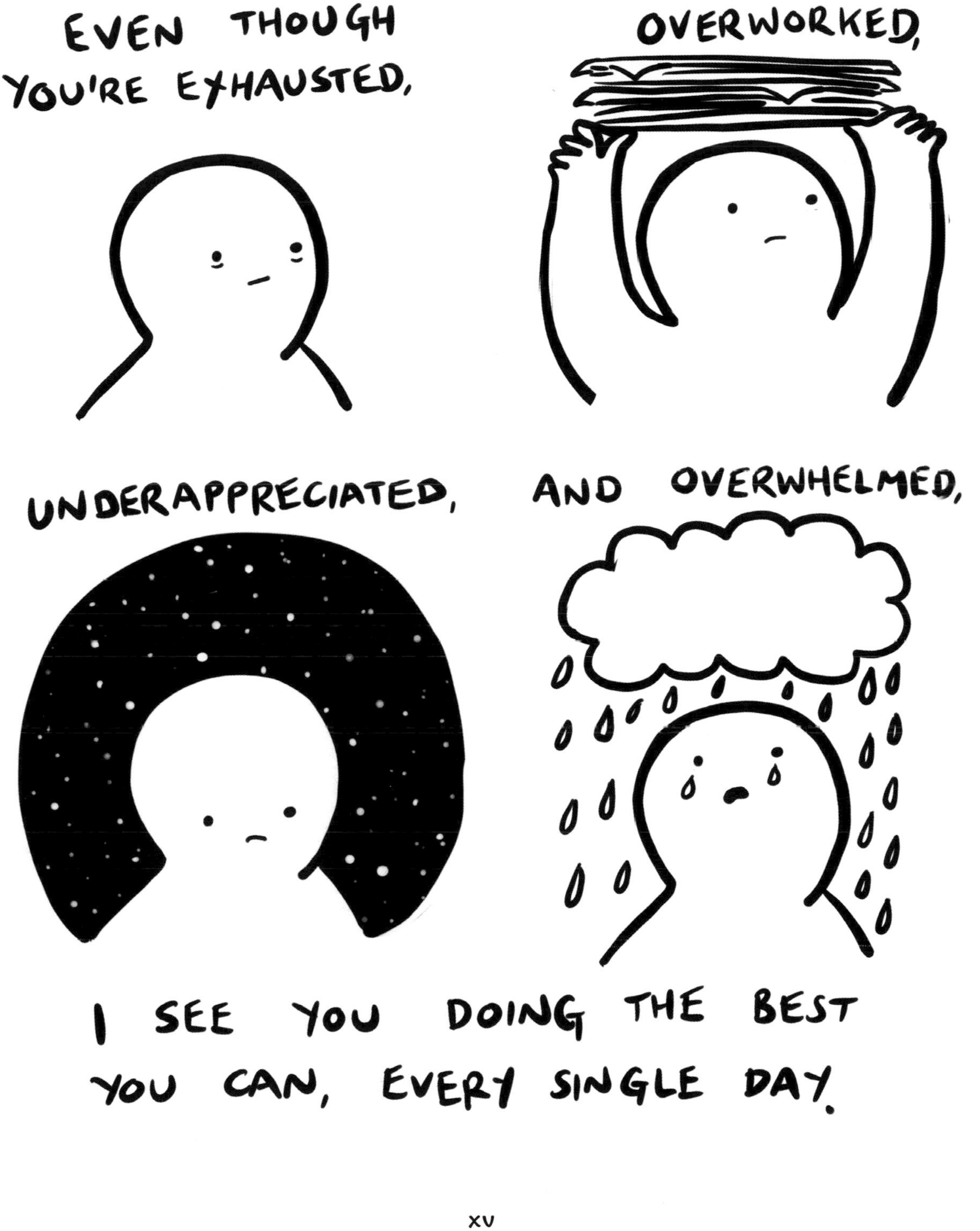
EVEN THOUGH YOU'RE EXHAUSTED,
OVERWORKED,
UNDERAPPRECIATED,
AND OVERWHELMED,
I SEE YOU DOING THE BEST YOU CAN, EVERY SINGLE DAY.

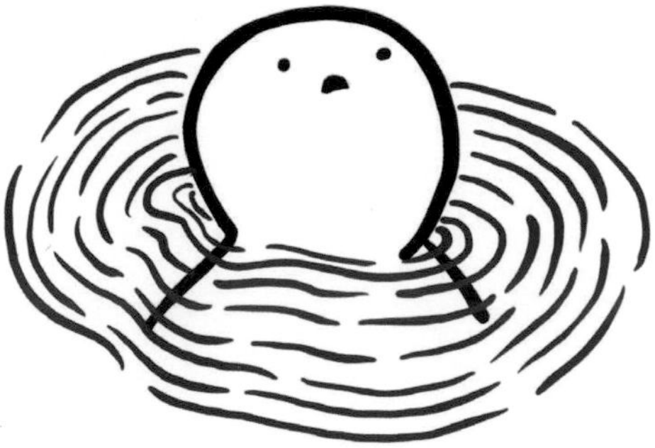

I SEE YOU TRYING
TO KEEP YOUR HEAD
ABOVE WATER,

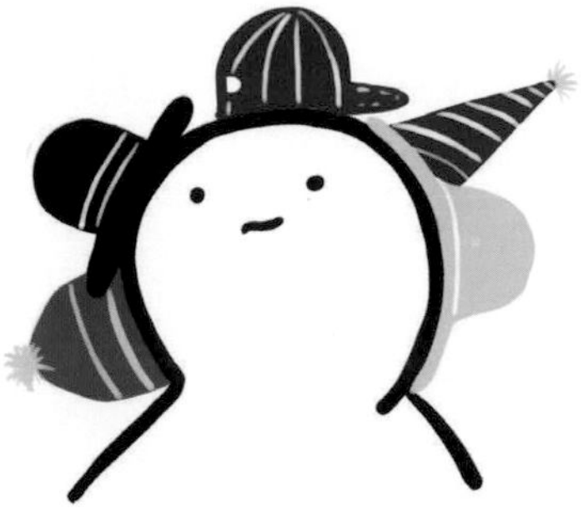

WEARING
MANY HATS,

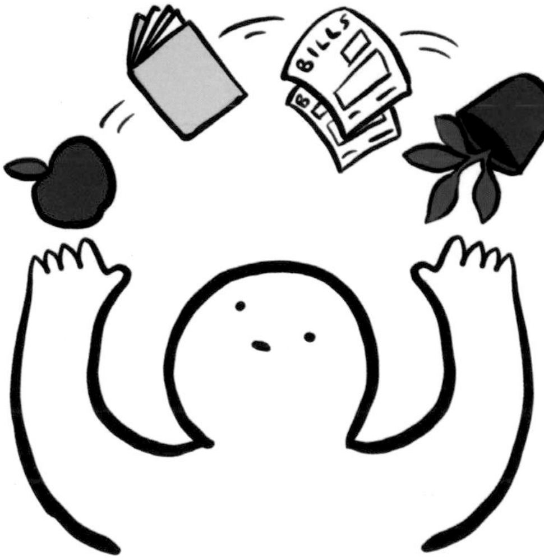
BILLS

JUGGLING
HEAPS OF
RESPONSIBILITIES,

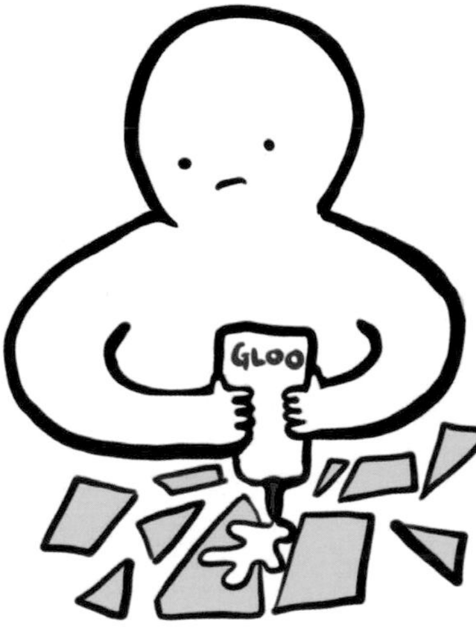
GLOO

AND GENERALLY
TRYING TO KEEP
IT TOGETHER AS
BEST AS YOU CAN.

TRUTHFULLY, I'M IN AWE OF YOU.

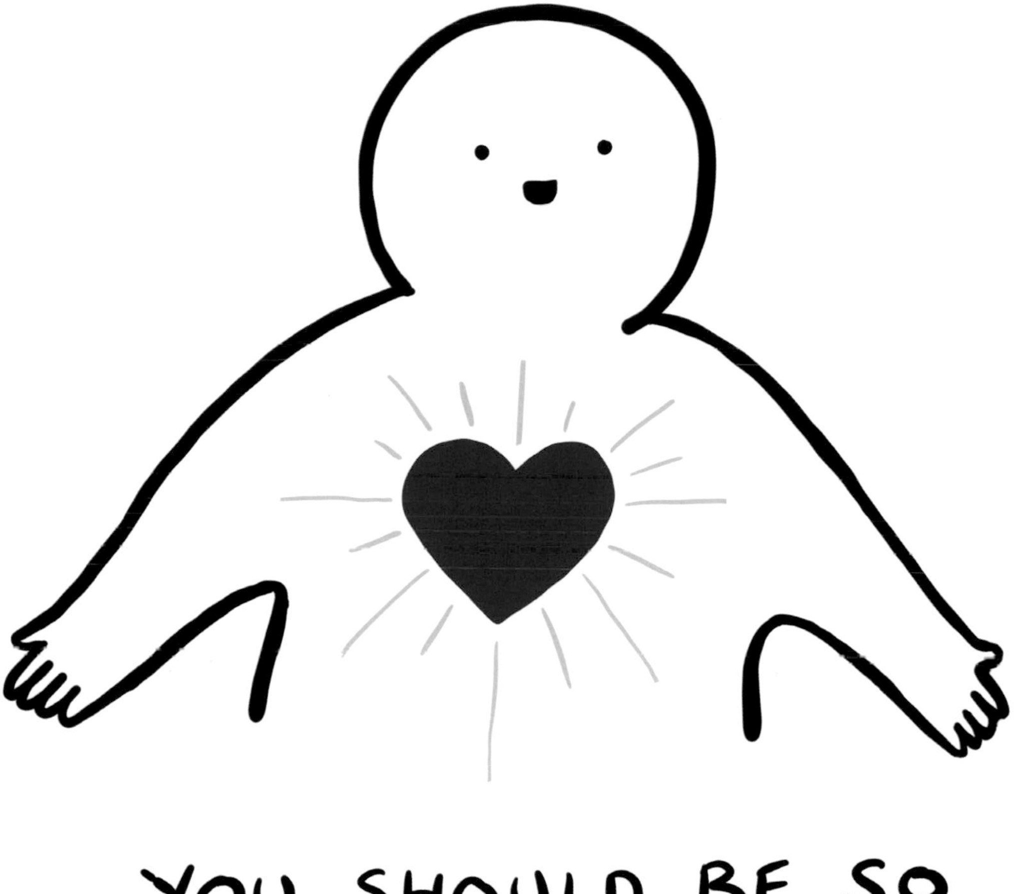

YOU SHOULD BE SO PROUD OF YOURSELF.

AND WHILE YOU DESERVE
A LIFE FULL OF

HIGH-
FIVING,

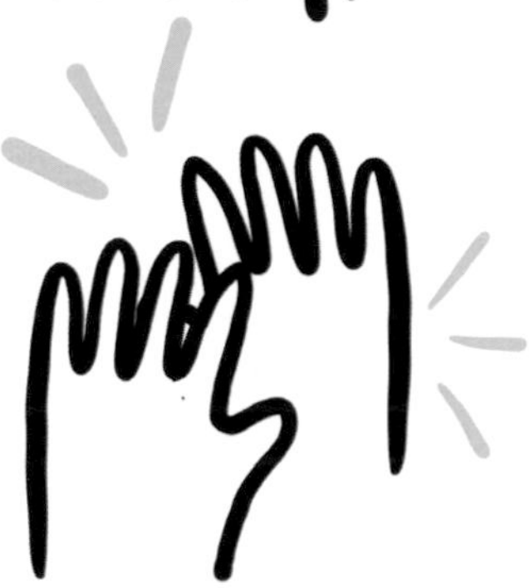

BEST-
FRIENDING,

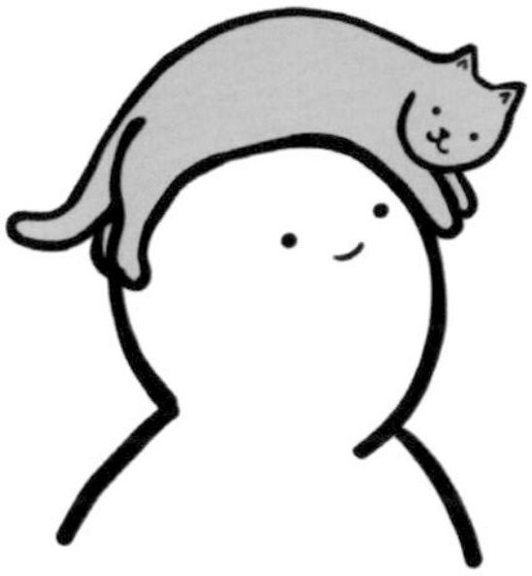

SUN-
SHINING,

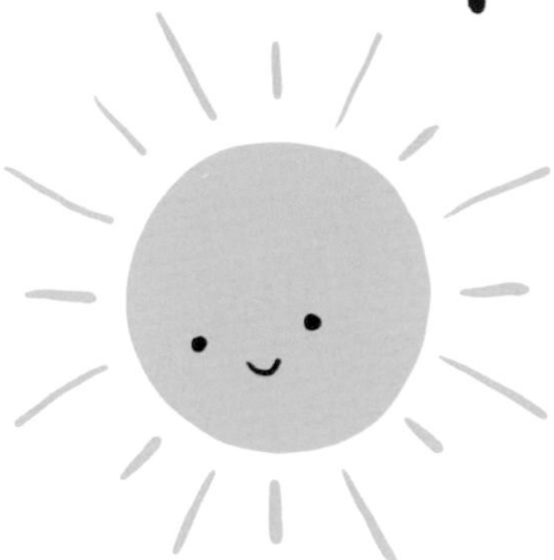

ICE-
CREAMING,

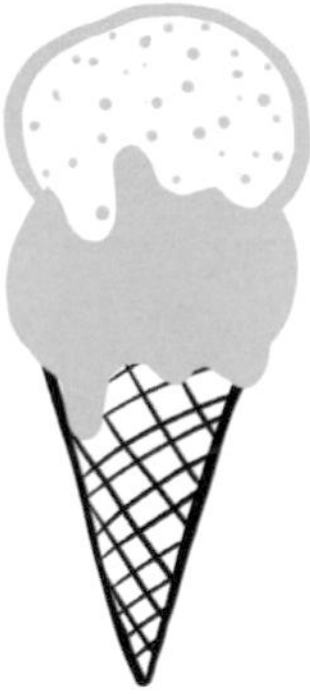

FAVOURITE-
SONGING,

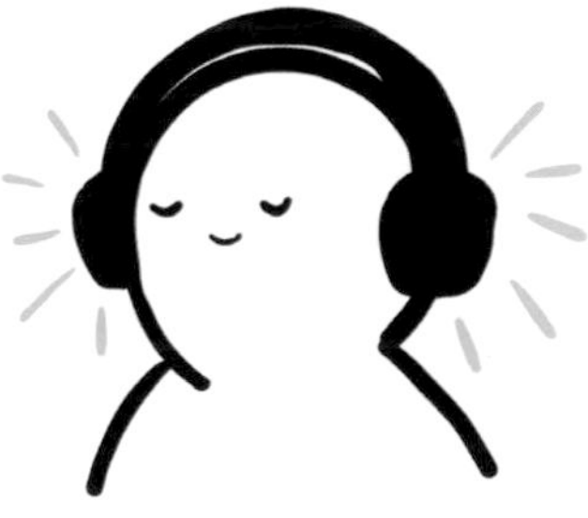

TEN-OUT-
OF-TEN
DAYS,

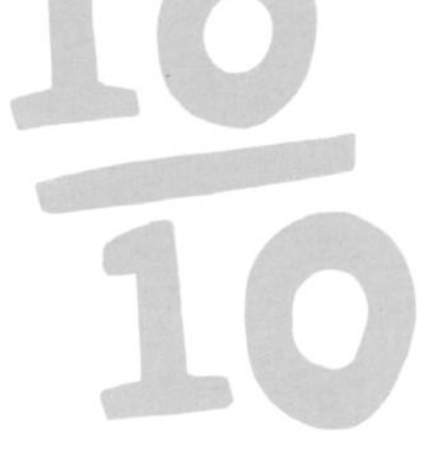
10
10

I STILL THINK...

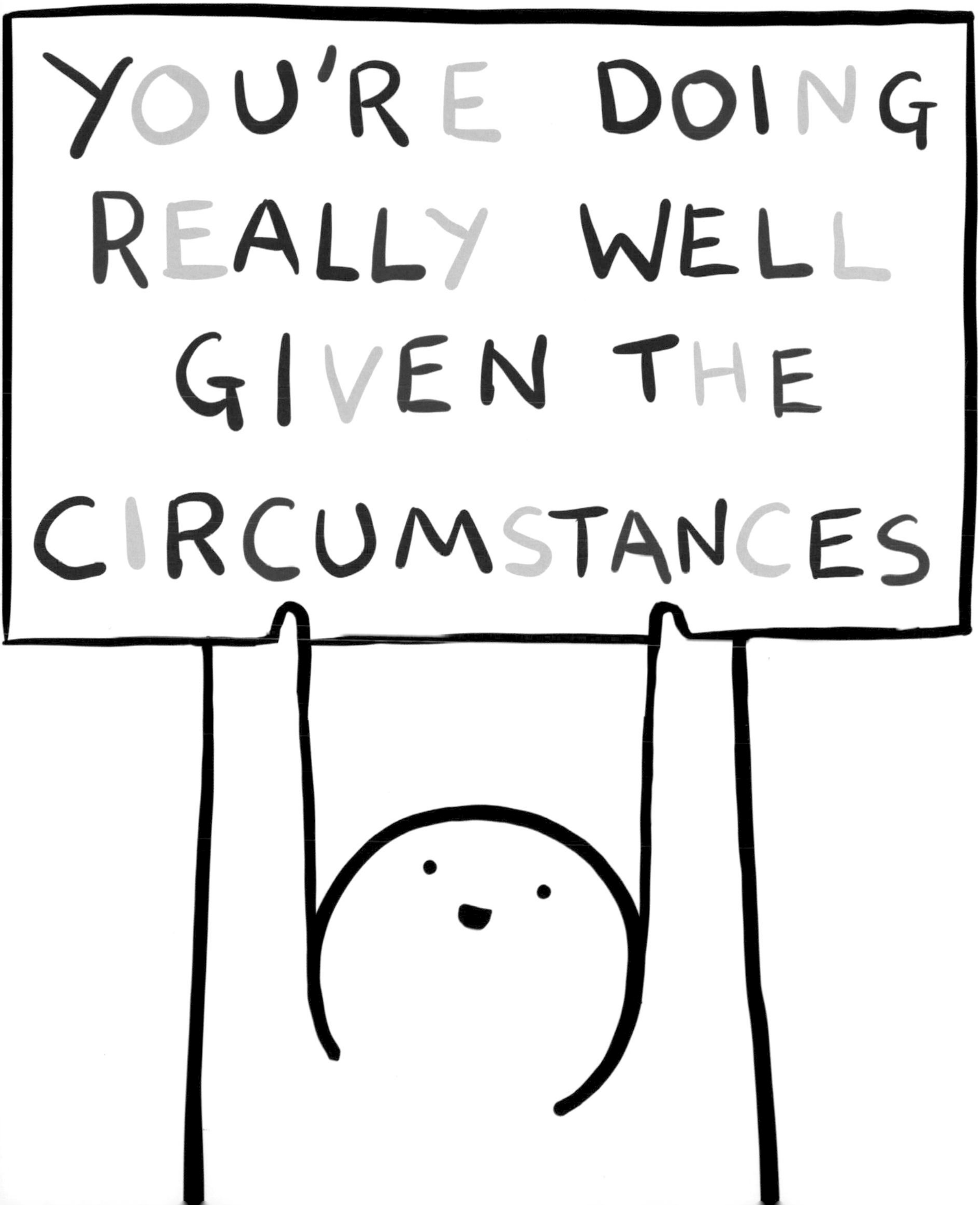
YOU'RE DOING
REALLY WELL
GIVEN THE
CIRCUMSTANCES

FEELING OUTSIDE THE LINES

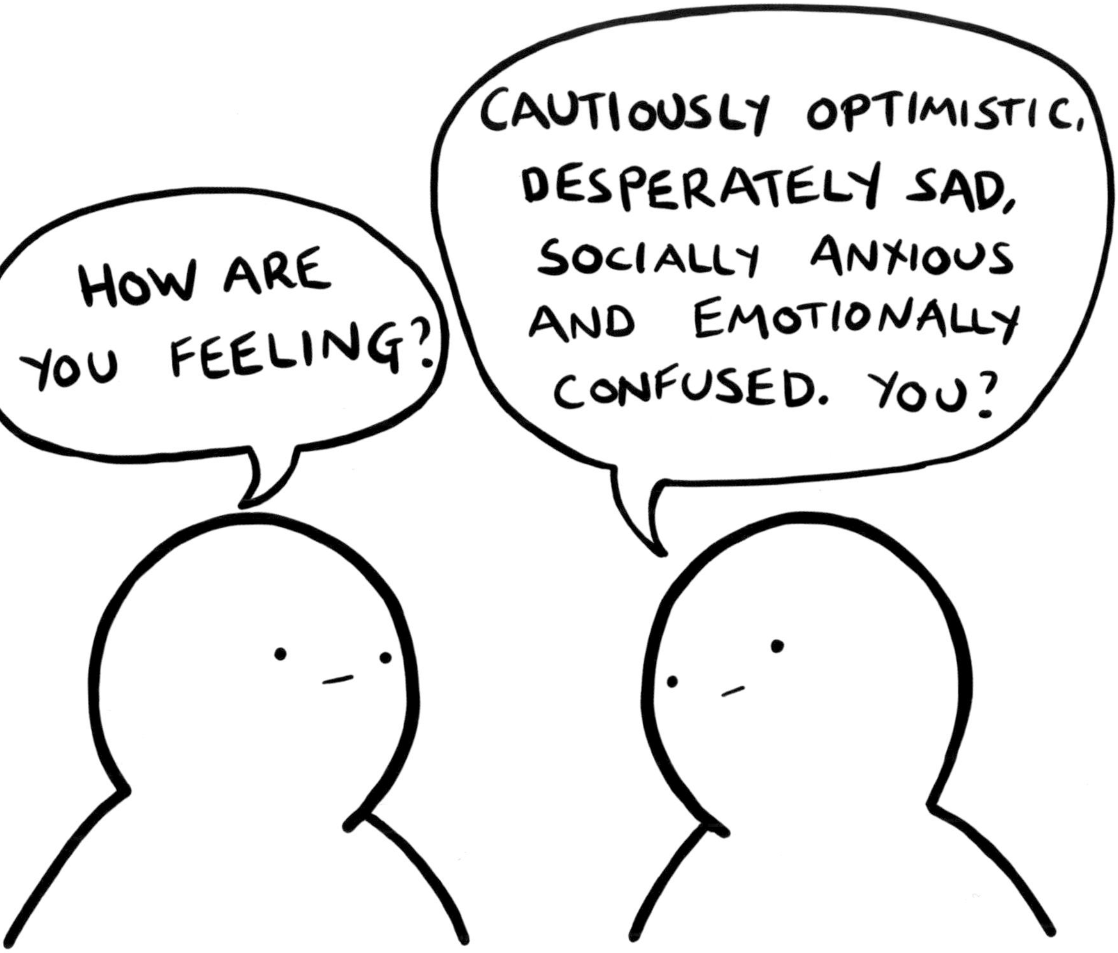
HOW ARE YOU FEELING?
CAUTIOUSLY OPTIMISTIC, DESPERATELY SAD, SOCIALLY ANXIOUS AND EMOTIONALLY CONFUSED. YOU?

HOW I'M SUPPOSED
TO FEEL:

HOW I FEEL:

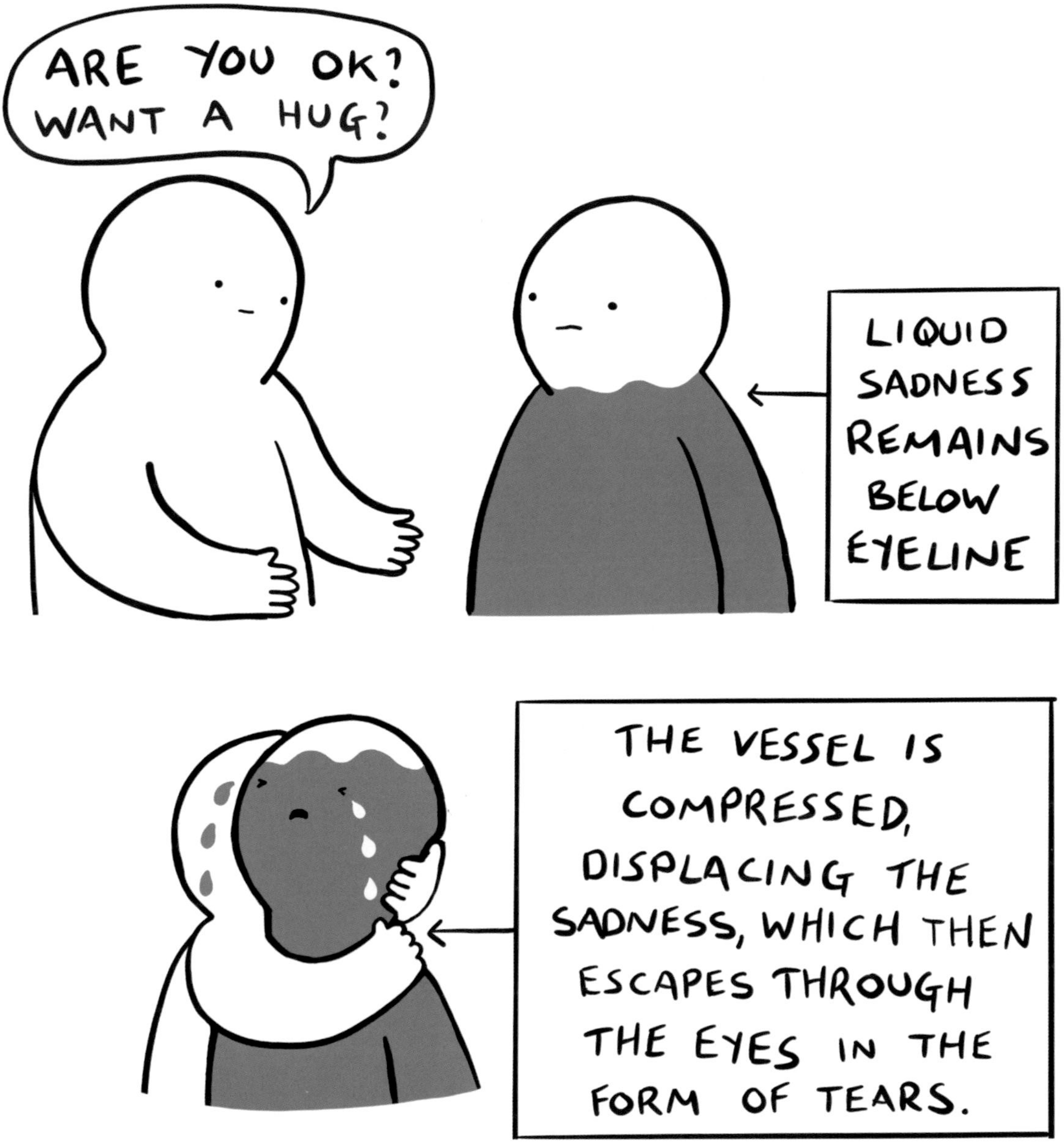
ARE YOU OK? WANT A HUG?
LIQUID SADNESS REMAINS BELOW EYELINE
THE VESSEL IS COMPRESSED, DISPLACING THE SADNESS, WHICH THEN ESCAPES THROUGH THE EYES IN THE FORM OF TEARS.

SOME PEOPLE FEEL THEIR FEELINGS IMMEDIATELY,
BUT I PREFER TO BOTTLE MINE UP
SADNESS
AND LET THEM MATURE FOR 10-15 YEARS
SADNESS
BEFORE SHARING THEM WITH A THERAPIST.
STRONG NOTES OF CLINICAL DEPRESSION!
SADNESS

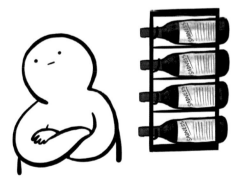

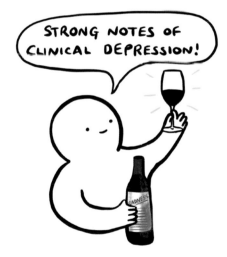

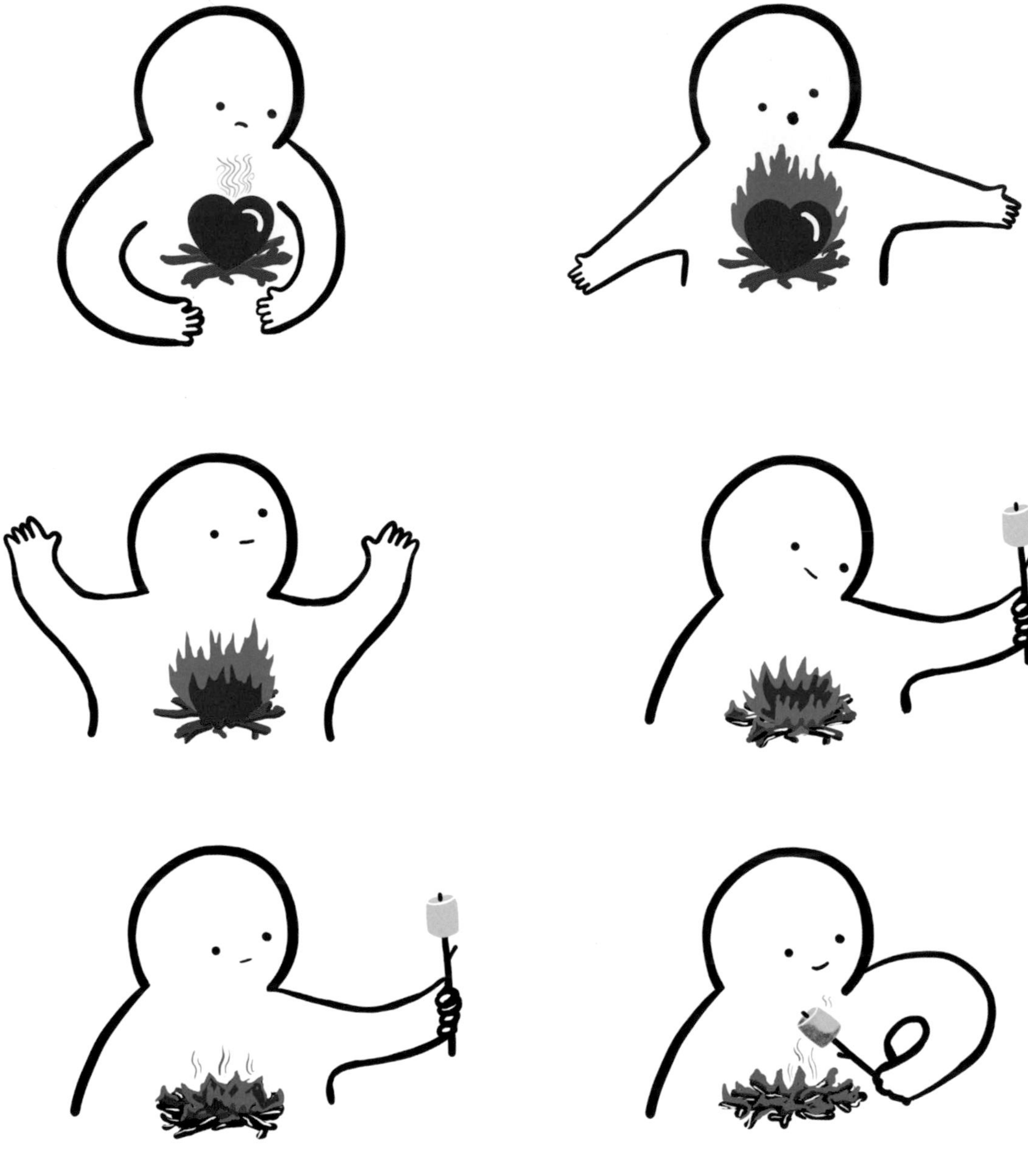

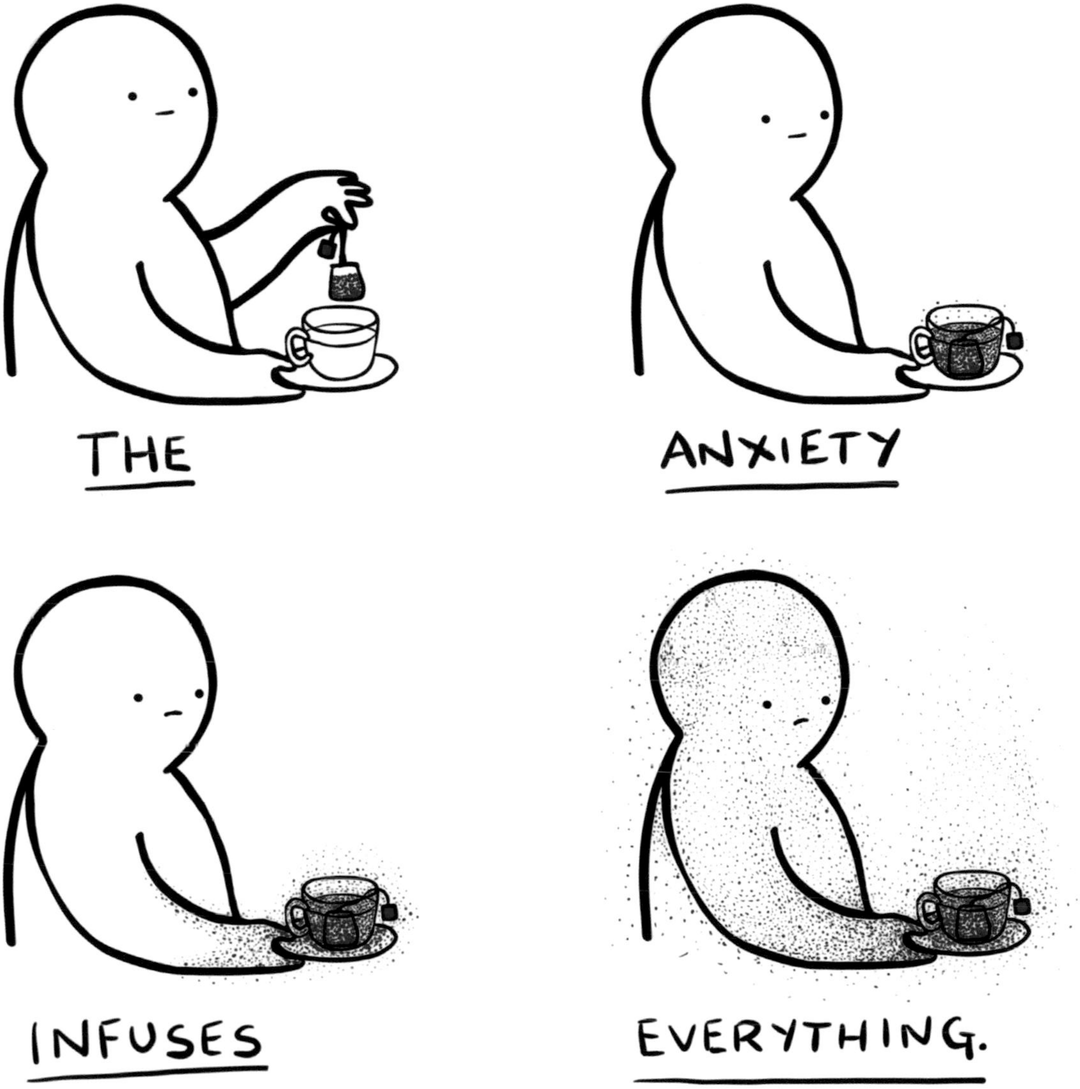
THE
ANXIETY
INFUSES
EVERYTHING.

WHILE IT'S IMPORTANT
TO ACKNOWLEDGE
YOUR FELINES,

TRY NOT TO
HOLD ON TO THEM
TOO TIGHTLY.

REMEMBER:
FELINES COME,

AND FELINES GO.

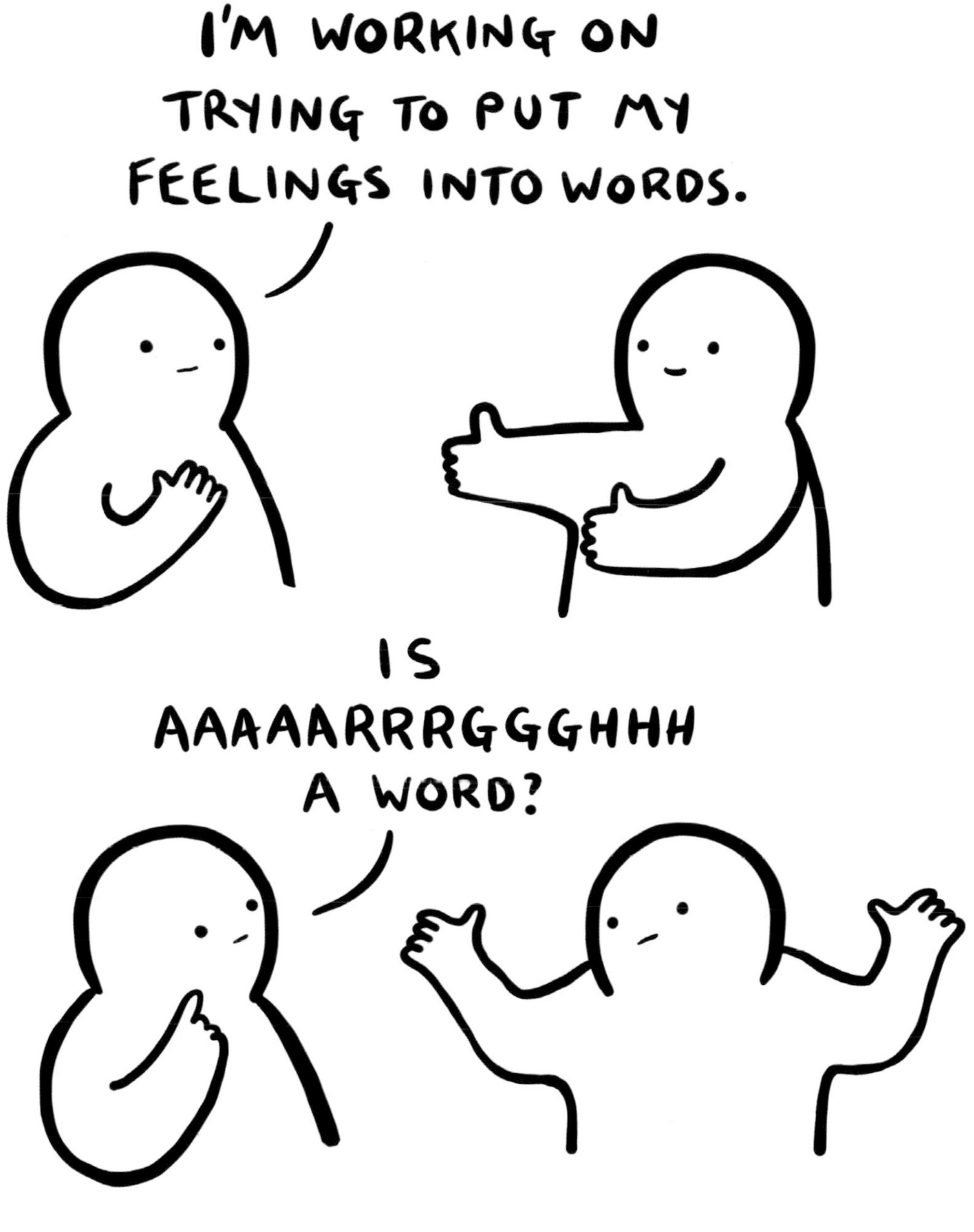
I'M WORKING ON TRYING TO PUT MY FEELINGS INTO WORDS.
IS AAAAARRRGGGHHH A WORD?

WHAT LOOKS STRAIGHTFORWARD ON THE OUTSIDE

CAN BE COMPLICATED ON THE INSIDE.

BIG SAD

SMALL SAD

LIGHT SPRINKLING
OF SAD

RISING SAD

SHARP SAD

CONFUSINGLY
BEAUTIFUL SAD

HEAVY SAD

CREEPING SAD

SAD ON TOAST

I AM A
BUNDLE OF
NERVES

I AM A
BALL OF
ENERGY

I AM A
BLOB OF
SADNESS

I AM A
HEART FULL
OF LOVE

I AM A PIT
OF DESPAIR

I AM A
RAY OF SUNSHINE

I AM GREEN
WITH ENVY

I AM A
CLOUD OF
DOUBT

I AM FULL
OF HOPE

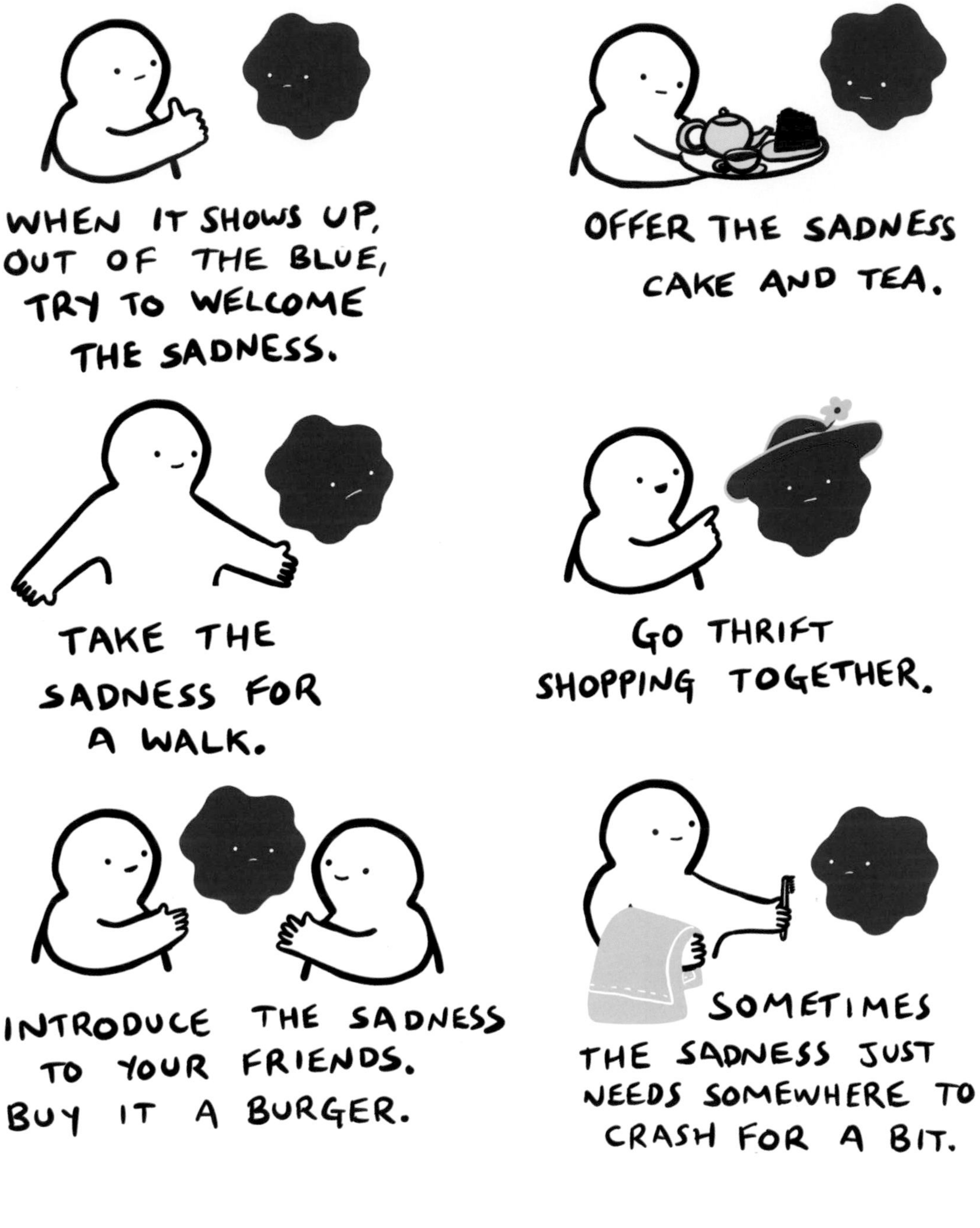
WHEN IT SHOWS UP, OUT OF THE BLUE, TRY TO WELCOME THE SADNESS.
OFFER THE SADNESS CAKE AND TEA.
TAKE THE SADNESS FOR A WALK.
GO THRIFT SHOPPING TOGETHER.
INTRODUCE THE SADNESS TO YOUR FRIENDS. BUY IT A BURGER.
SOMETIMES THE SADNESS JUST NEEDS SOMEWHERE TO CRASH FOR A BIT.

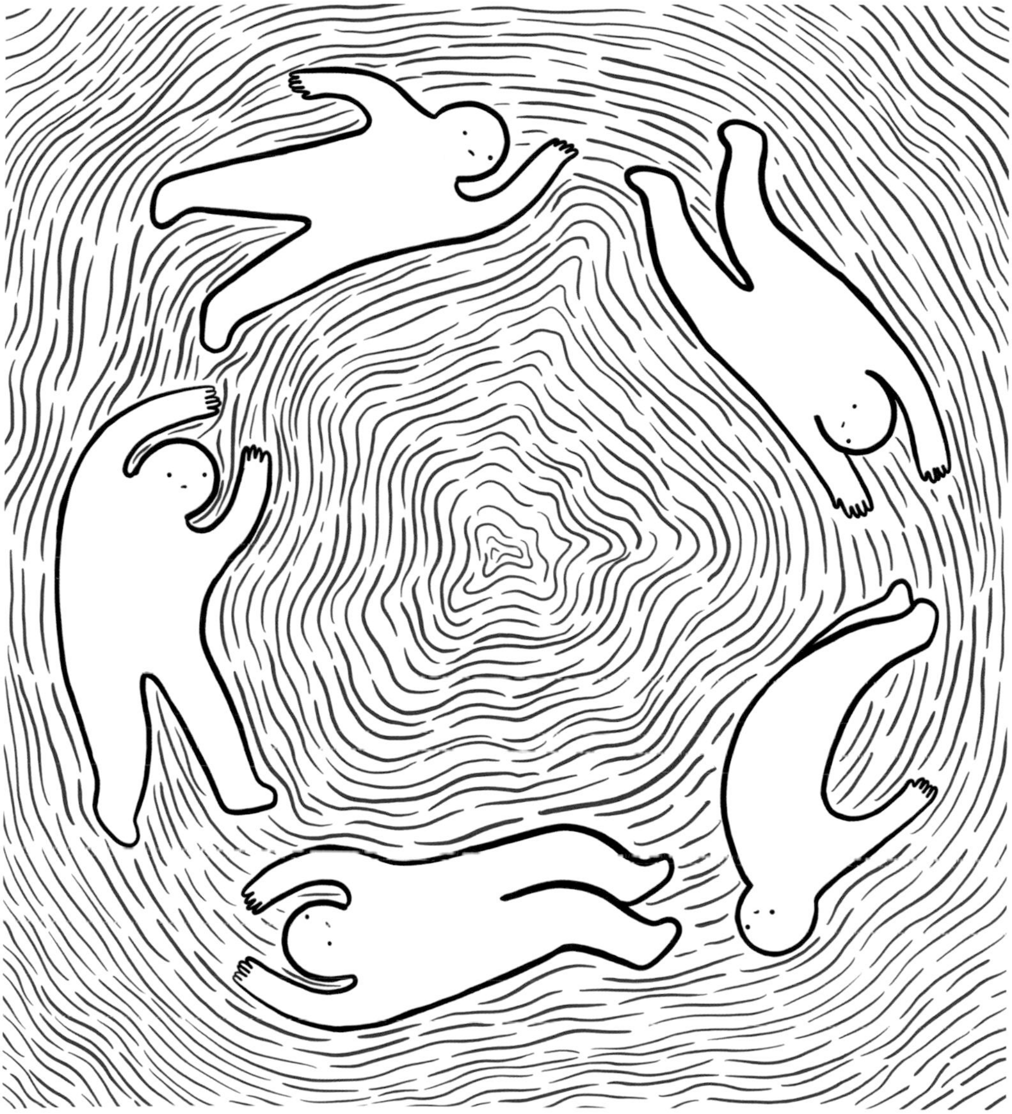

YOU CAN'T THINK YOURSELF OUT OF YOUR FEELINGS.

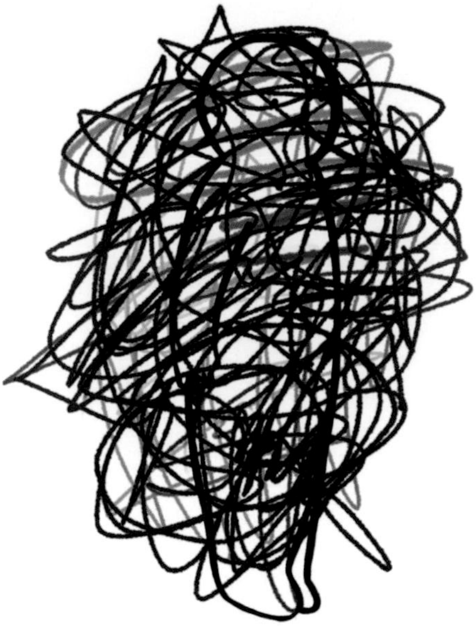

TAKE A STEP BACK.

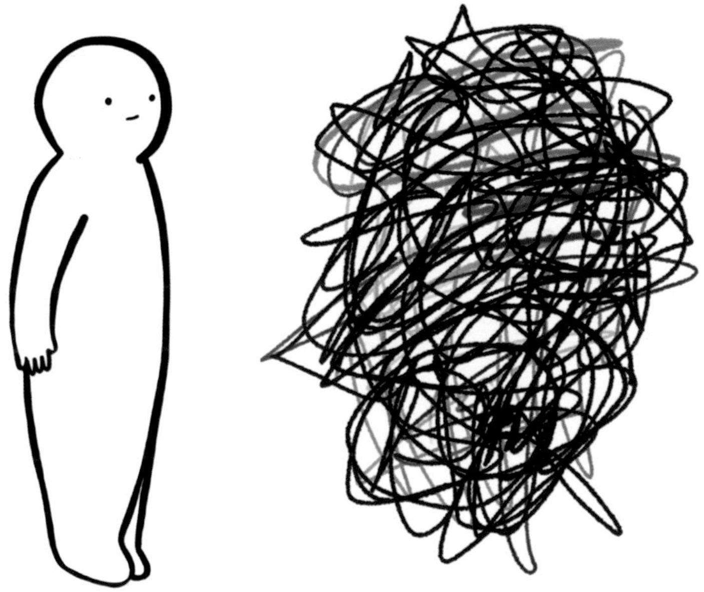

OBSERVE THE EMOTION.

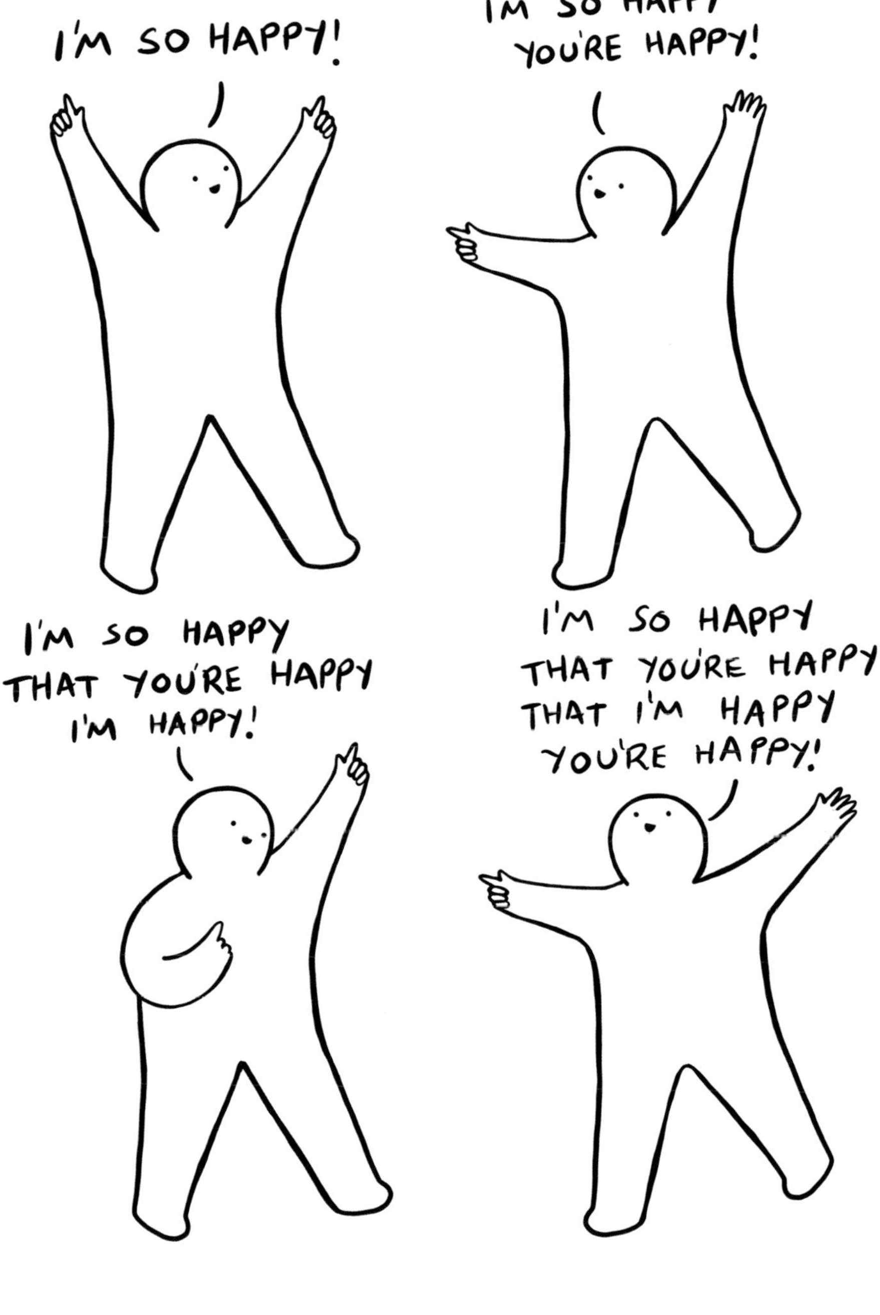
I'M SO HAPPY!
I'M SO HAPPY YOU'RE HAPPY!
I'M SO HAPPY THAT YOU'RE HAPPY I'M HAPPY!
I'M SO HAPPY THAT YOU'RE HAPPY THAT I'M HAPPY YOU'RE HAPPY!

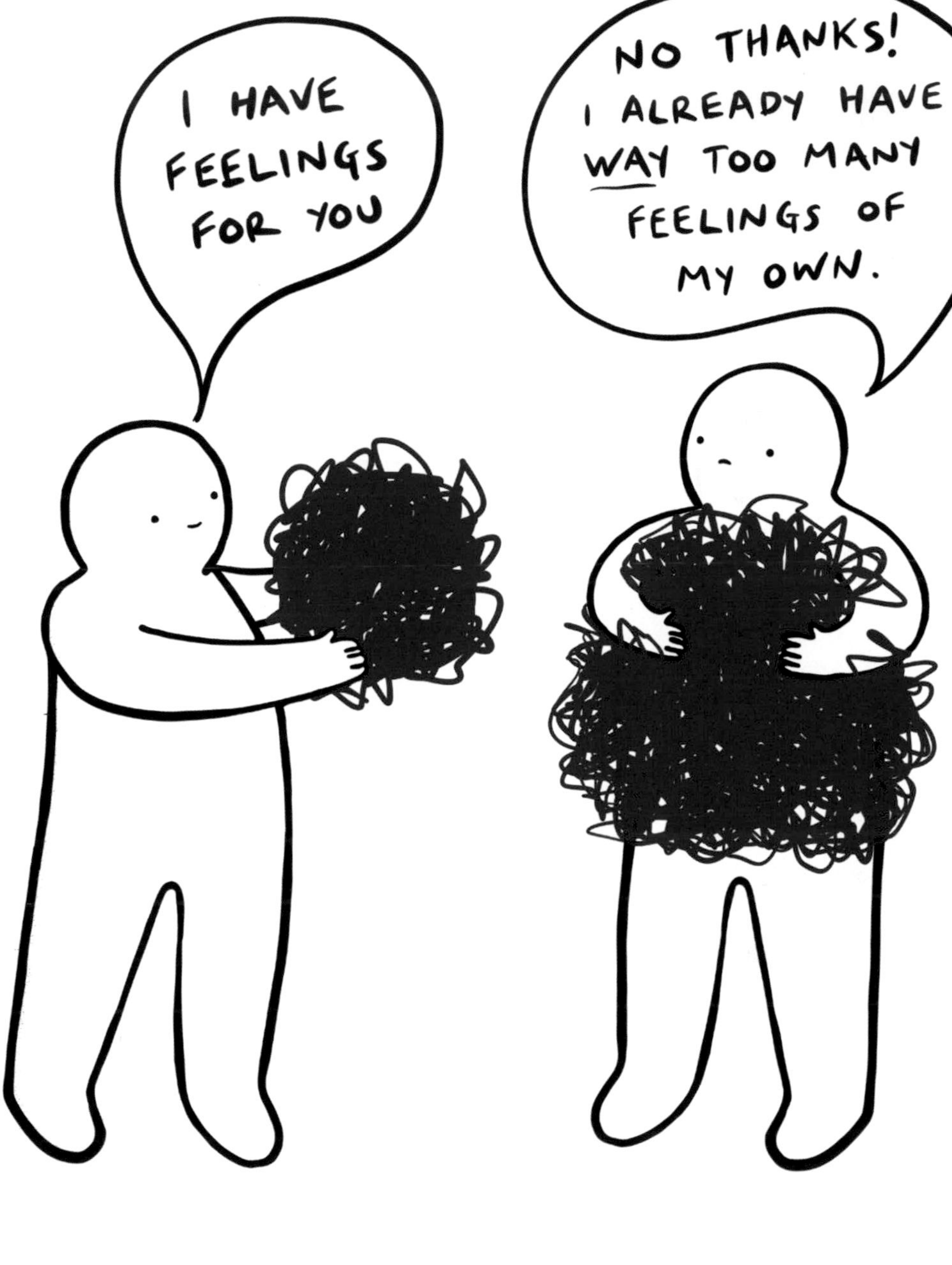
I HAVE FEELINGS FOR YOU
NO THANKS! I ALREADY HAVE WAY TOO MANY FEELINGS OF MY OWN.

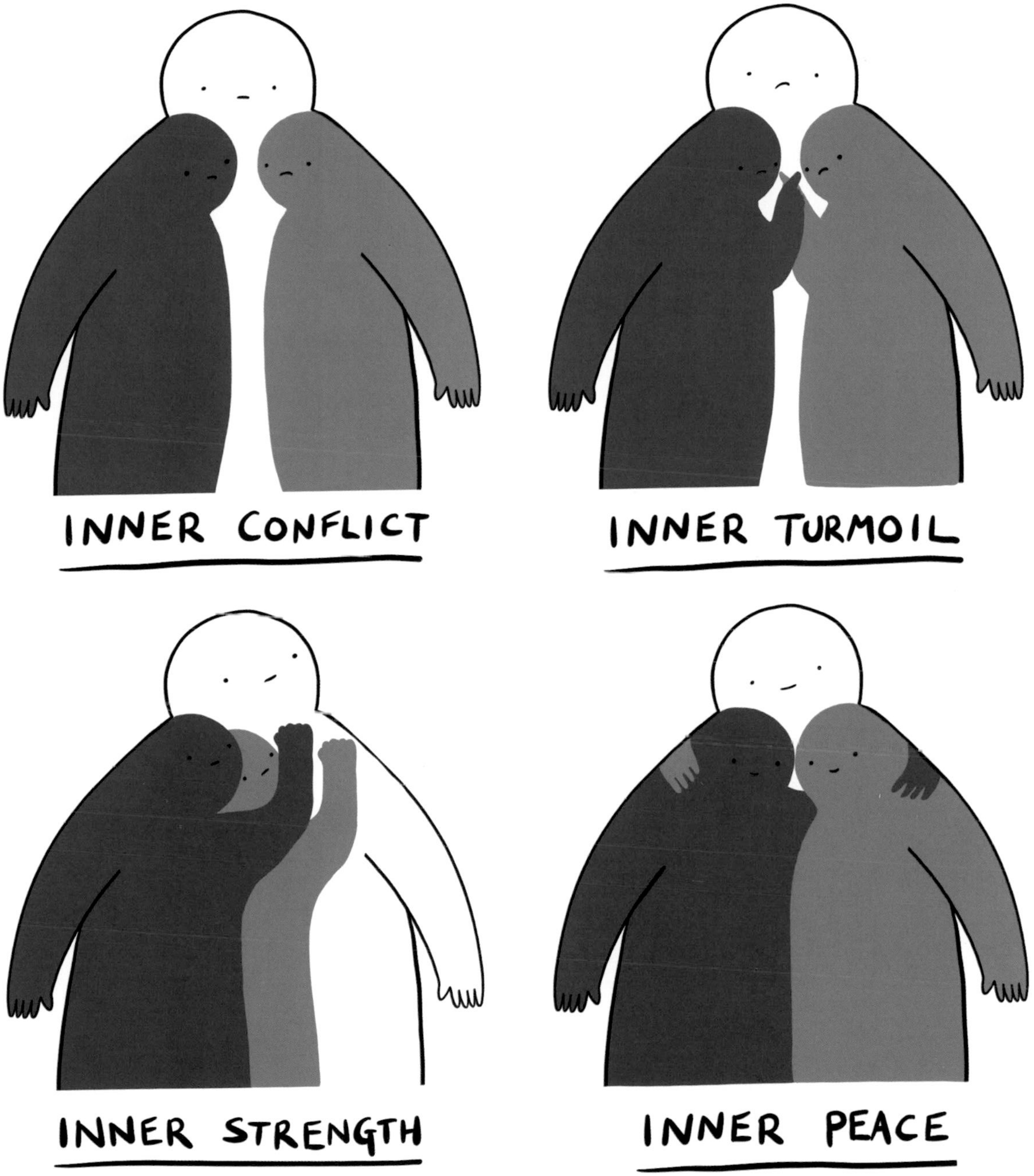
INNER CONFLICT
INNER TURMOIL
INNER STRENGTH
INNER PEACE

TRYING TO FIT ALL MY FEELINGS
INTO MY ANSWER TO THE QUESTION
"HOW ARE YOU?"

SOMETIMES THE SAD
IS VERY BIG

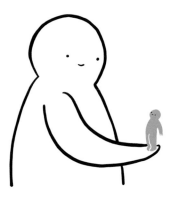

SOMETIMES THE SAD
IS VERY SMALL

SOMETIMES THE SAD
FADES A BIT

BUT IT'S RARE THAT
IT'S NOT THERE AT ALL.

TRYING TO WORK OUT HOW I'M FEELING TODAY:

x =
MOOD²
HOW LONG AGO I ATE
HOURS SLEEP
× θ (10/4 − b)
WEATHER
TRAUMA
TIME
Δ
π ×
1701084
(VALIDATION)³
− x̄ ANXIETY − Σ
472.8
36
y
#
SUCCESS ≥ FAILURE?
− t² + JOY (23/7 ×
? × HEALTH ∞

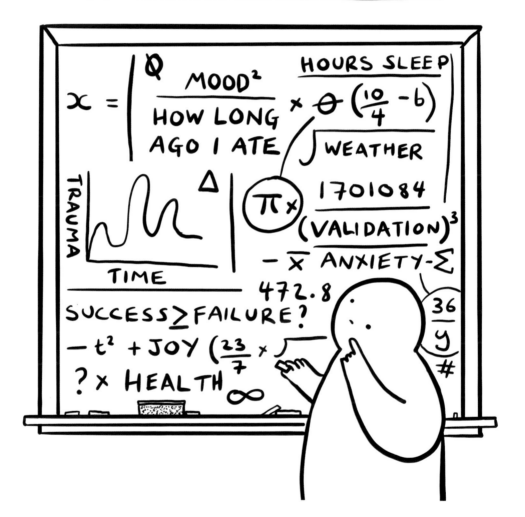

EMOTIONS
ARE STORED
IN THE BODY

IF YOU RUN OUT OF
SPACE, ALL LOGIC
CAN BE CLEARED
FROM THIS AREA TO
MAKE ROOM FOR
MORE EMOTIONS.

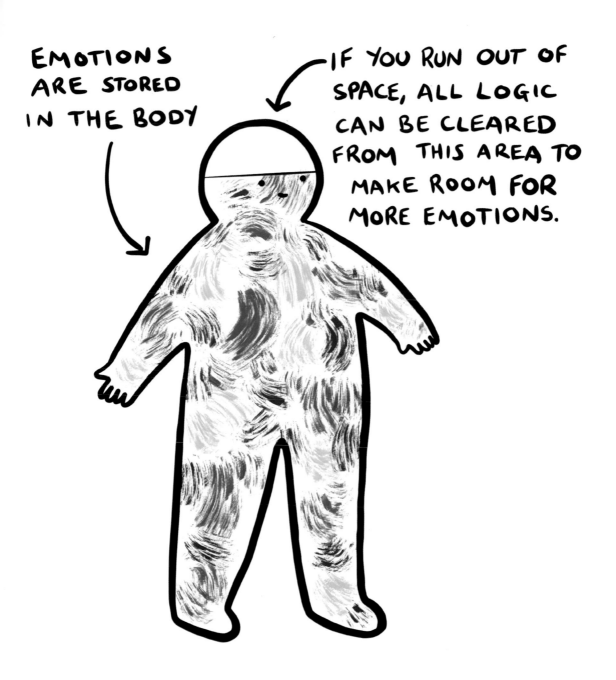

THE FEELING
JUST WAITING
TO BE
ACKNOWLEDGED.

ME JUST
WAITING FOR
IT TO GO
AWAY.

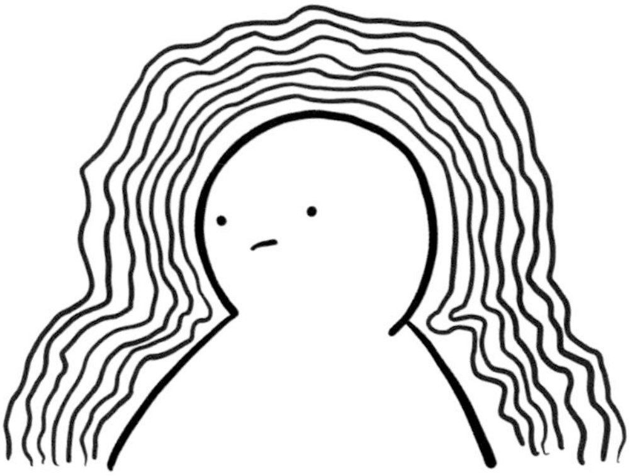

AM I NERVOUS?

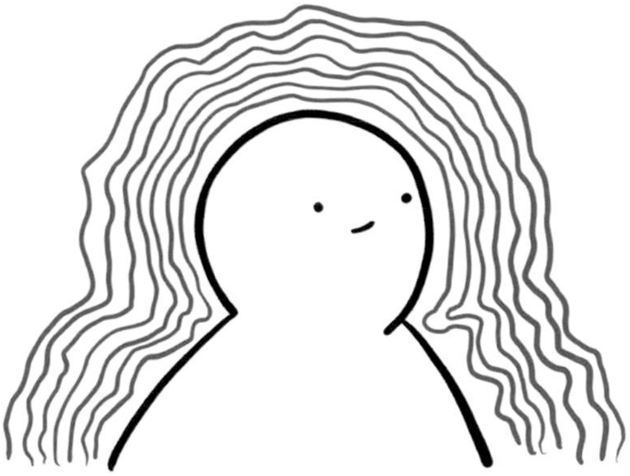

OR AM I EXCITED?

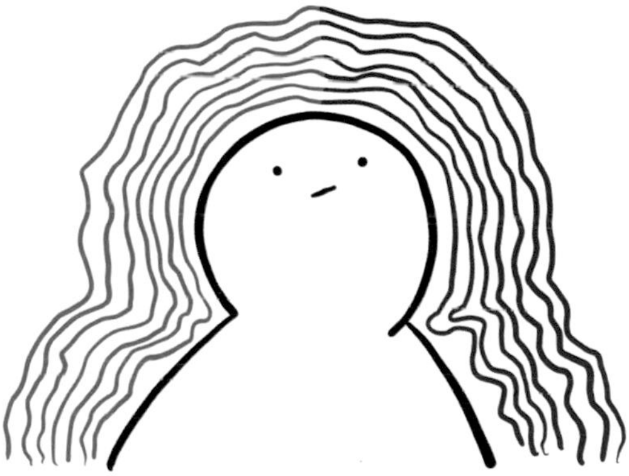

OR HALF NERVOUS,
HALF EXCITED?

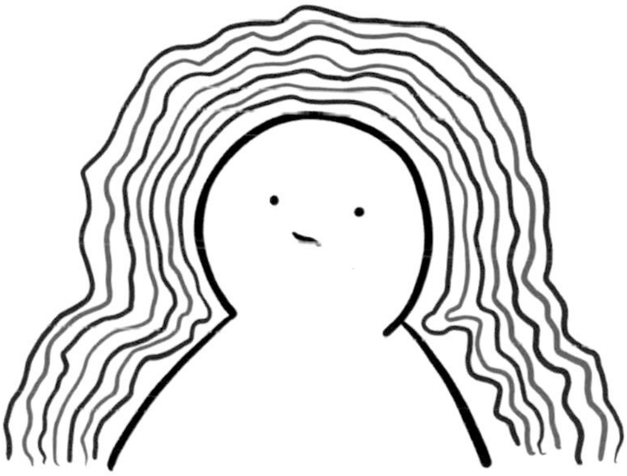

OR BOTH NERVOUS
AND EXCITED?

BEST FRONDS FOREVER

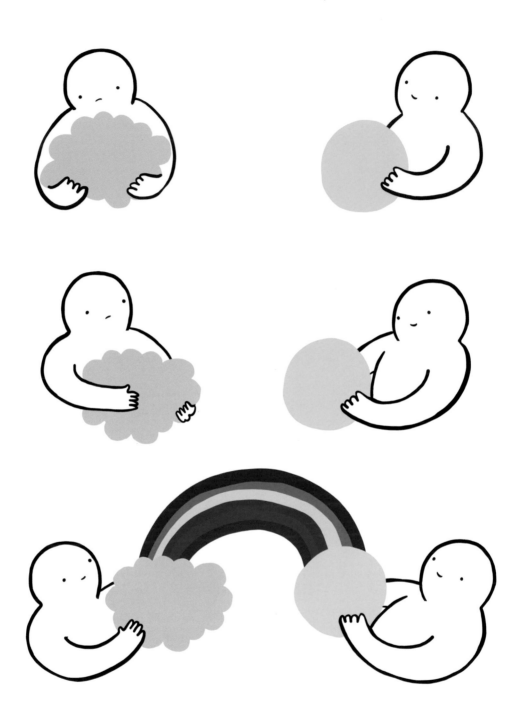

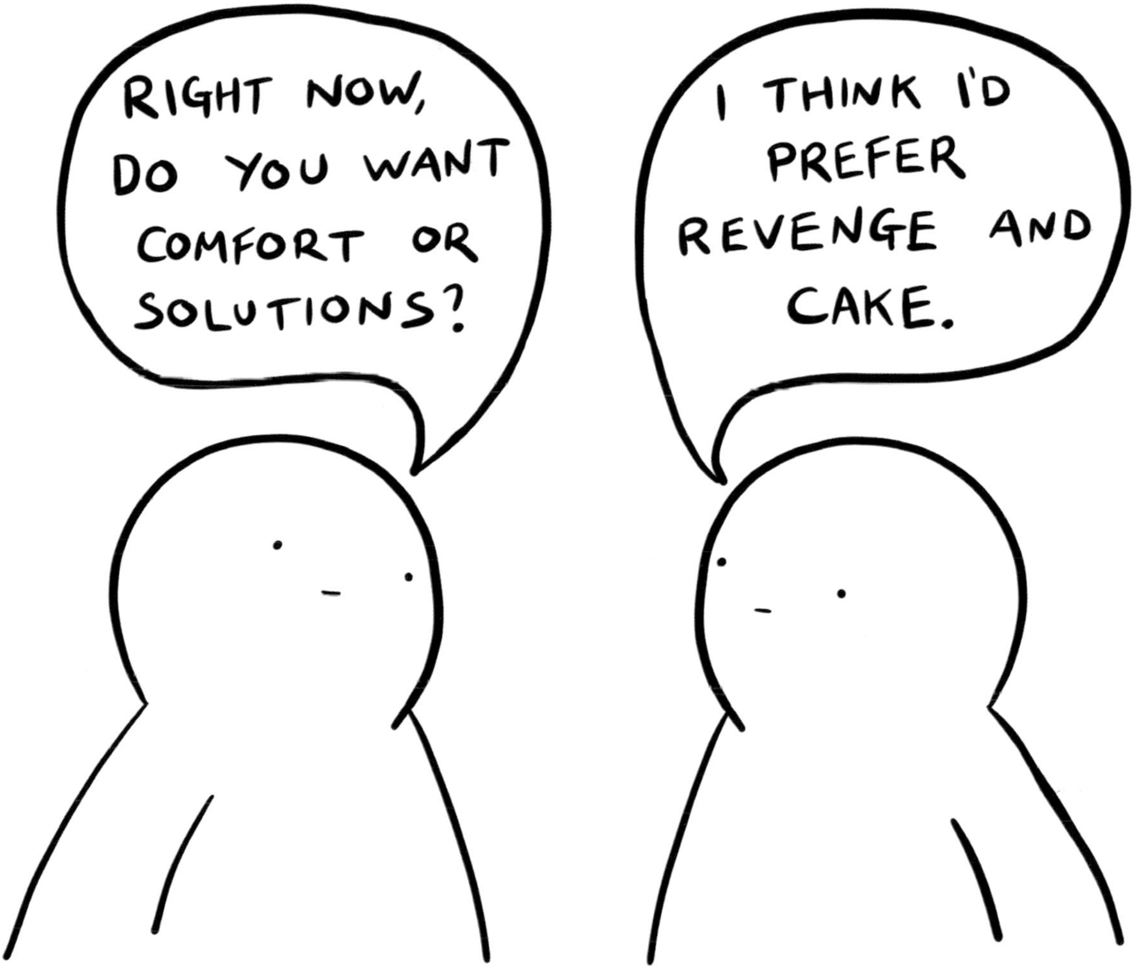
RIGHT NOW, DO YOU WANT COMFORT OR SOLUTIONS?
I THINK I'D PREFER REVENGE AND CAKE.

ME
E
E
WE

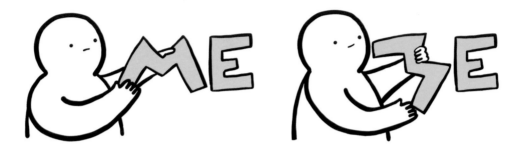

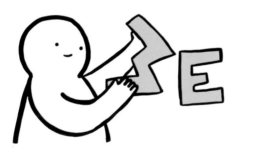

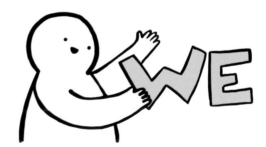

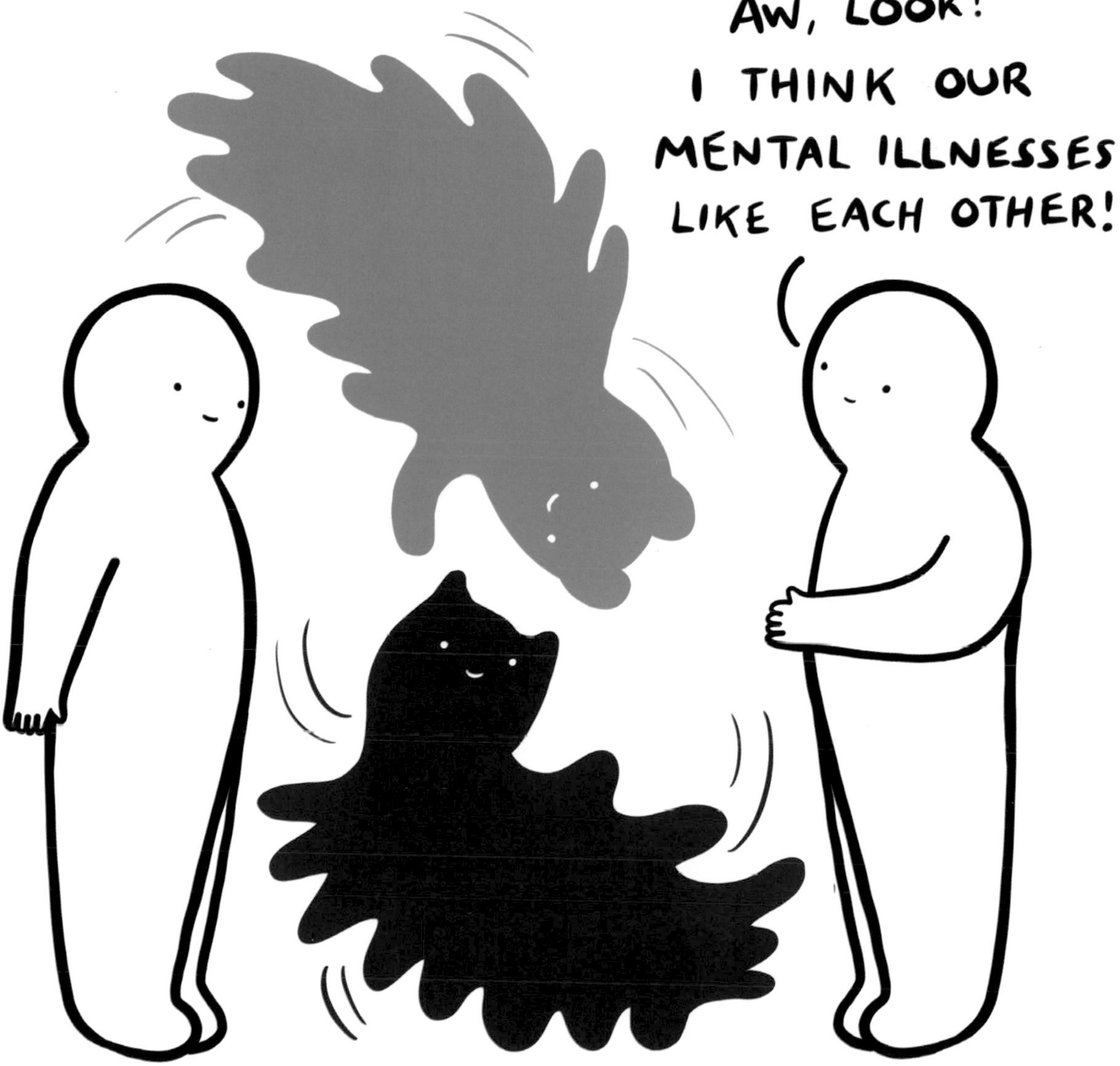
AW, LOOK!
I THINK OUR
MENTAL ILLNESSES
LIKE EACH OTHER!

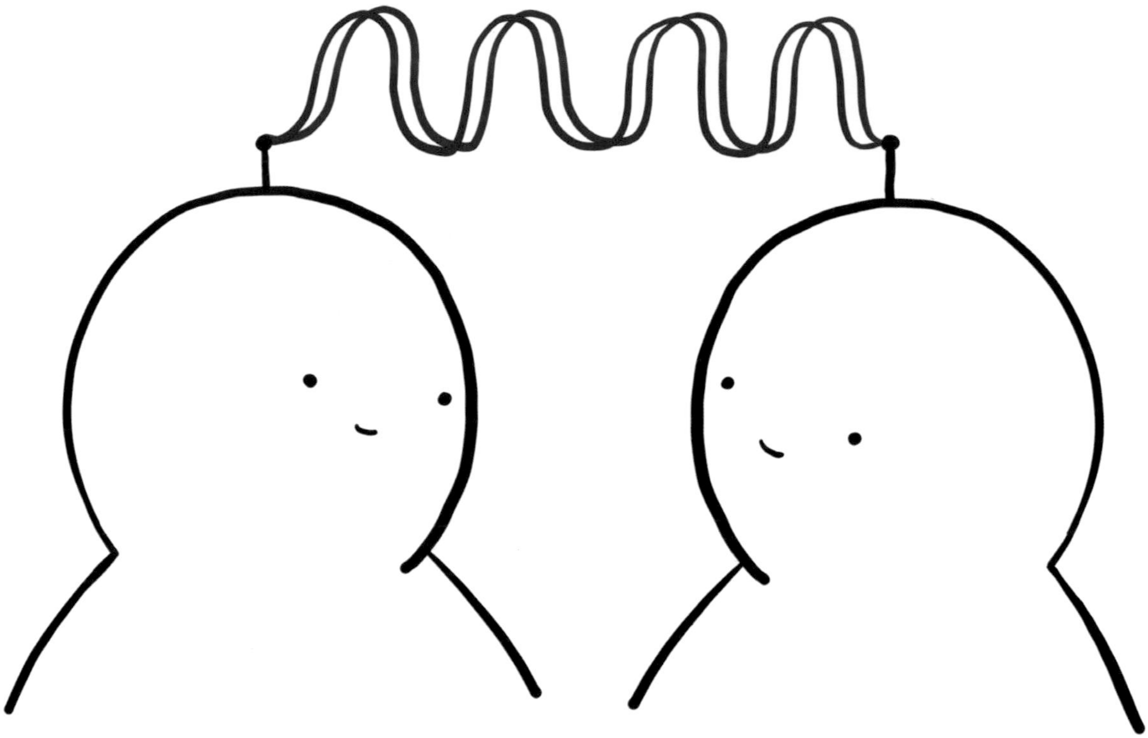

I LIKE BEING ON THE SAME WAVELENGTH AS YOU

OMG SAME HERE!

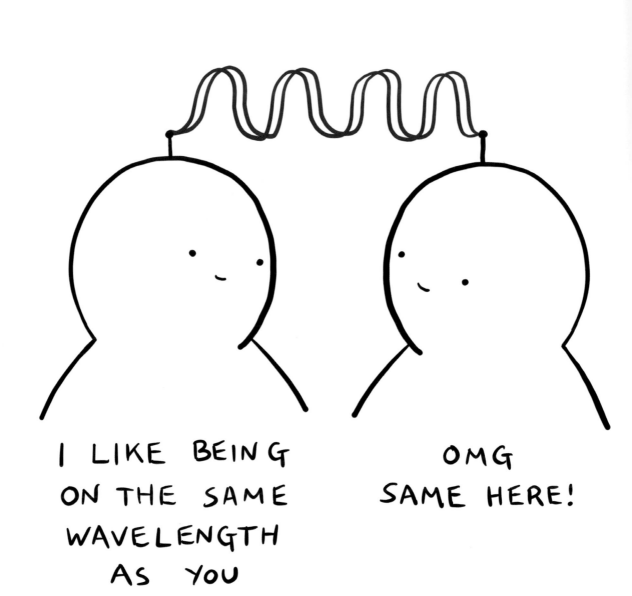

PAT
PAT
PAT
PAT

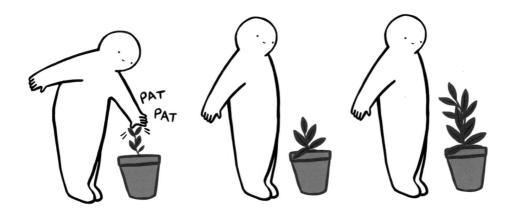

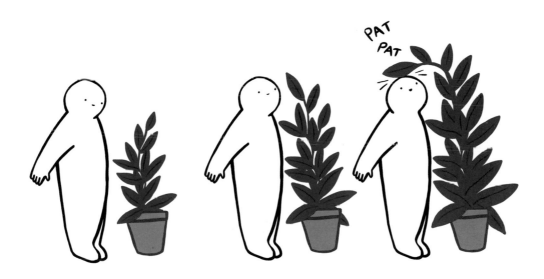

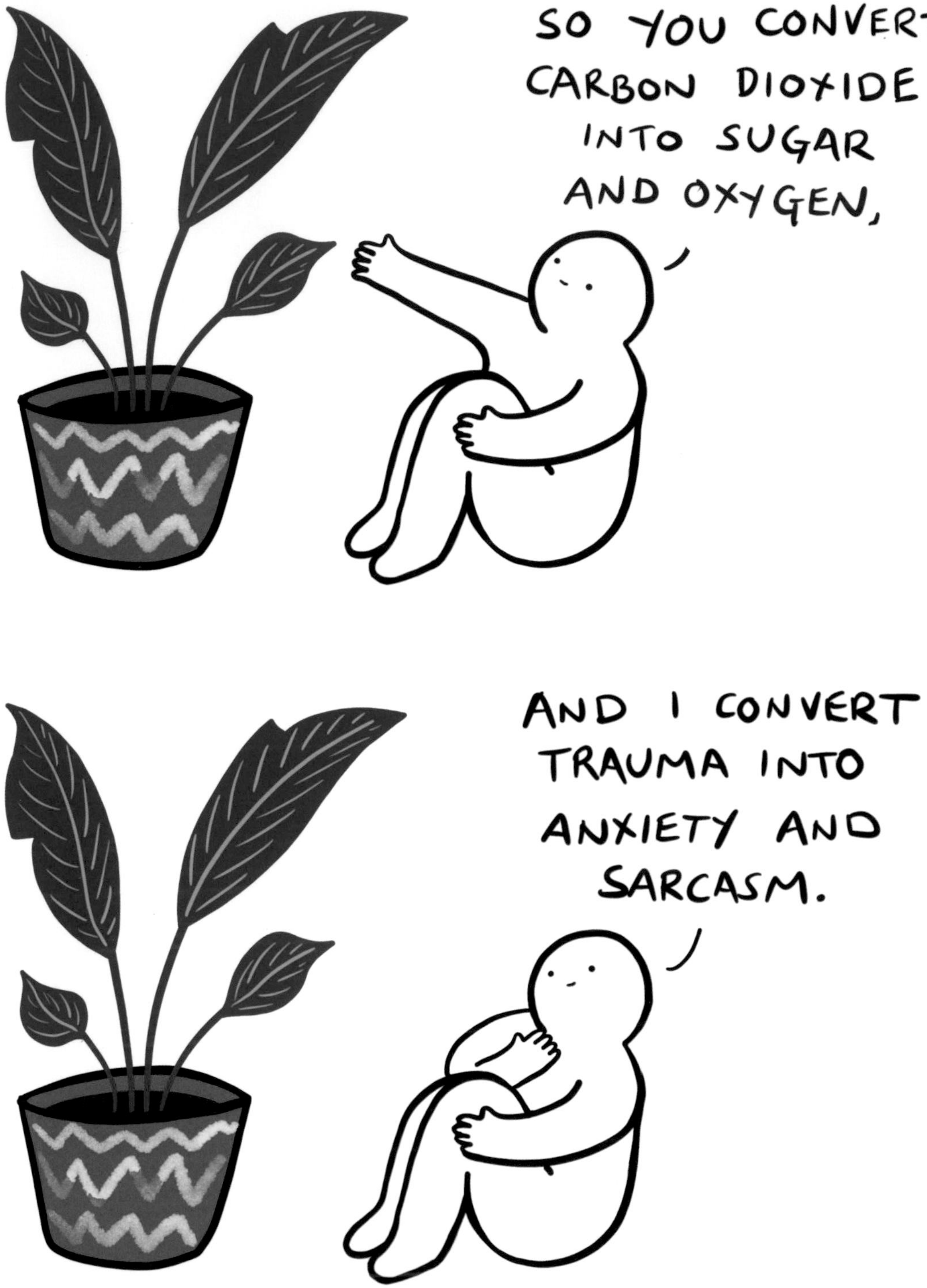
SO YOU CONVERT CARBON DIOXIDE INTO SUGAR AND OXYGEN,
AND I CONVERT TRAUMA INTO ANXIETY AND SARCASM.

YOU TOUCH MY HEART

YOU TOUCH MY MIND

BUT IF YOU TOUCH MY FRIES,

IT'S OVER.

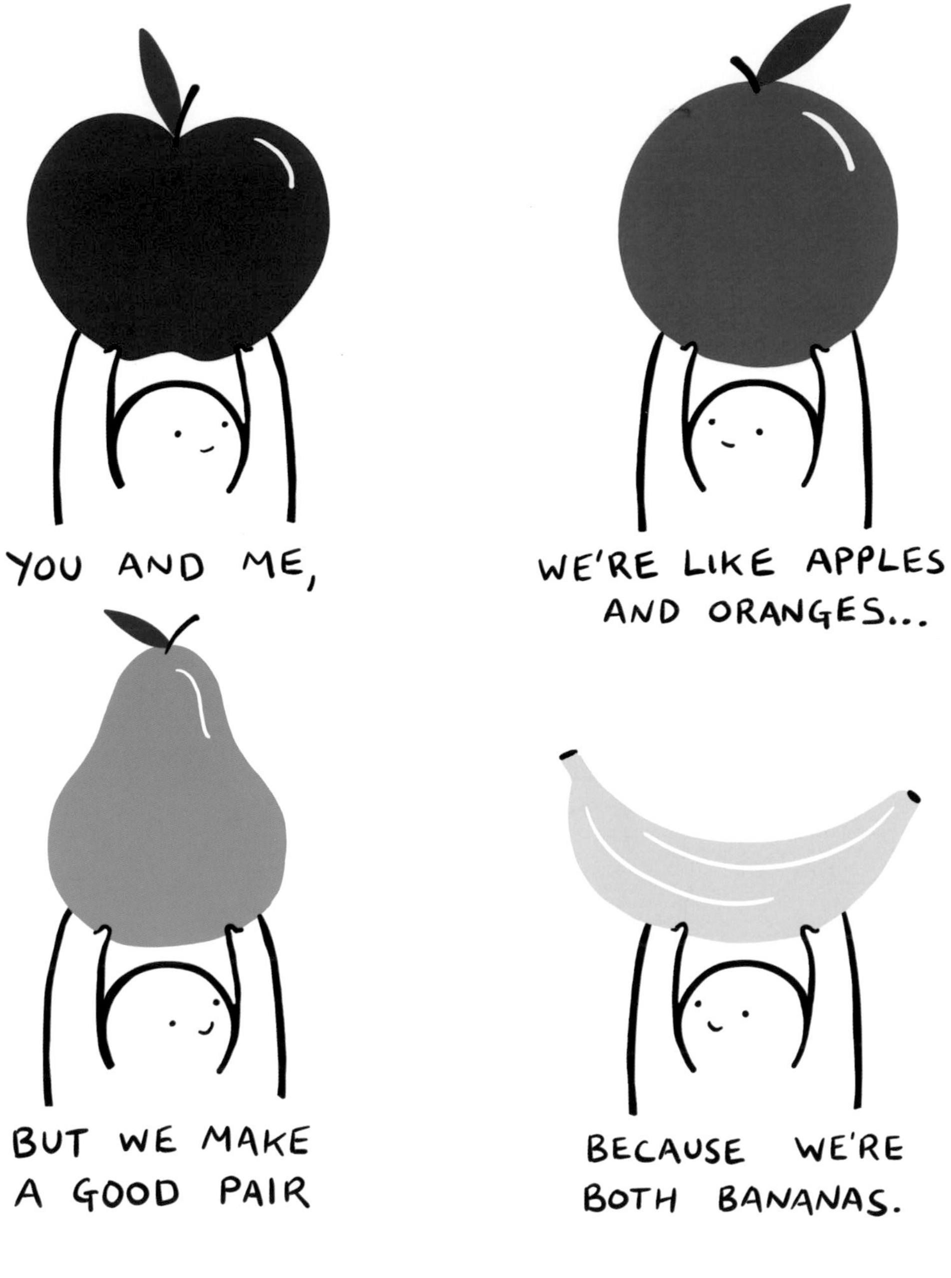
YOU AND ME,
WE'RE LIKE APPLES AND ORANGES...
BUT WE MAKE A GOOD PAIR
BECAUSE WE'RE BOTH BANANAS.

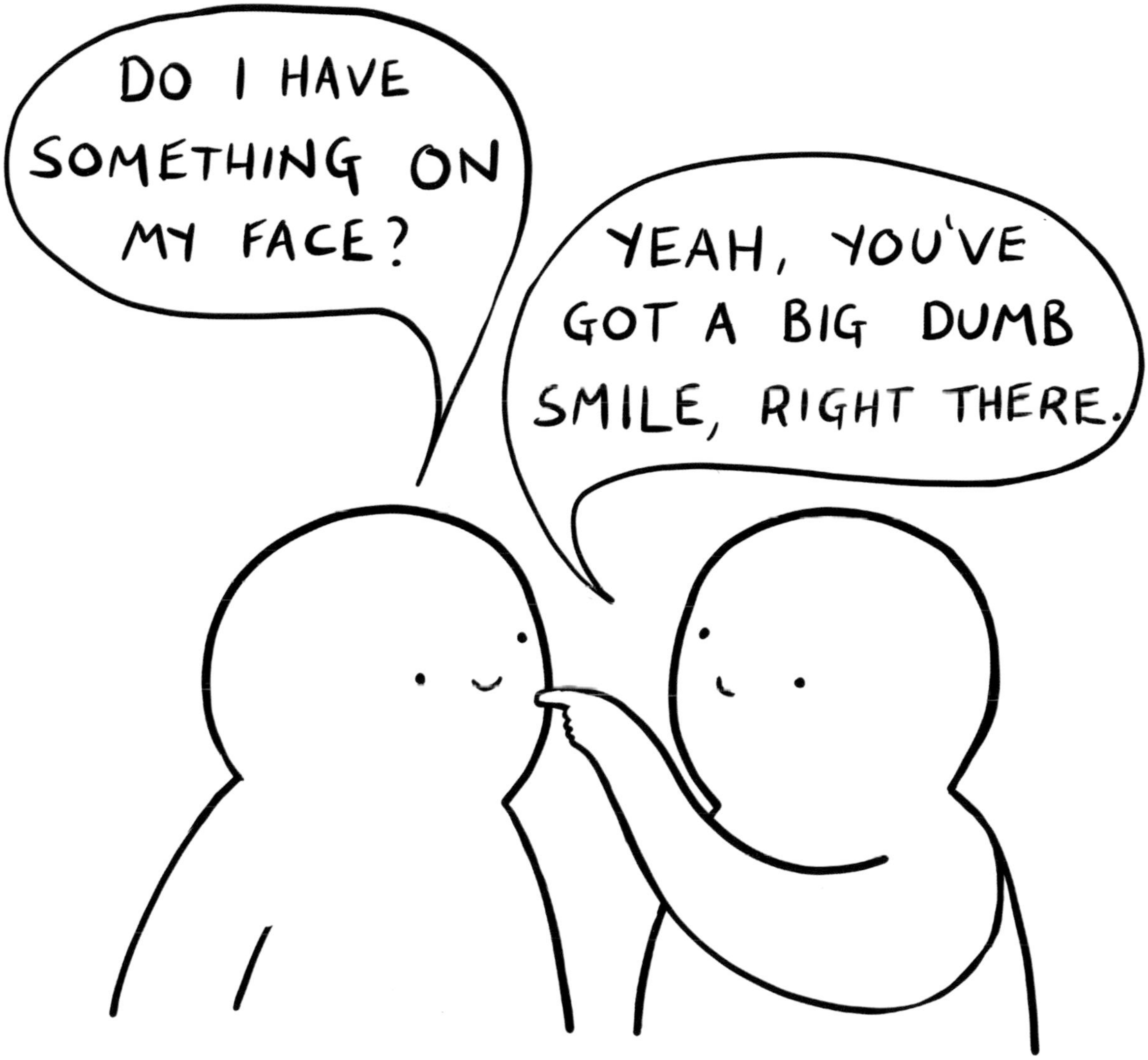
DO I HAVE SOMETHING ON MY FACE?
YEAH, YOU'VE GOT A BIG DUMB SMILE, RIGHT THERE.

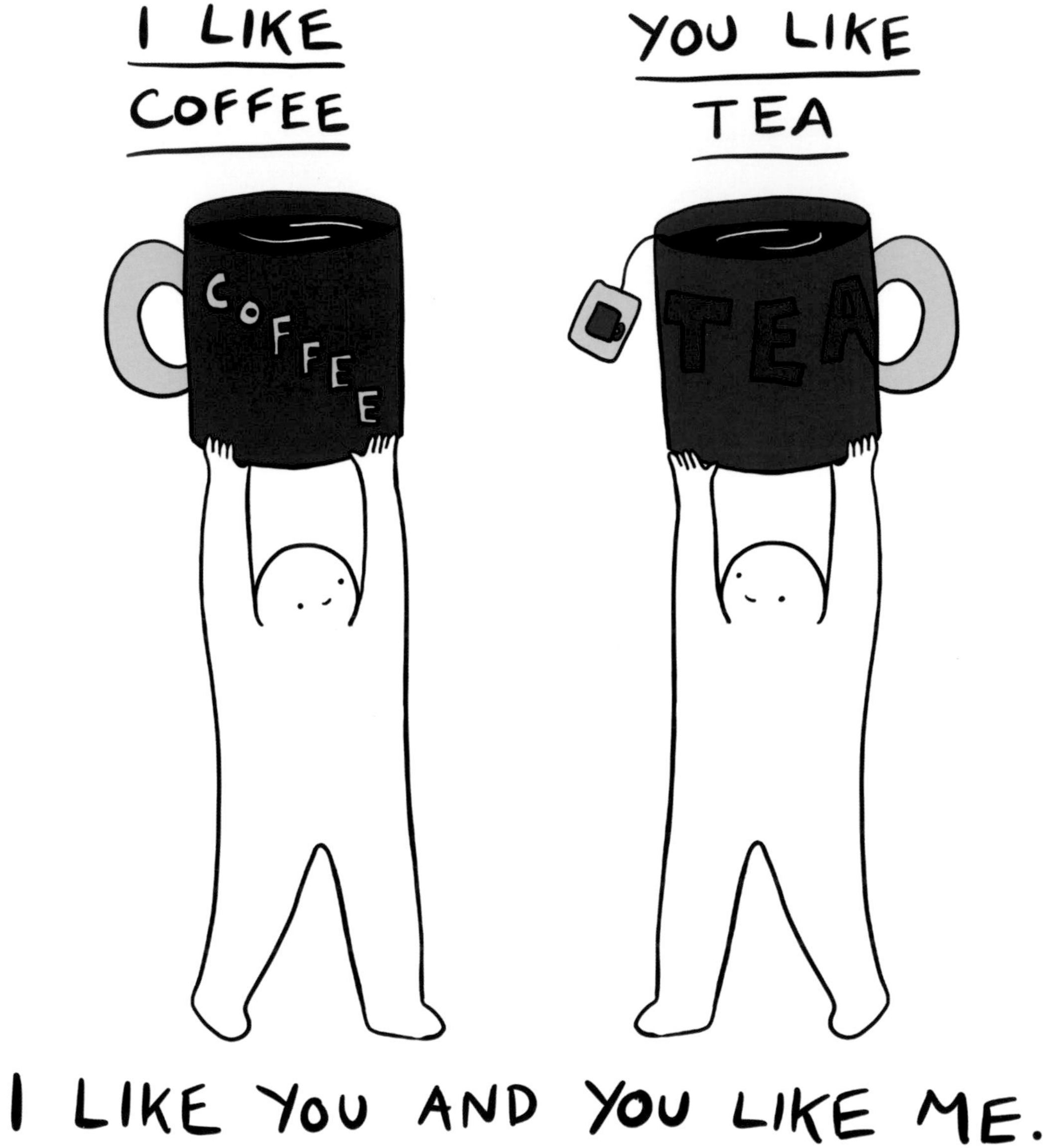
I LIKE COFFEE
YOU LIKE TEA
COFFEE
TEA
I LIKE YOU AND YOU LIKE ME.

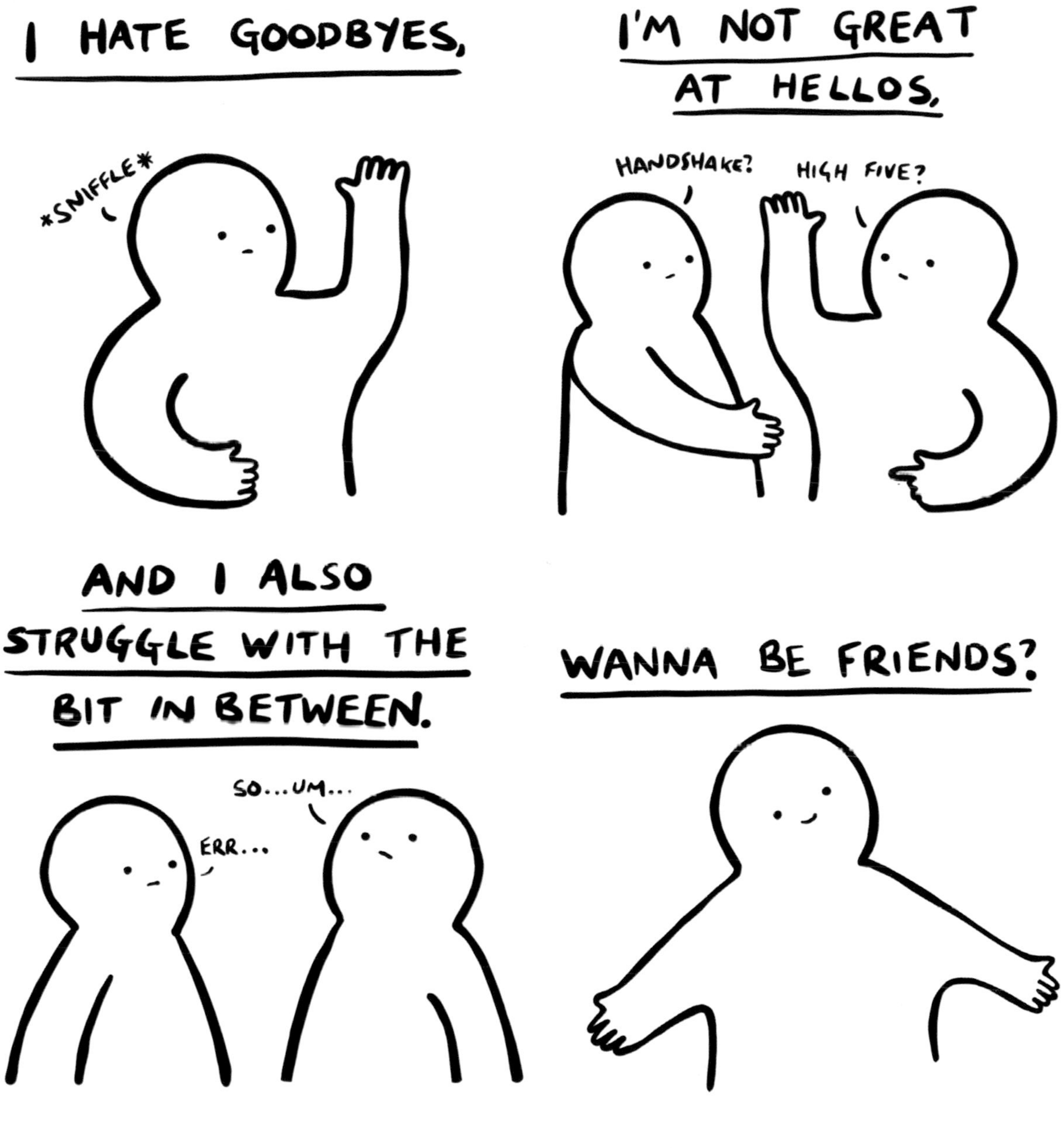
I HATE GOODBYES,
SNIFFLE
I'M NOT GREAT AT HELLOS,
HANDSHAKE?
HIGH FIVE?
AND I ALSO STRUGGLE WITH THE BIT IN BETWEEN.
ERR...
SO...UM...
WANNA BE FRIENDS?

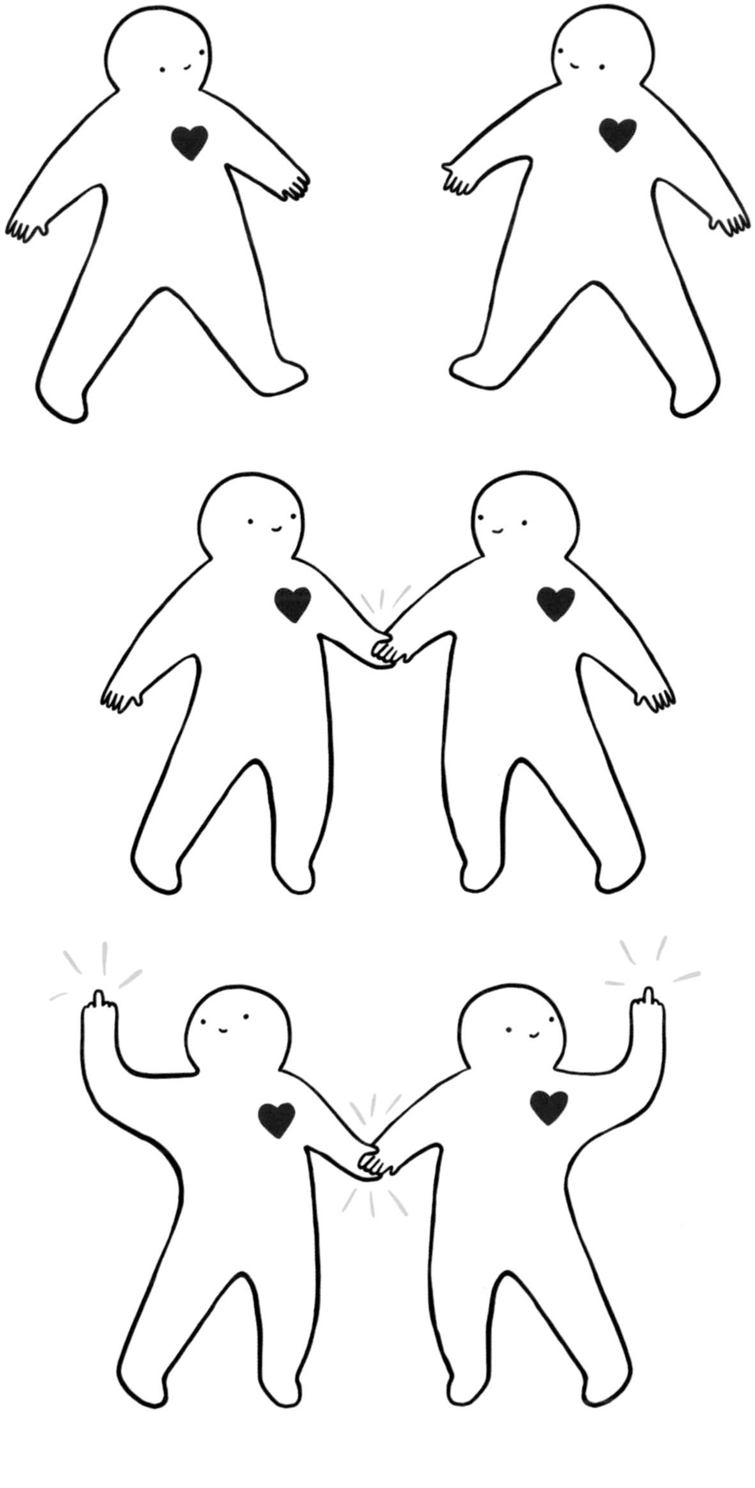

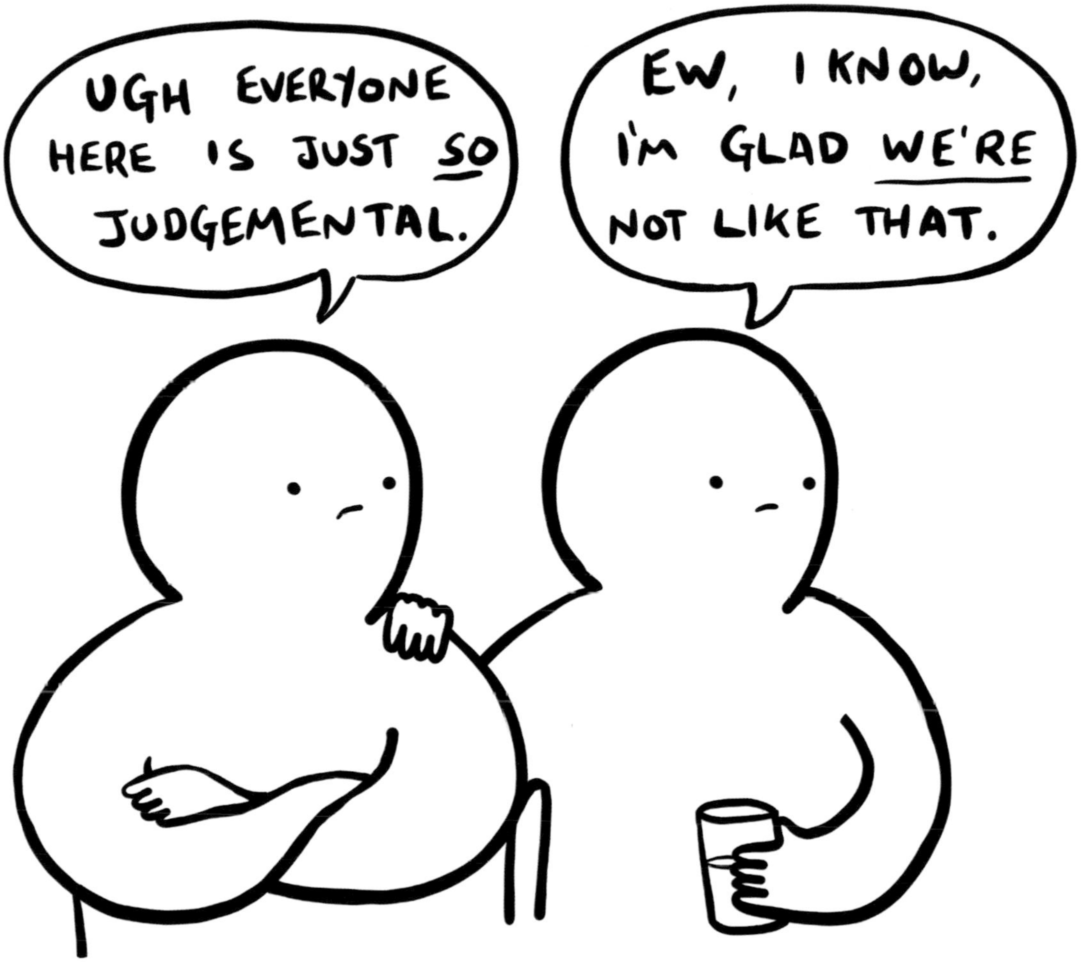
UGH EVERYONE HERE IS JUST SO JUDGEMENTAL.
EW, I KNOW, I'M GLAD WE'RE NOT LIKE THAT.

WHO LEFT ME IN CHARGE OF ME?

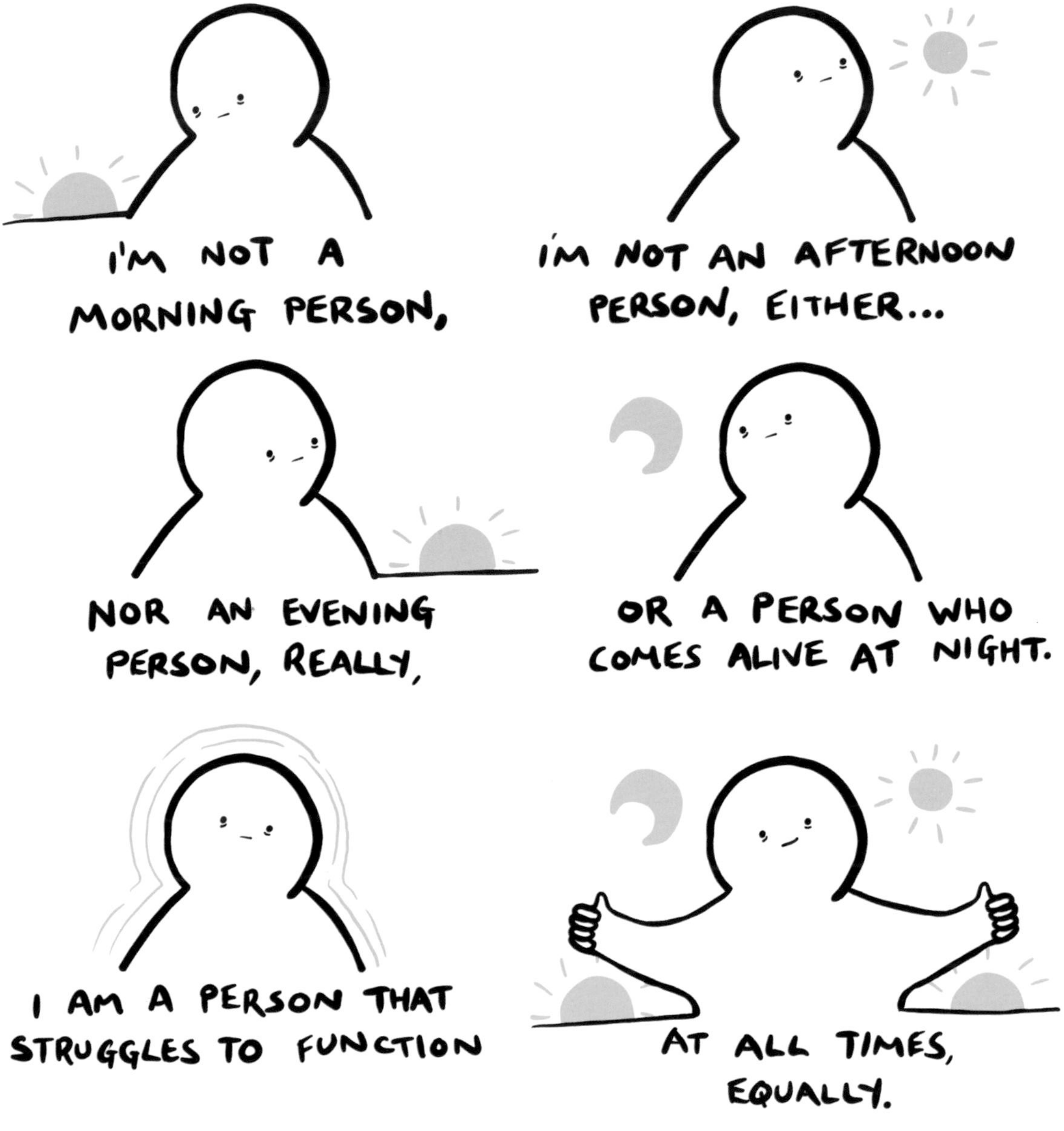
I'M NOT A MORNING PERSON,
I'M NOT AN AFTERNOON PERSON, EITHER...
NOR AN EVENING PERSON, REALLY,
OR A PERSON WHO COMES ALIVE AT NIGHT.
I AM A PERSON THAT STRUGGLES TO FUNCTION
AT ALL TIMES, EQUALLY.

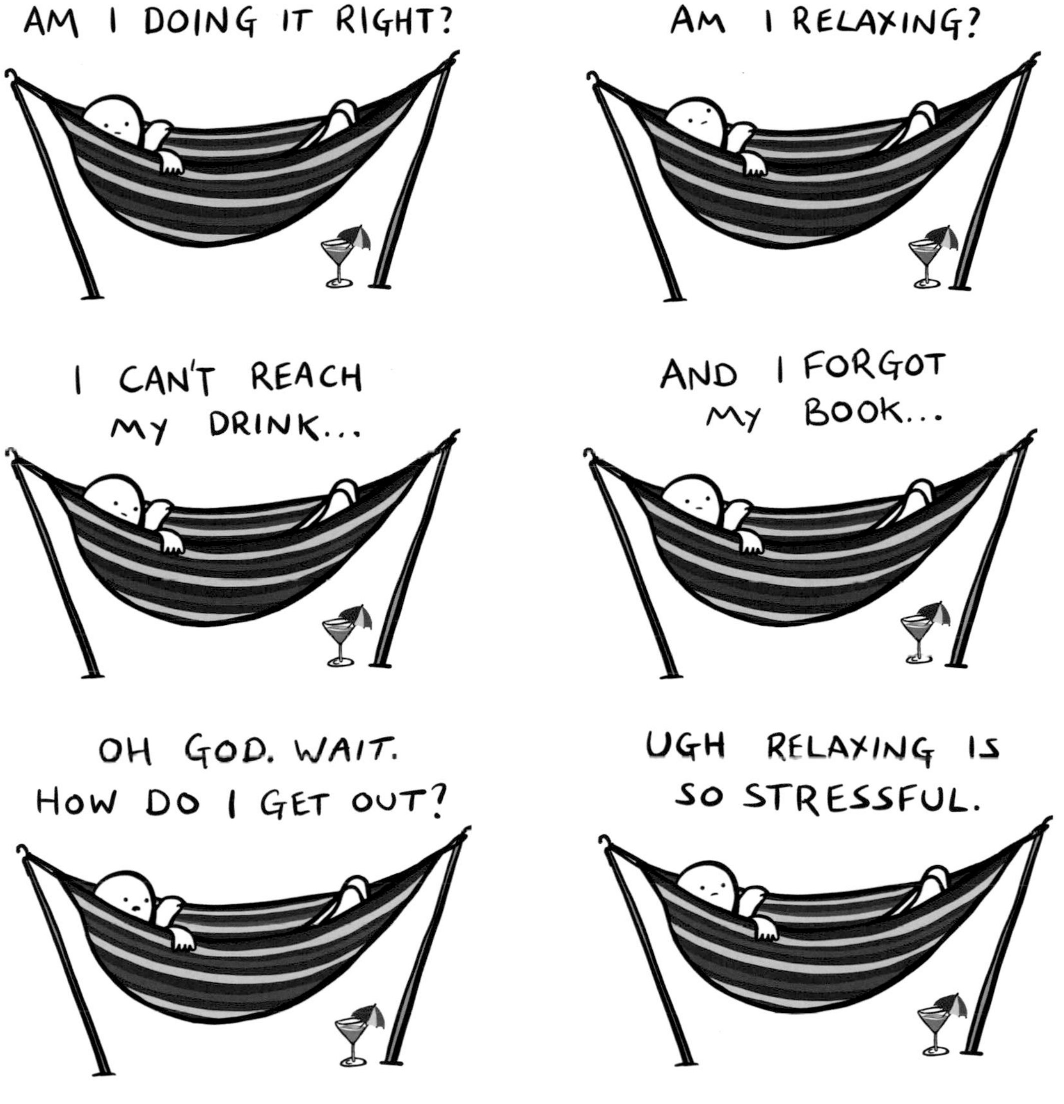
AM I DOING IT RIGHT?
AM I RELAXING?
I CAN'T REACH MY DRINK...
AND I FORGOT MY BOOK...
OH GOD. WAIT. HOW DO I GET OUT?
UGH RELAXING IS SO STRESSFUL.

ME TRYING TO SET A BOUNDARY:

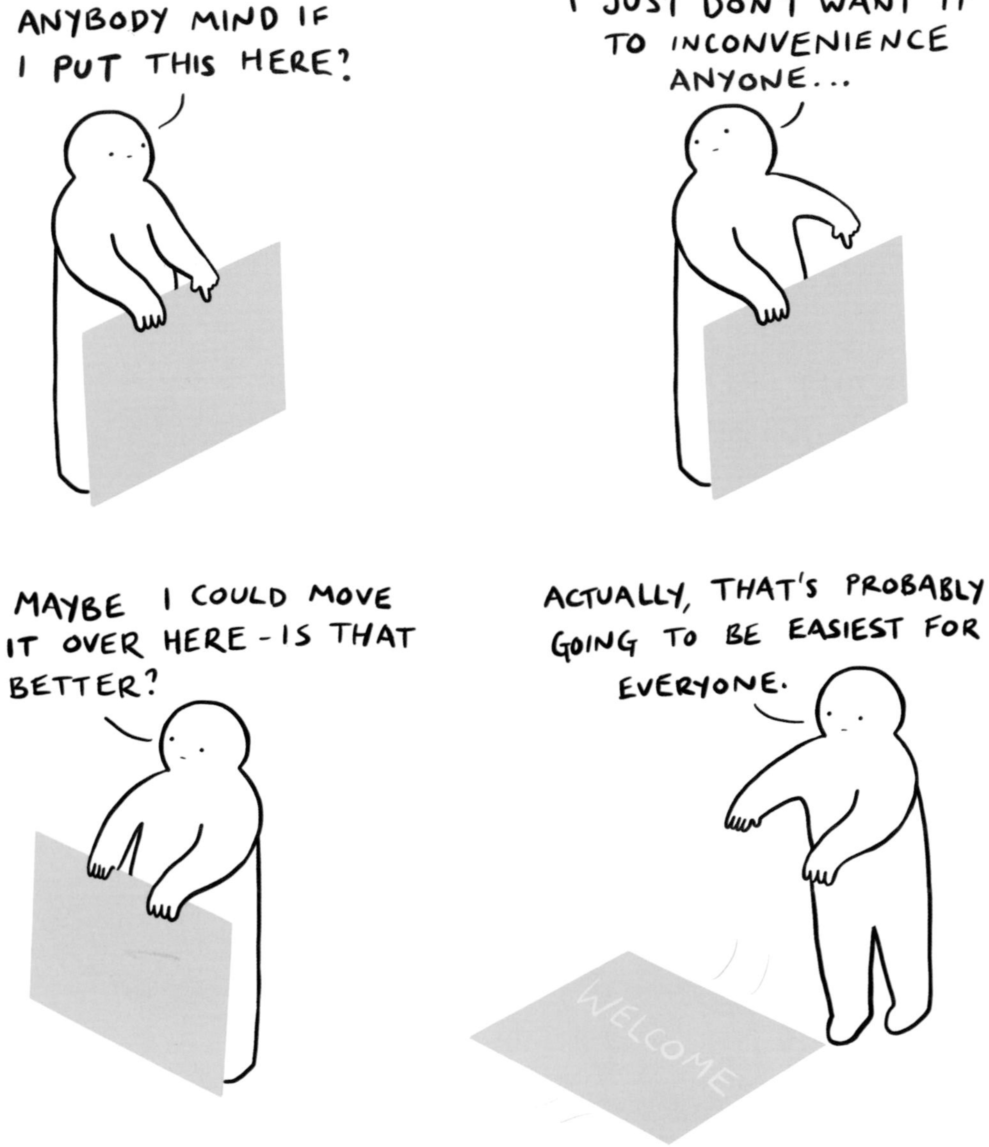
ANYBODY MIND IF I PUT THIS HERE?
I JUST DON'T WANT IT TO INCONVENIENCE ANYONE...
MAYBE I COULD MOVE IT OVER HERE - IS THAT BETTER?
ACTUALLY, THAT'S PROBABLY GOING TO BE EASIEST FOR EVERYONE.
WELCOME

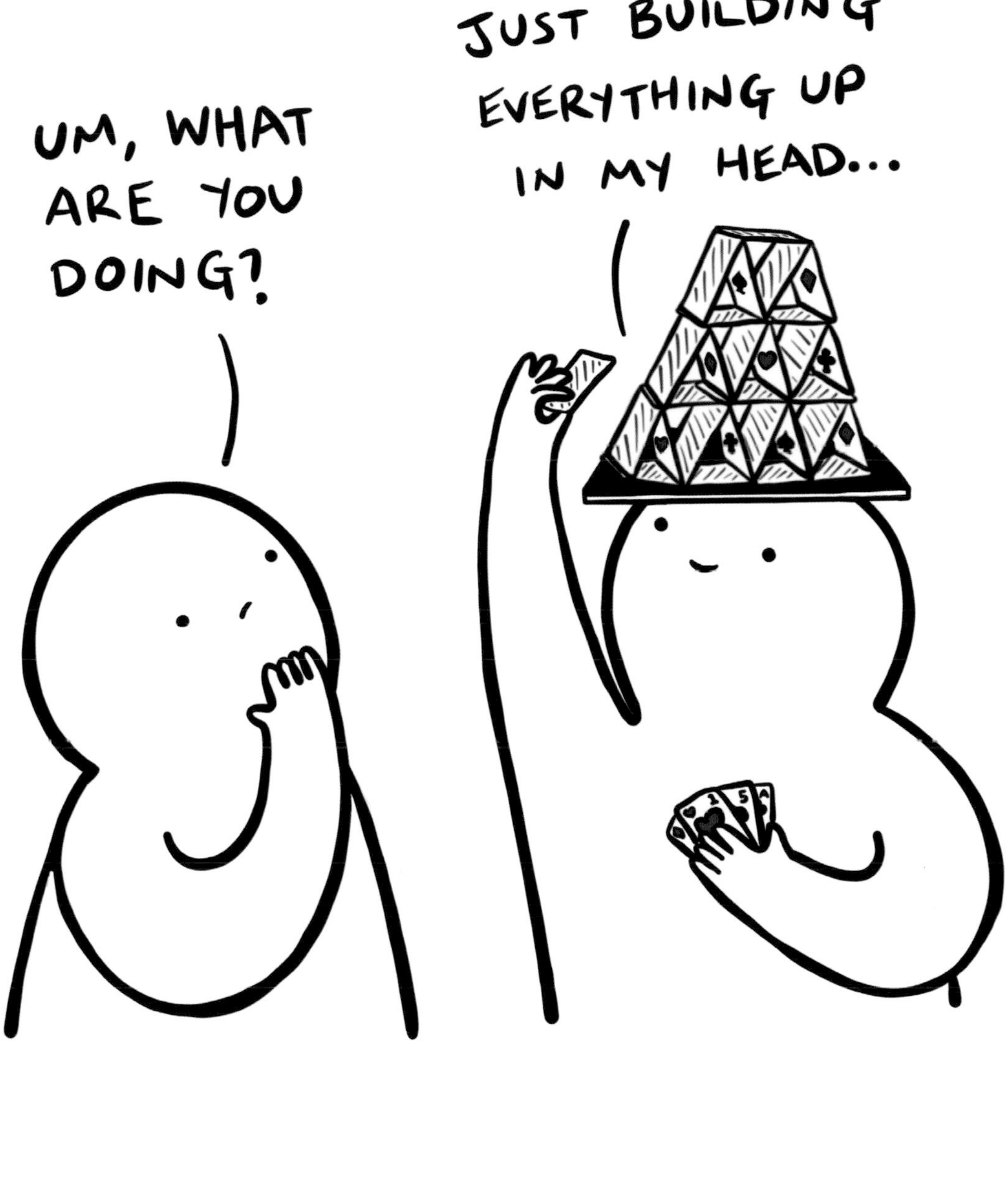
UM, WHAT ARE YOU DOING?
JUST BUILDING EVERYTHING UP IN MY HEAD...

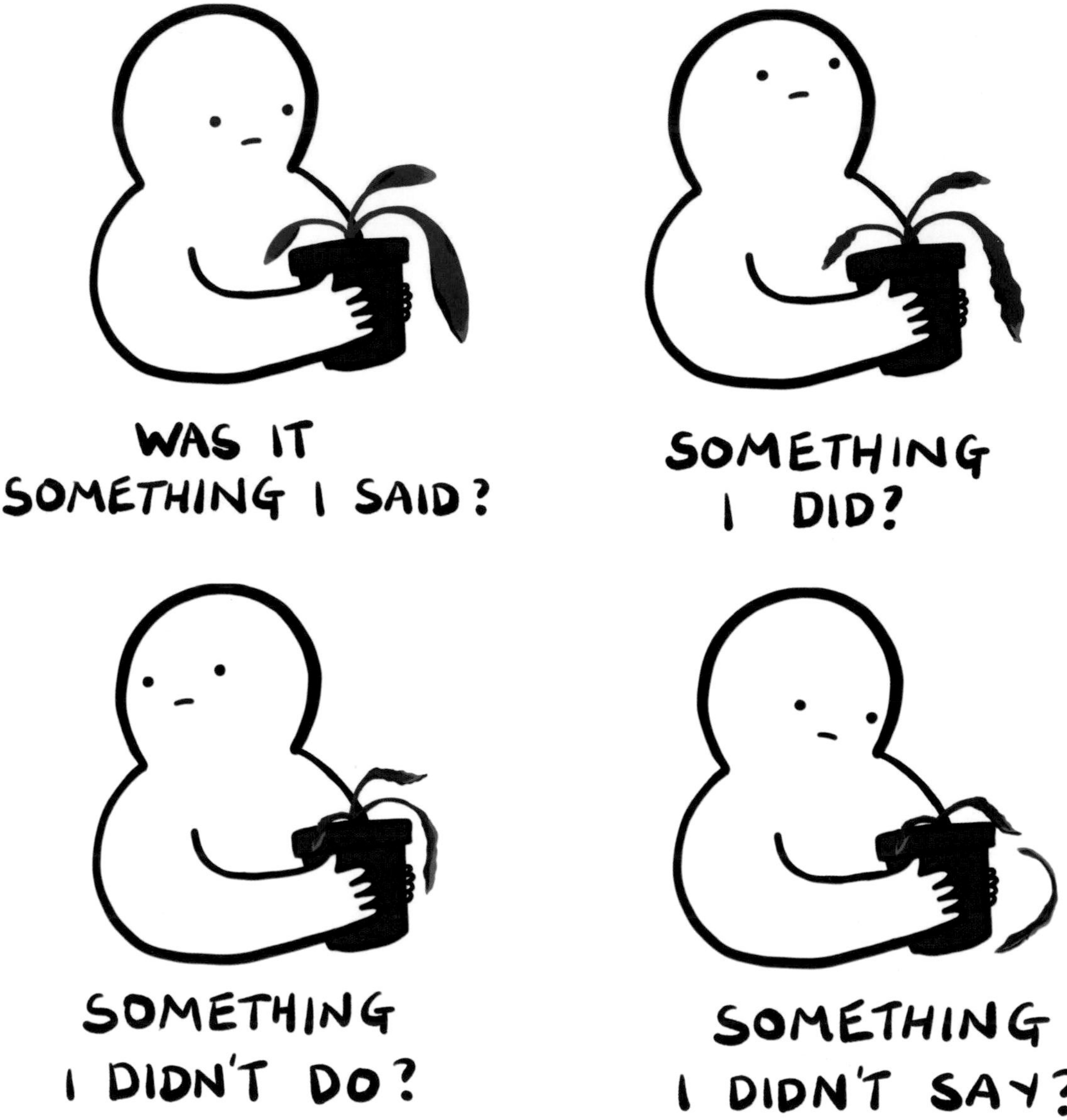
WAS IT SOMETHING I SAID?
SOMETHING I DID?
SOMETHING I DIDN'T DO?
SOMETHING I DIDN'T SAY?

ME, EVERY 5 MINUTES:

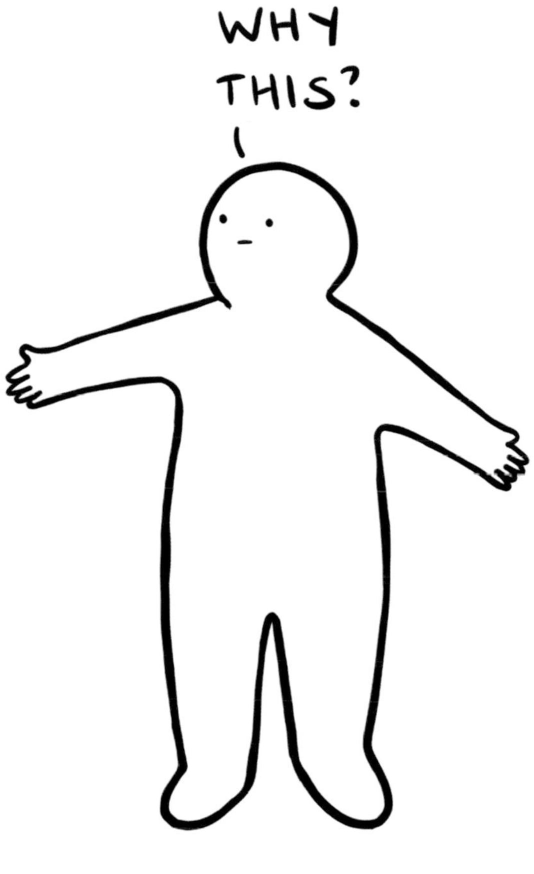
WHY THIS?
WHY NOW?
WHY ME?

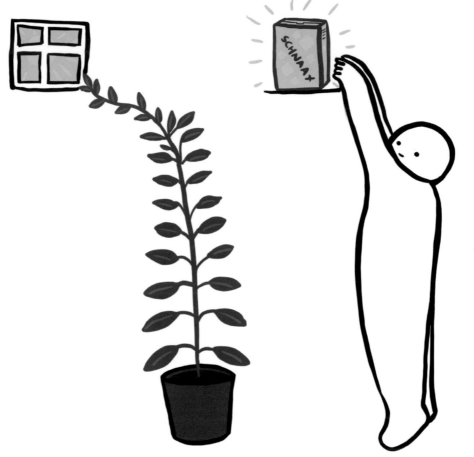

JUST AS
PLANTS REACH
FOR THE SUN,

I REACH FOR
THE SNACKS YOU
HIDE FROM ME ON
TOP OF THE FRIDGE.

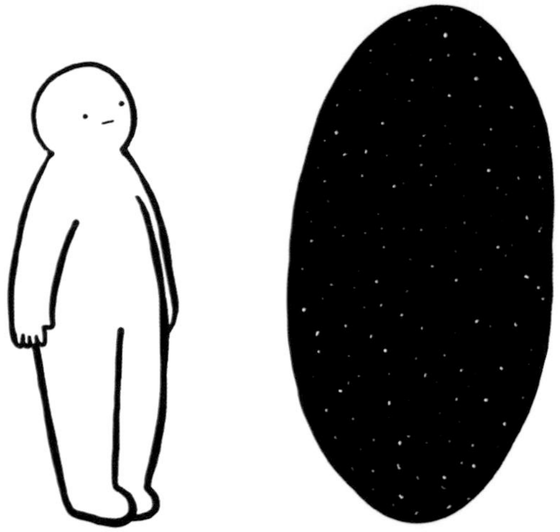

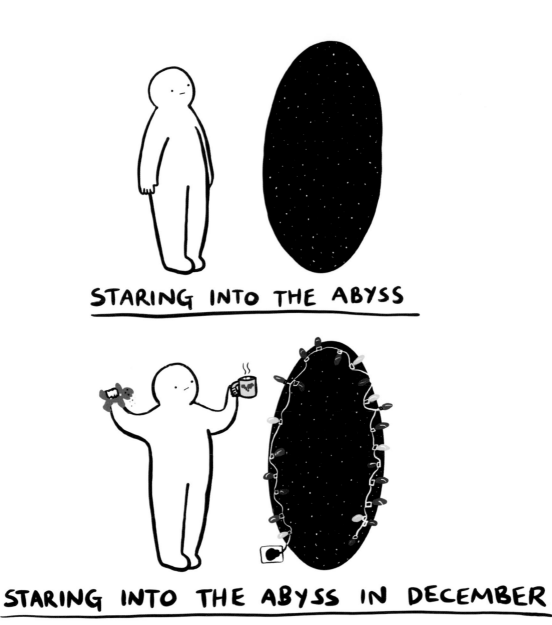

STARING INTO THE ABYSS

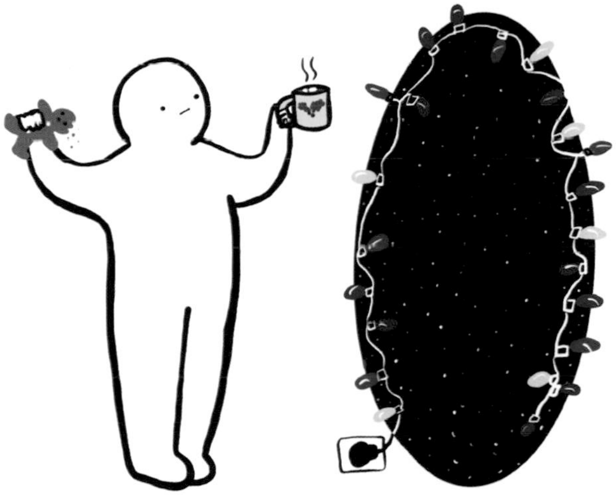

STARING INTO THE ABYSS IN DECEMBER

BETTER STAY HYDRATED,

GONNA DO A LOOOOT
OF CRYING TODAY.

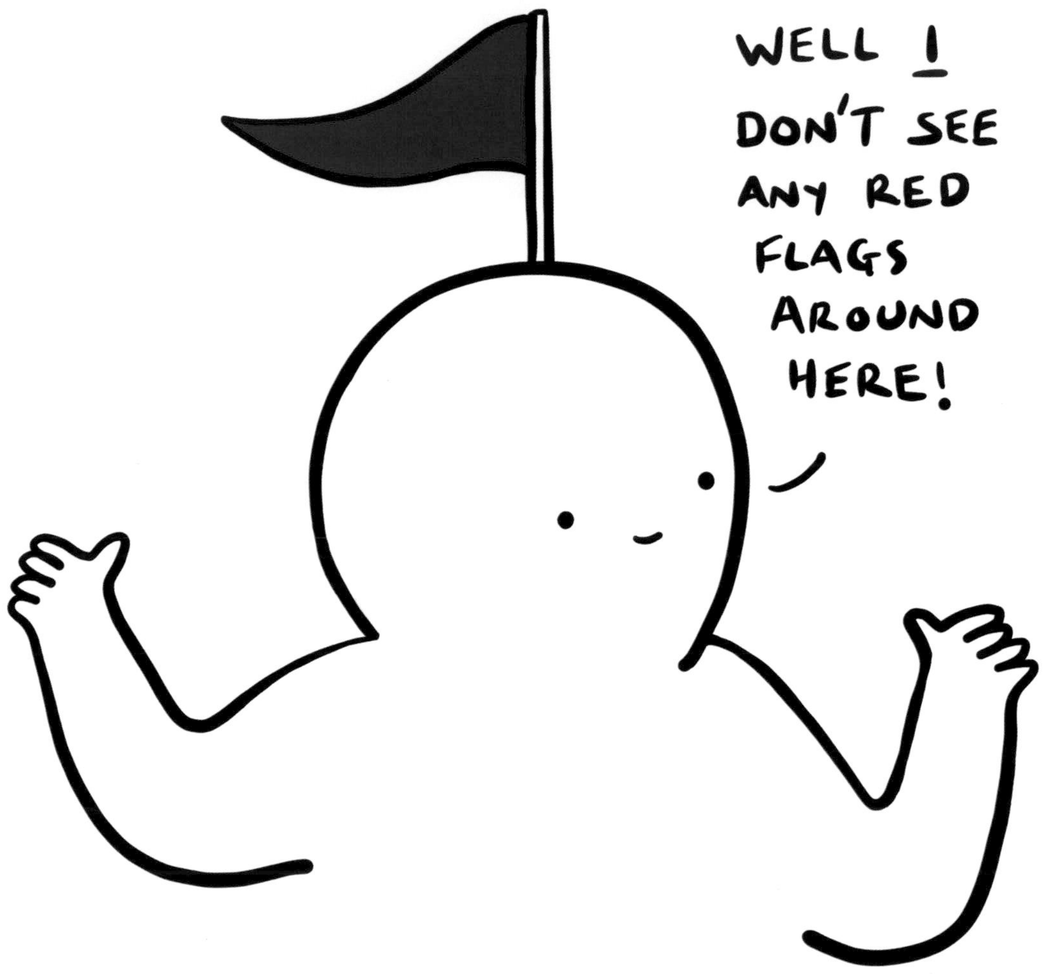
WELL I DON'T SEE ANY RED FLAGS AROUND HERE!

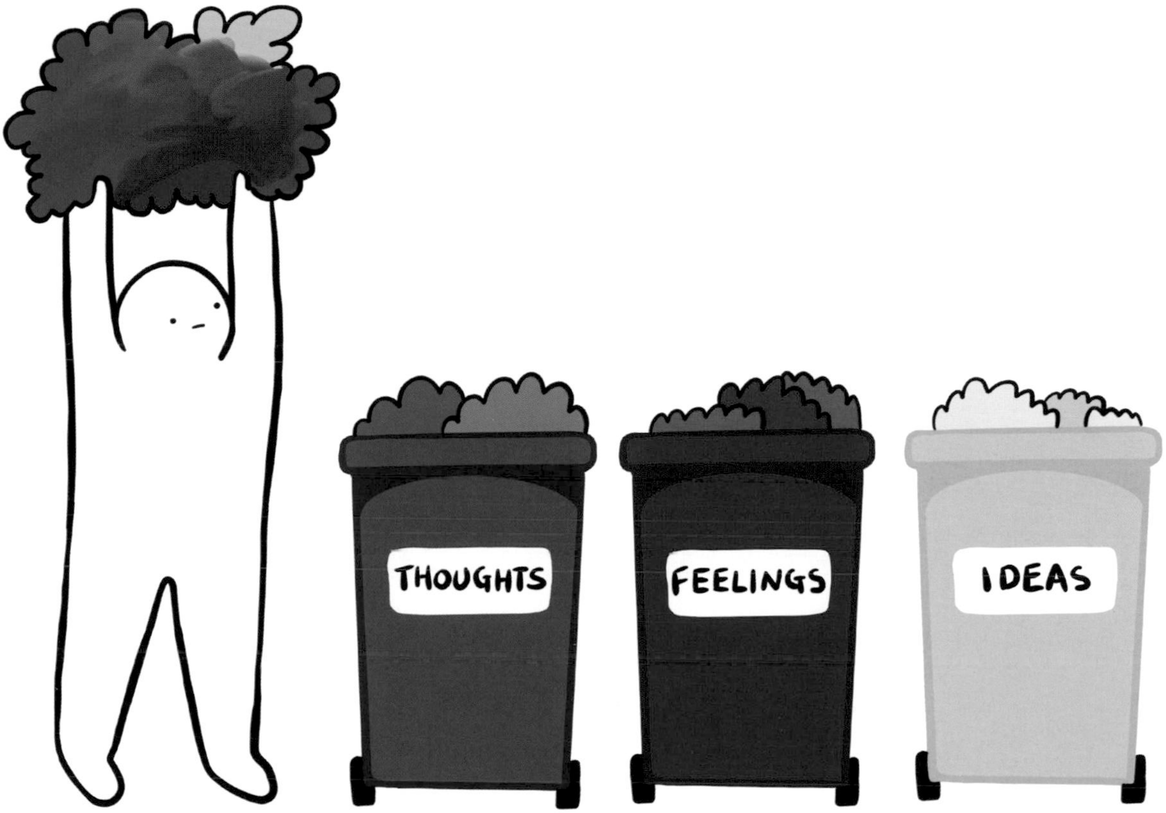
THOUGHTS
FEELINGS
IDEAS

TRYING TO SORT MYSELF OUT

THIS LOOKS LIKE A JOB FOR...

SOMEONE WITH MORE SELF-ESTEEM THAN ME.

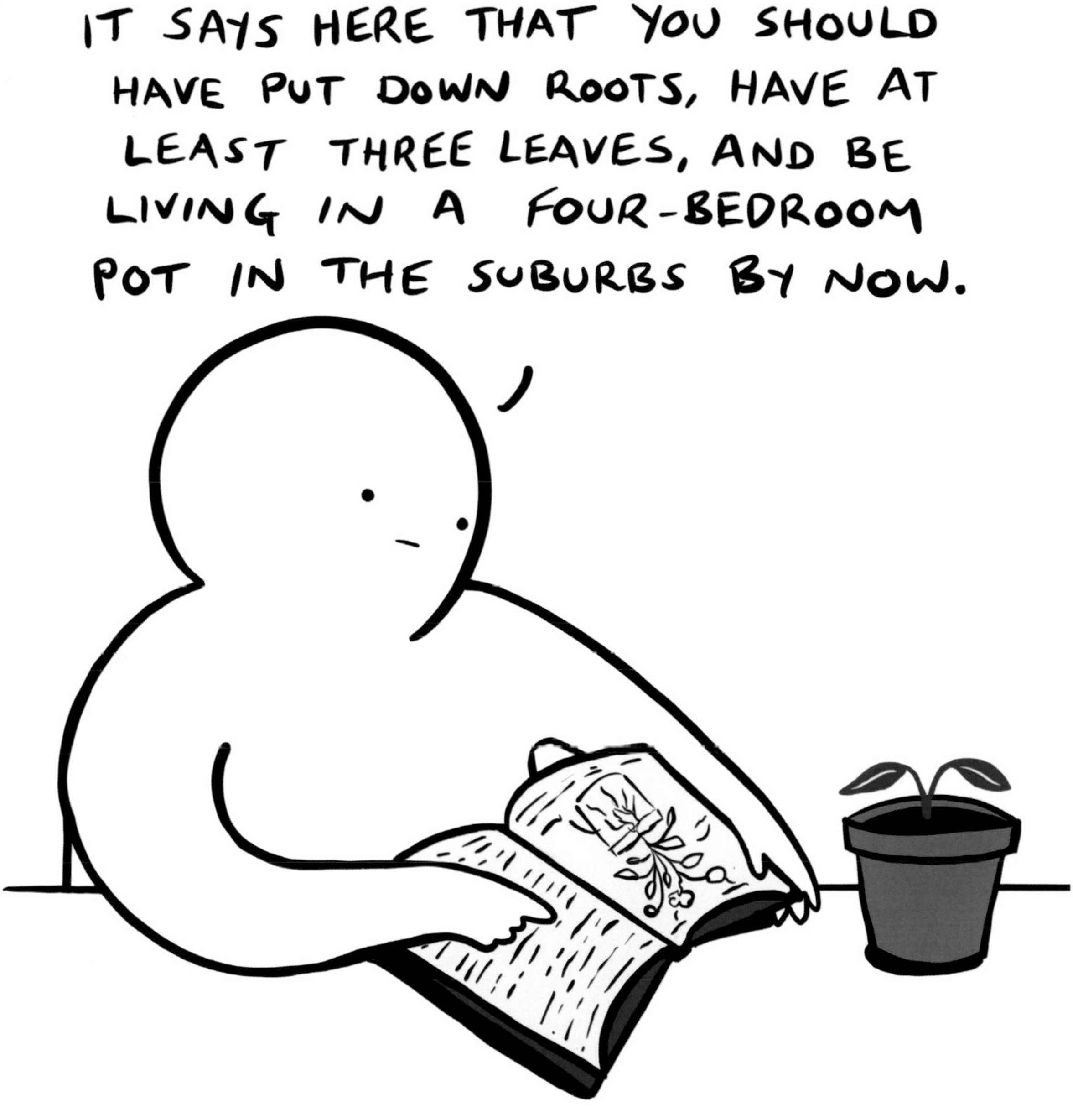
IT SAYS HERE THAT YOU SHOULD HAVE PUT DOWN ROOTS, HAVE AT LEAST THREE LEAVES, AND BE LIVING IN A FOUR-BEDROOM POT IN THE SUBURBS BY NOW.

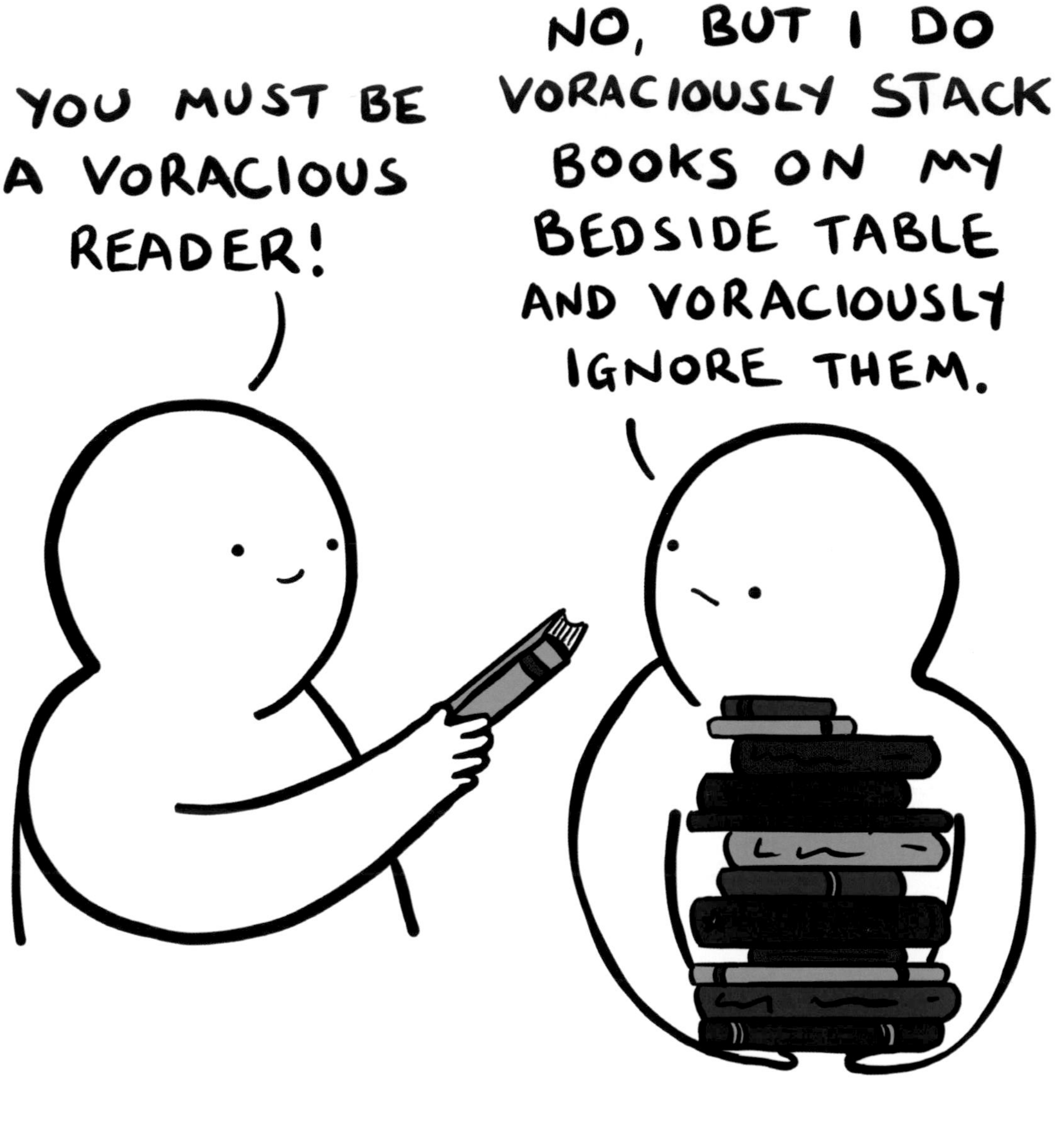
YOU MUST BE A VORACIOUS READER!
NO, BUT I DO VORACIOUSLY STACK BOOKS ON MY BEDSIDE TABLE AND VORACIOUSLY IGNORE THEM.

OF ALL MY QUESTIONABLE COPING STRATEGIES,

COFFEE IS MY FAVOURITE.

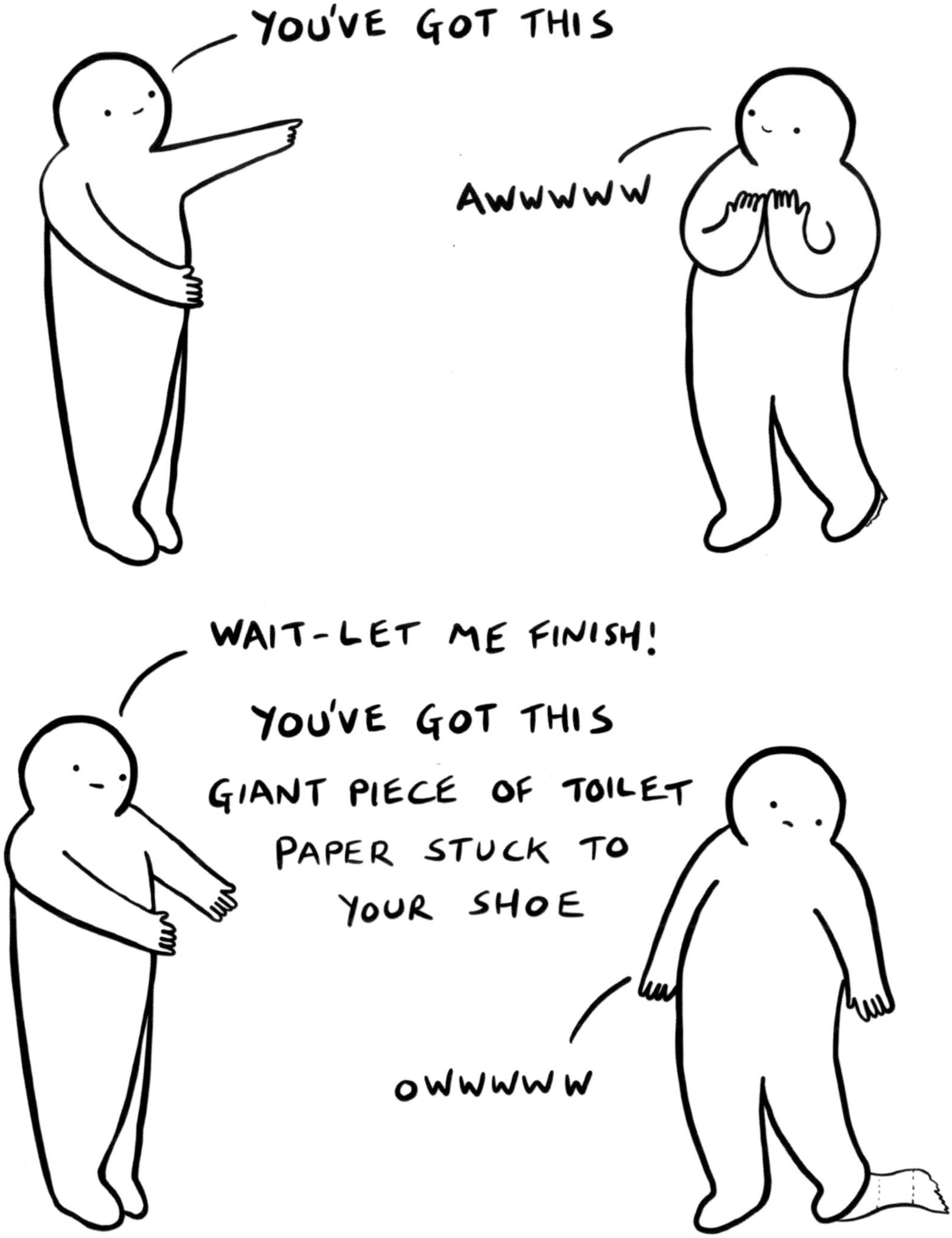
YOU'VE GOT THIS
AWWWWW
WAIT-LET ME FINISH!
YOU'VE GOT THIS
GIANT PIECE OF TOILET
PAPER STUCK TO
YOUR SHOE
OWWWWW

IF ADOPTING THE LIFESTYLE
OF THE THREE-TOED SLOTH
IS WRONG, I DON'T WANT
TO BE RIGHT.

I DID IT! I HAD A GROWN-UP CONVERSATION!
I SET BOUNDARIES! I EXPRESSED NEEDS!
I WAS OPEN AND HONEST ABOUT MY FEELINGS!
OH MY GOD IT WAS SO STRESSFUL! NEVER AGAIN!

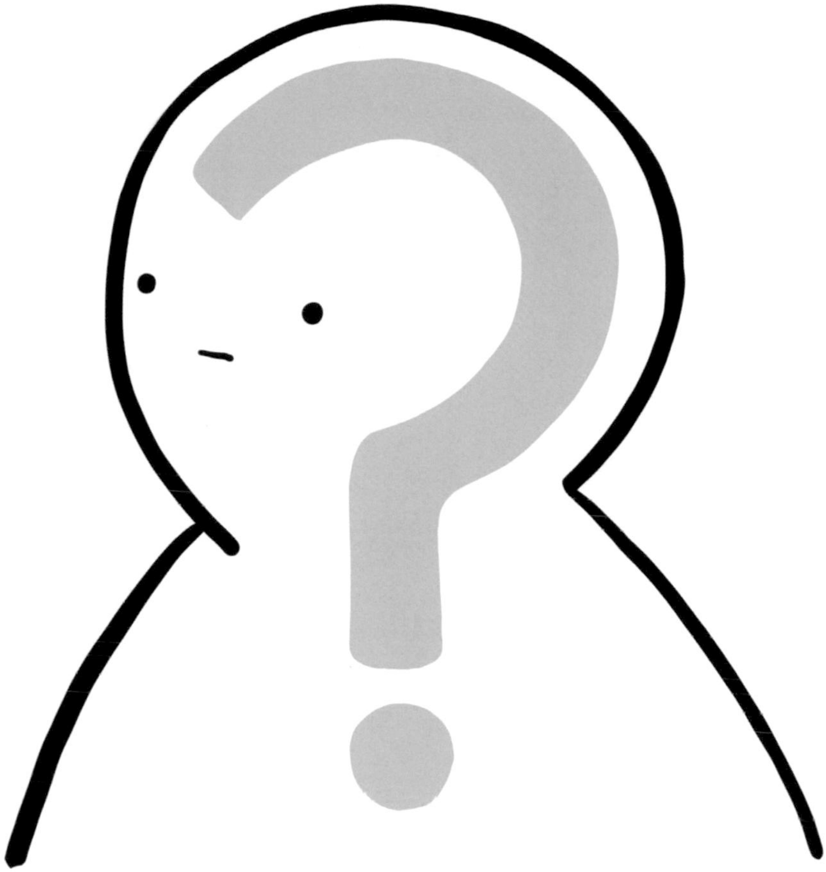

DOES ANYONE ACTUALLY KNOW WHAT THEY'RE DOING, OR IS EVERYONE PRETENDING?

ROSES ARE RED AND SO ARE FLAGS

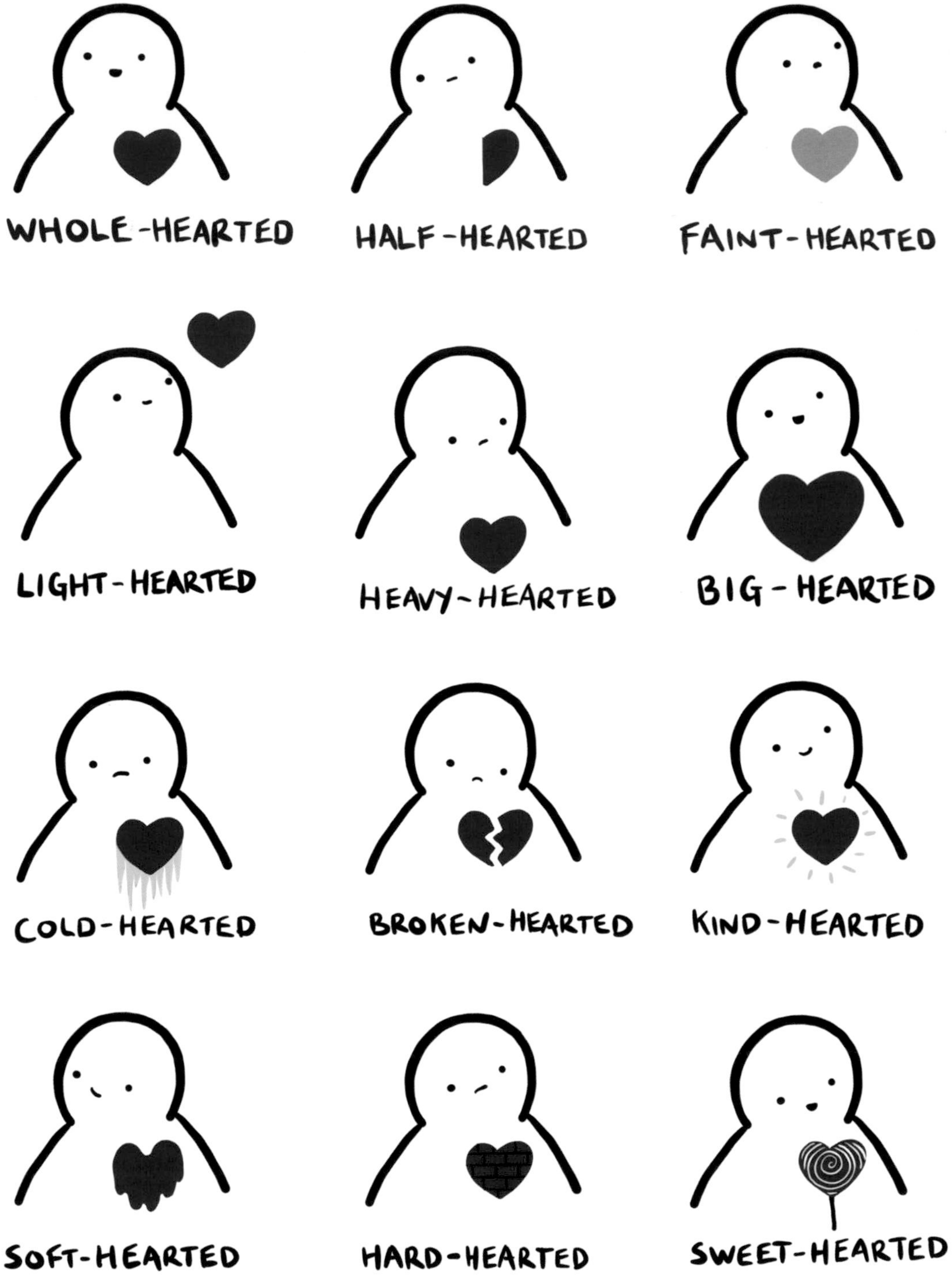
WHOLE-HEARTED
HALF-HEARTED
FAINT-HEARTED
LIGHT-HEARTED
HEAVY-HEARTED
BIG-HEARTED
COLD-HEARTED
BROKEN-HEARTED
KIND-HEARTED
SOFT-HEARTED
HARD-HEARTED
SWEET-HEARTED

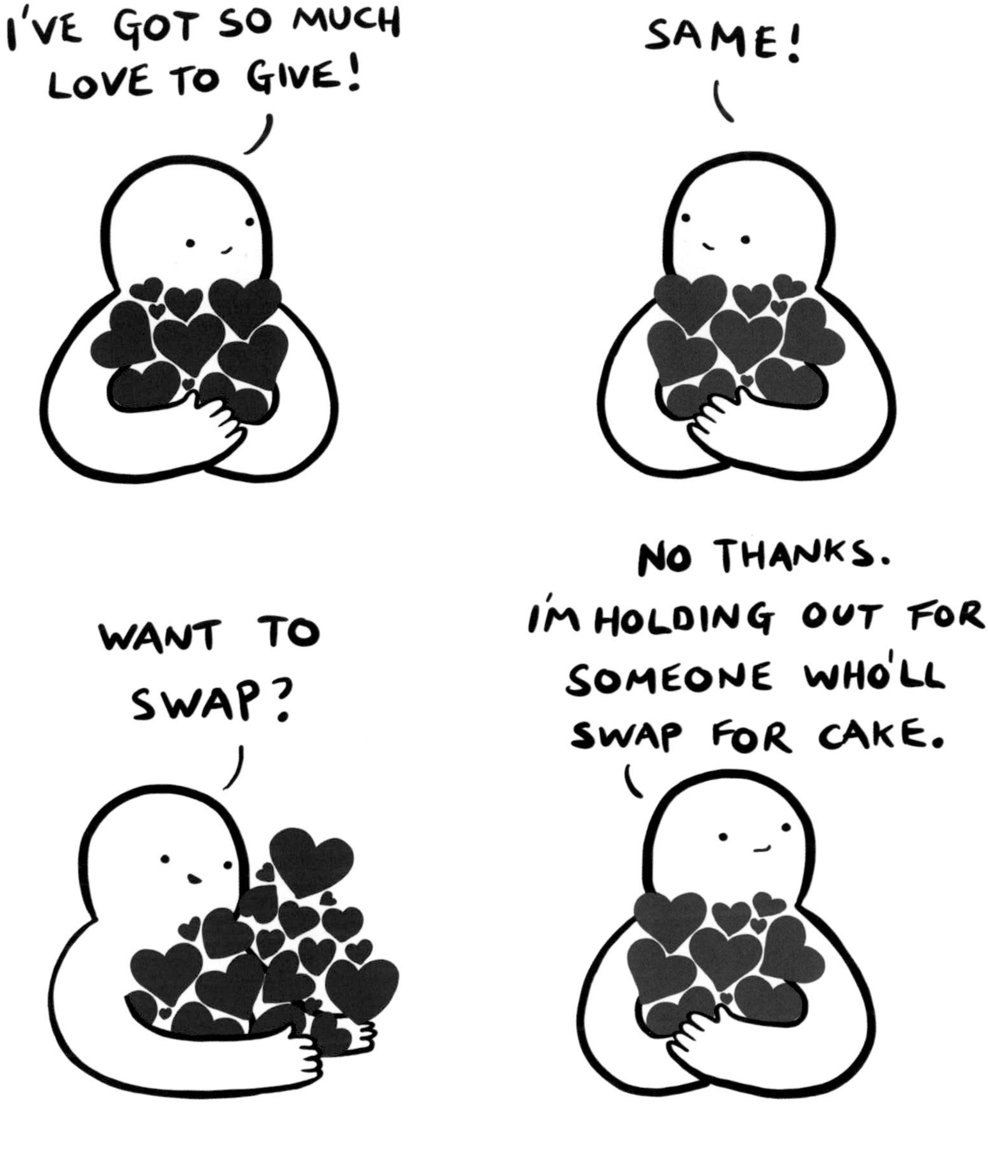
I'VE GOT SO MUCH LOVE TO GIVE!
SAME!
WANT TO SWAP?
NO THANKS. I'M HOLDING OUT FOR SOMEONE WHO'LL SWAP FOR CAKE.

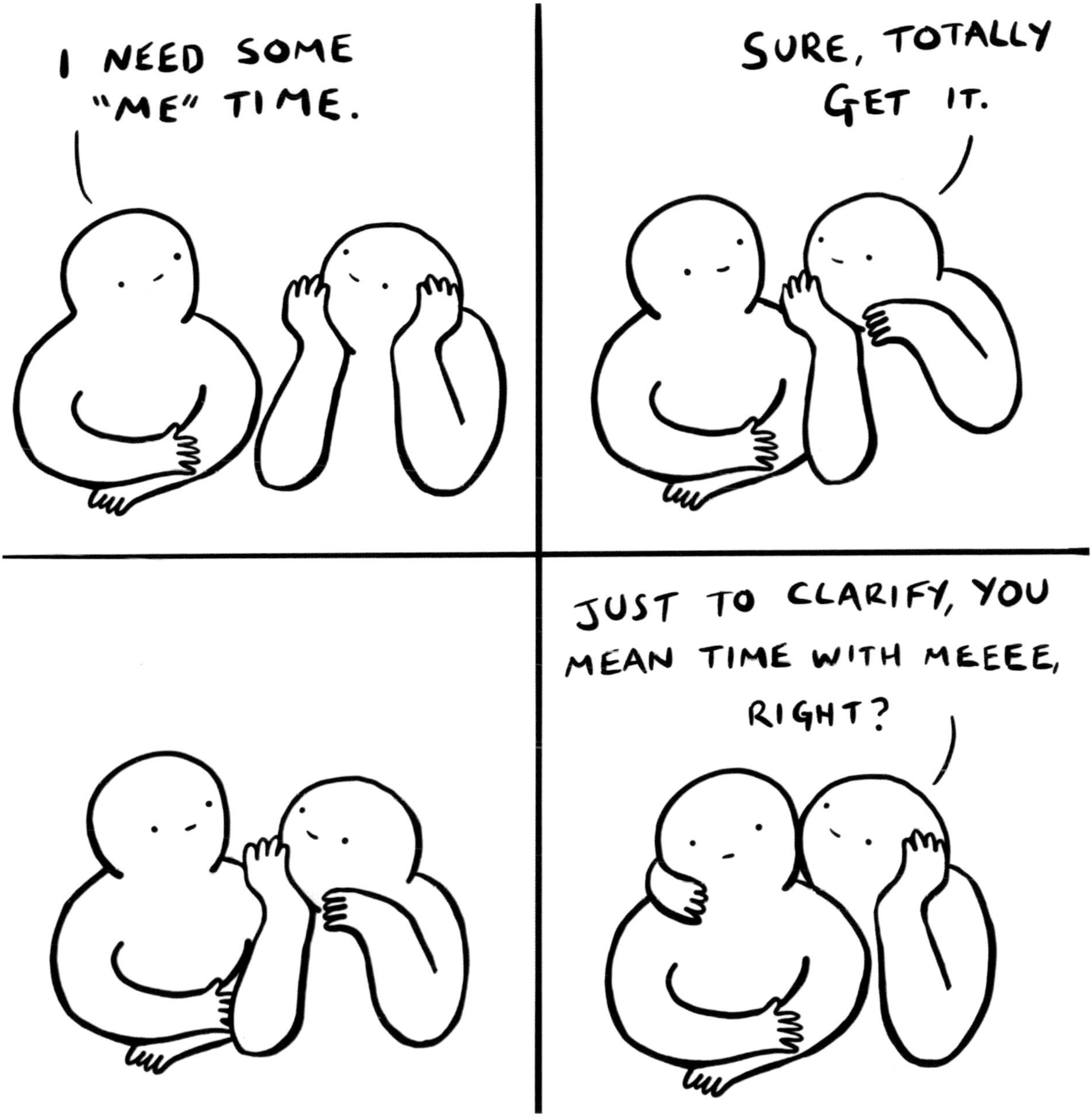
I NEED SOME "ME" TIME.
SURE, TOTALLY GET IT.
JUST TO CLARIFY, YOU MEAN TIME WITH MEEEE, RIGHT?

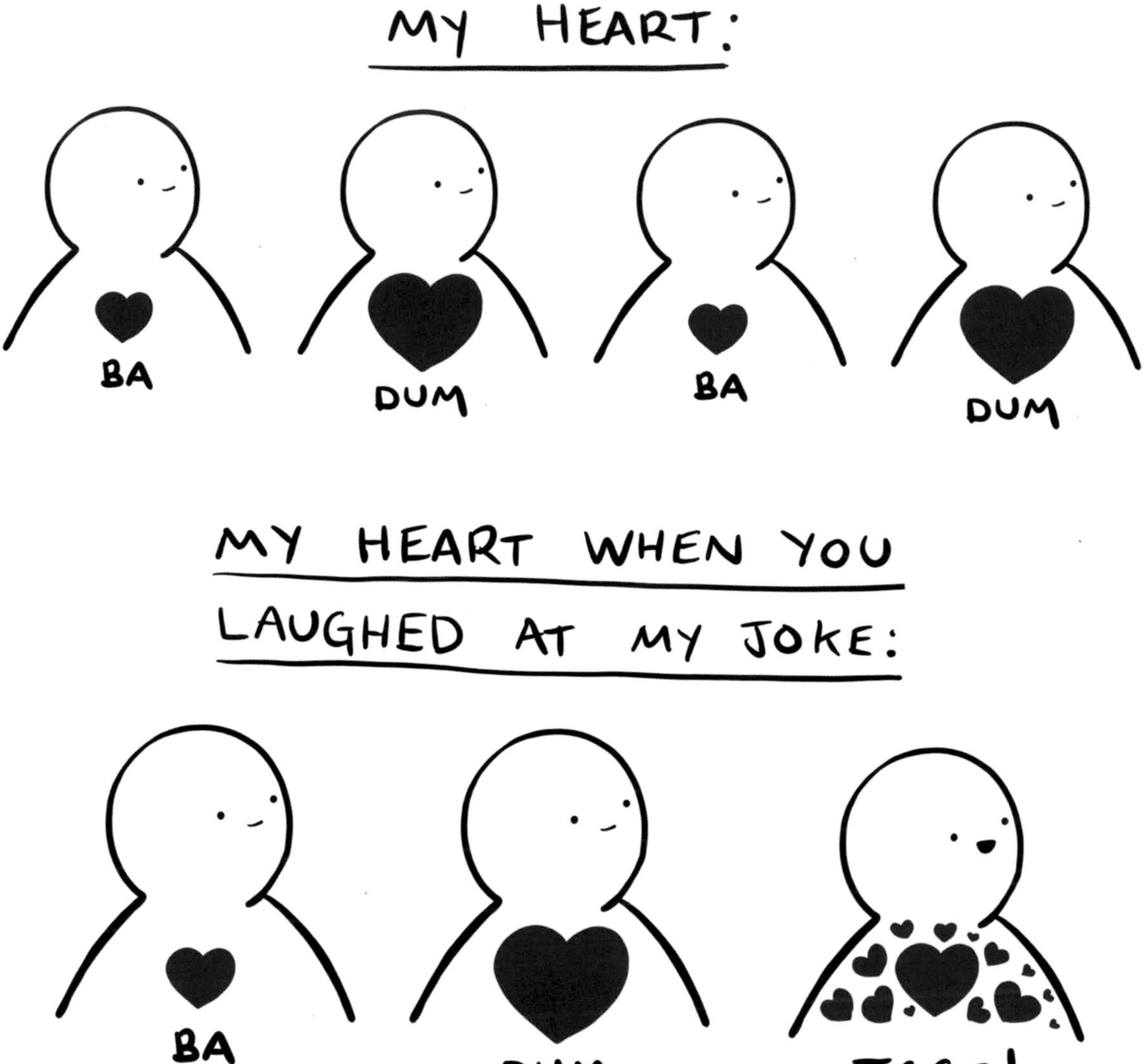
MY HEART:
BA
DUM
BA
DUM
MY HEART WHEN YOU LAUGHED AT MY JOKE:
BA
DUM
TSSS!

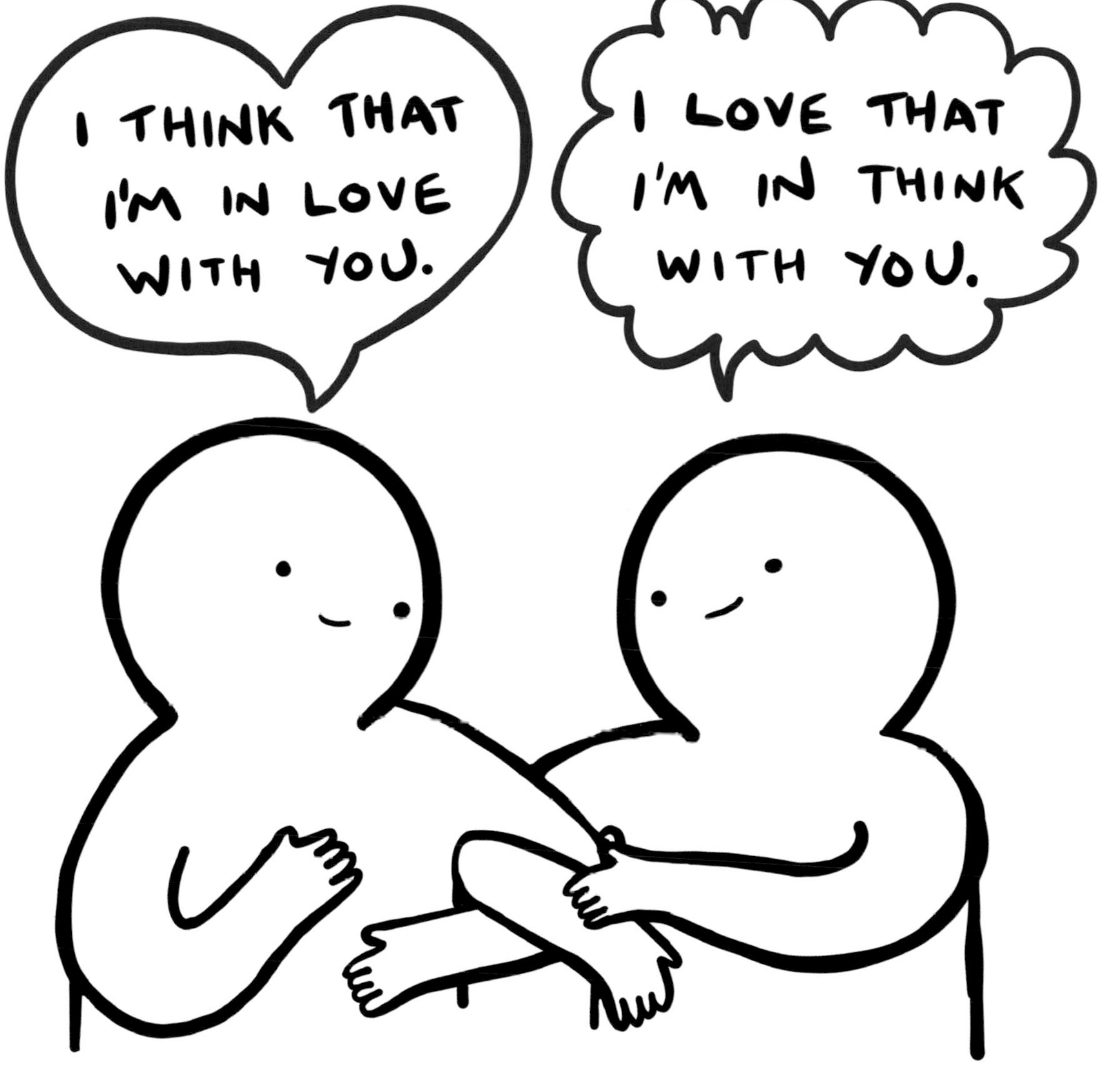
I THINK THAT I'M IN LOVE WITH YOU.
I LOVE THAT I'M IN THINK WITH YOU.

PLEASE STAND STILL—
I'M TRYING TO PROJECT ALL
MY INSECURITIES ONTO YOU.

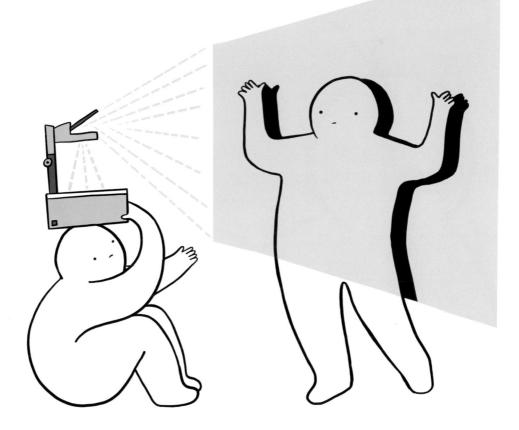

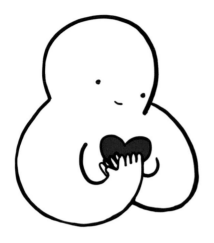

LOVE

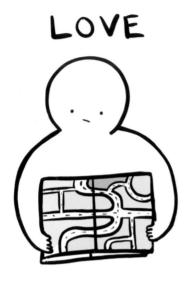

WILL

FIND

A WAY.

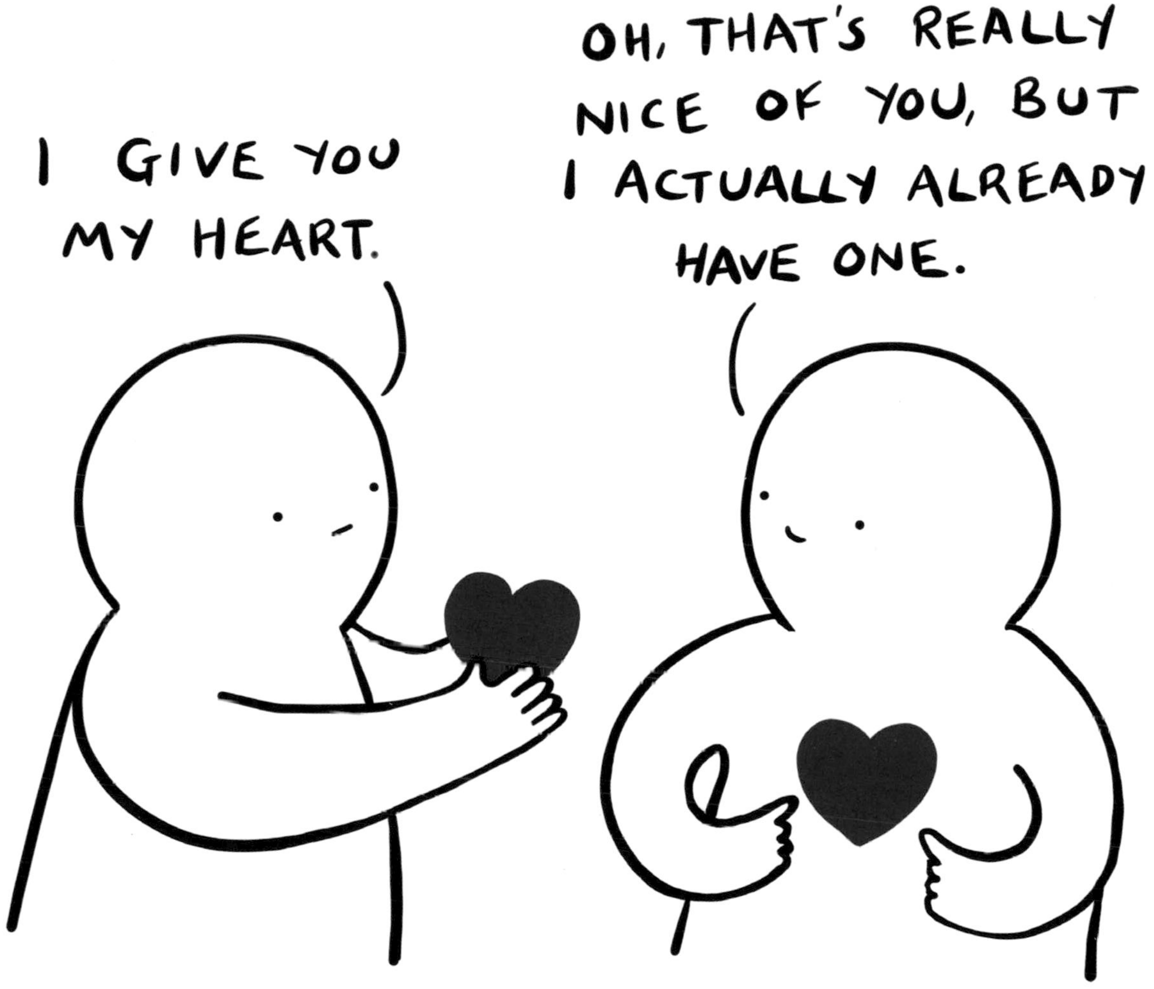
I GIVE YOU MY HEART.
OH, THAT'S REALLY NICE OF YOU, BUT I ACTUALLY ALREADY HAVE ONE.

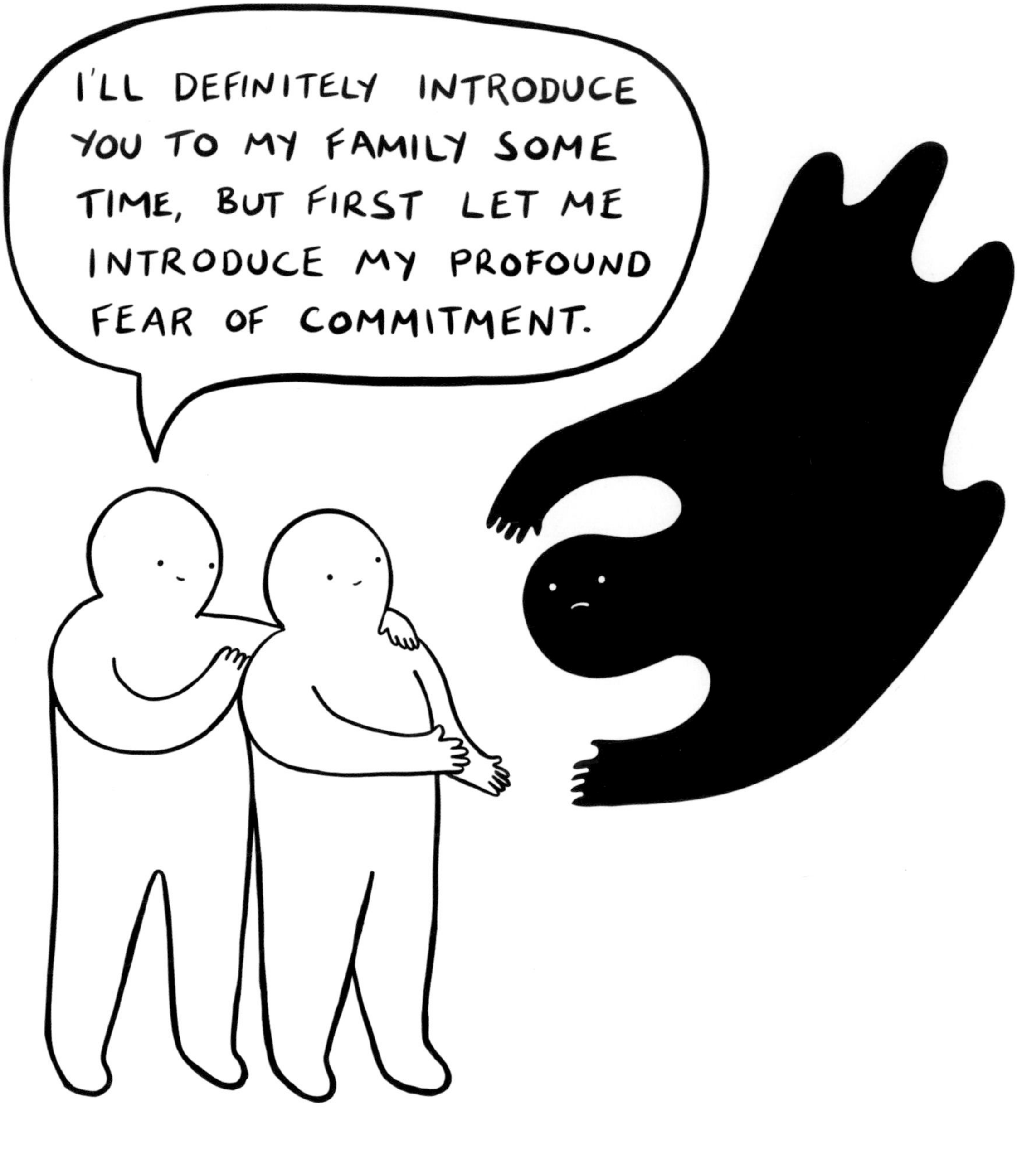
I'LL DEFINITELY INTRODUCE YOU TO MY FAMILY SOME TIME, BUT FIRST LET ME INTRODUCE MY PROFOUND FEAR OF COMMITMENT.

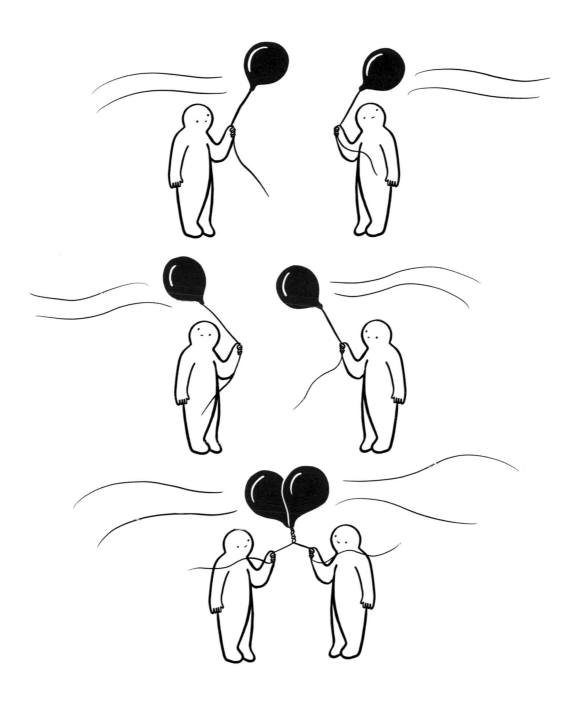

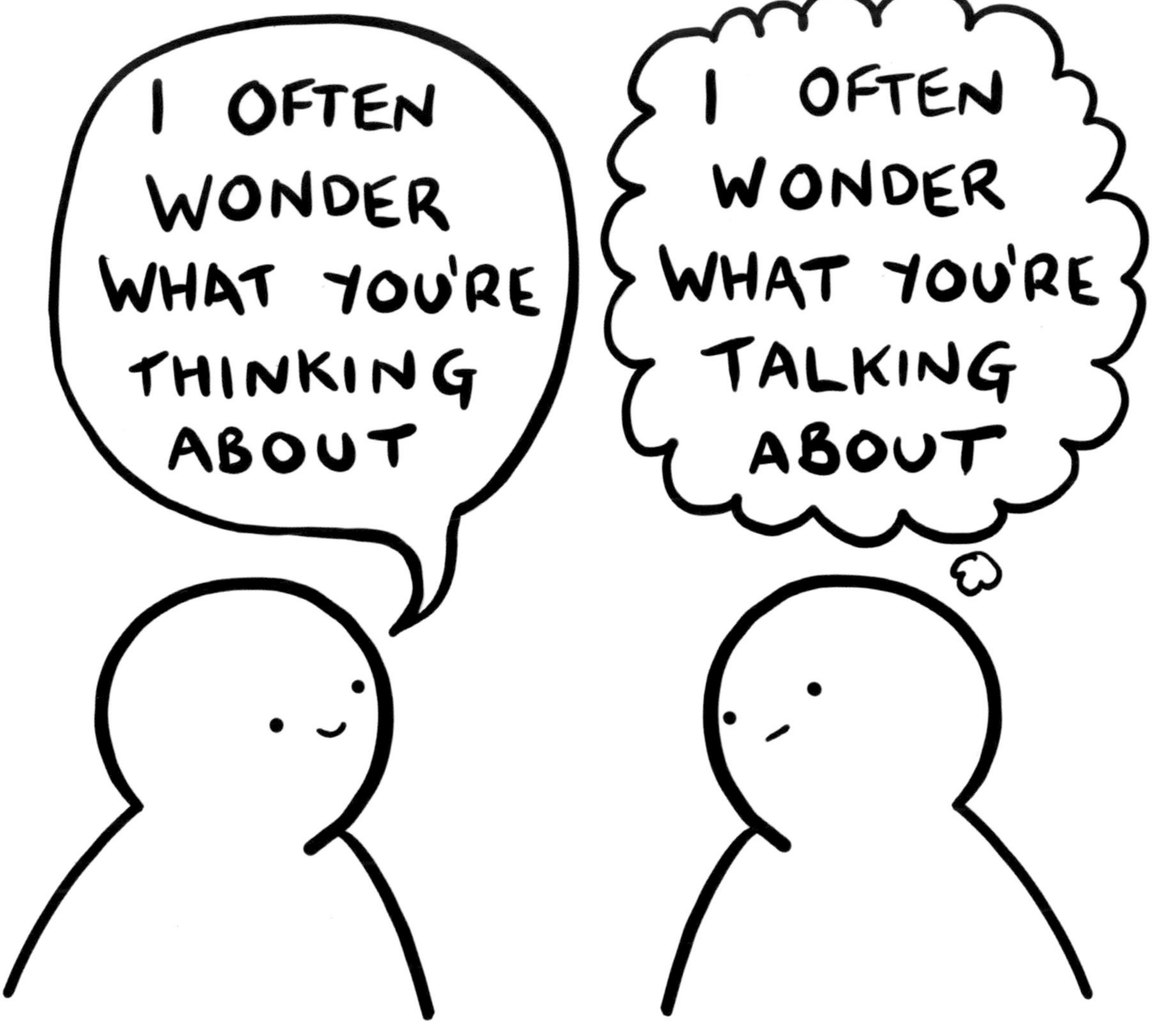
I OFTEN WONDER WHAT YOU'RE THINKING ABOUT
I OFTEN WONDER WHAT YOU'RE TALKING ABOUT

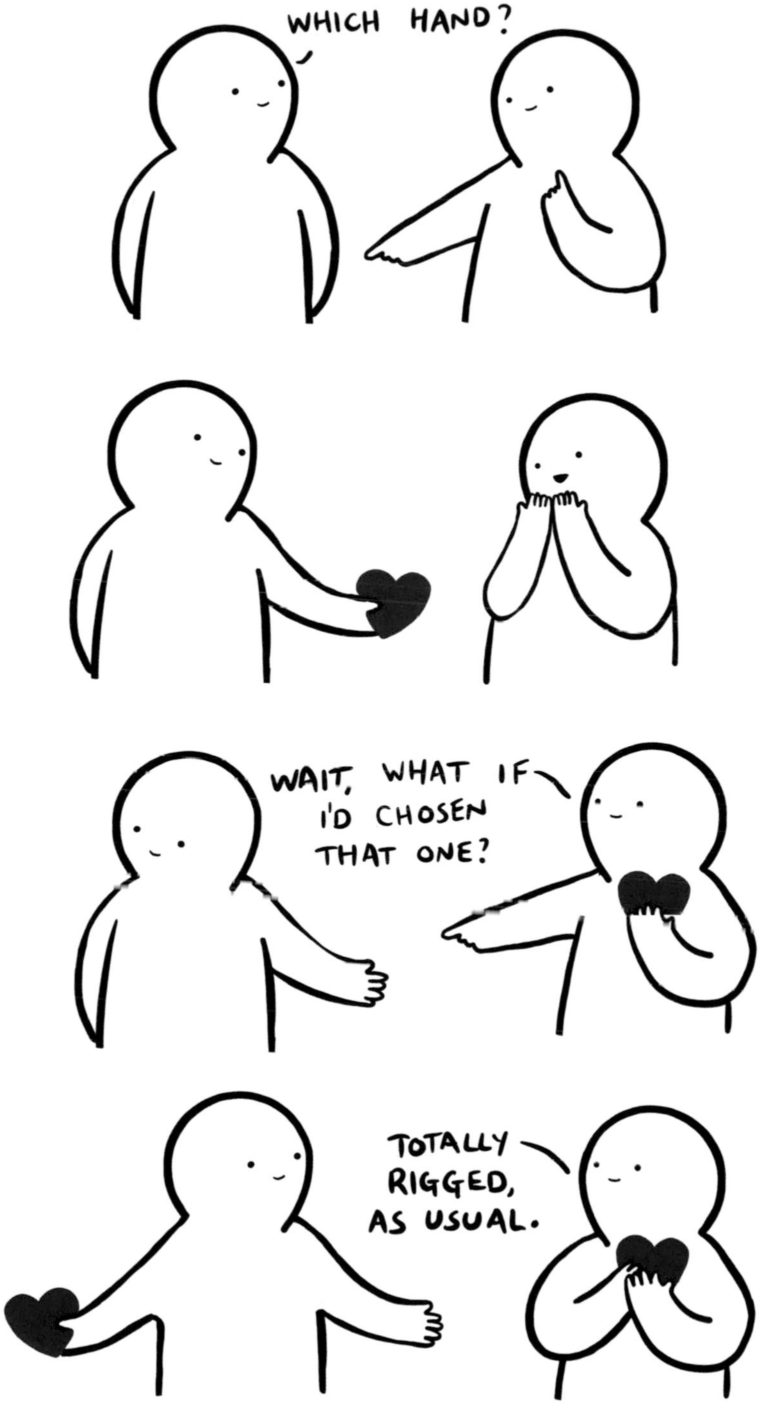
WHICH HAND?
WAIT, WHAT IF I'D CHOSEN THAT ONE?
TOTALLY RIGGED, AS USUAL.

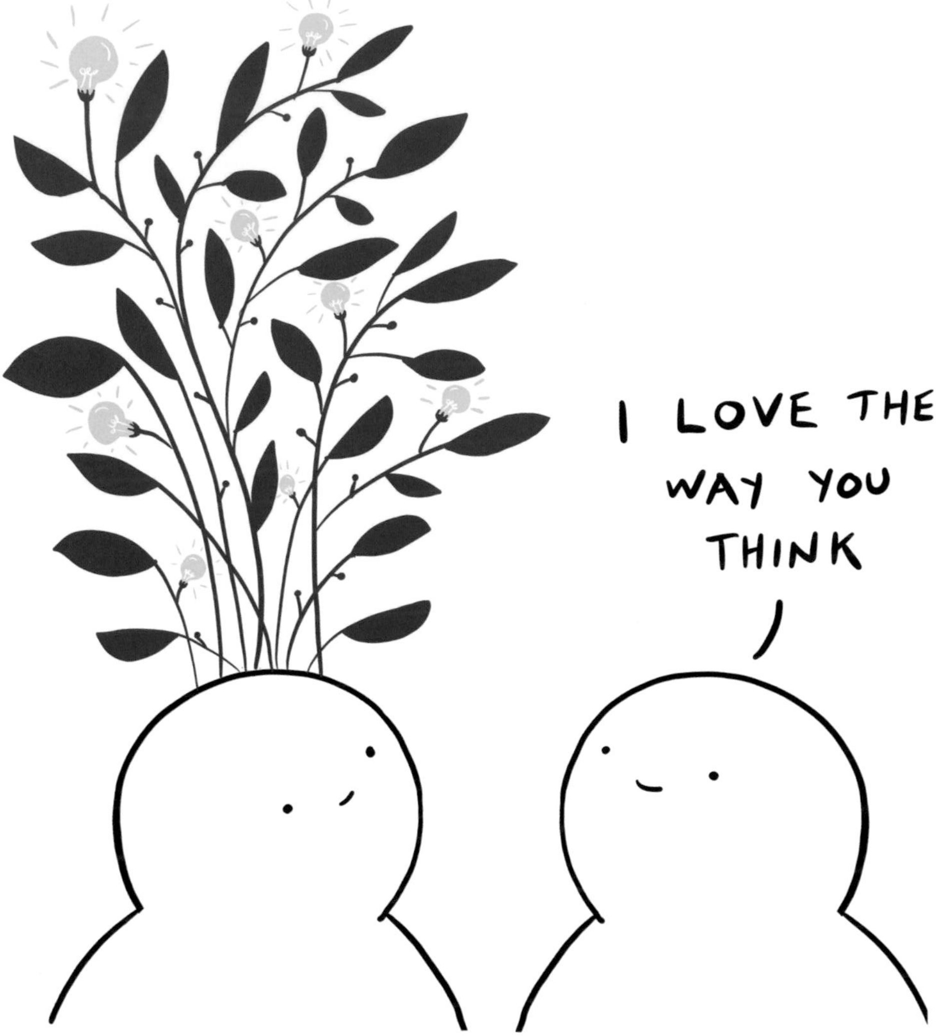
I LOVE THE WAY YOU THINK

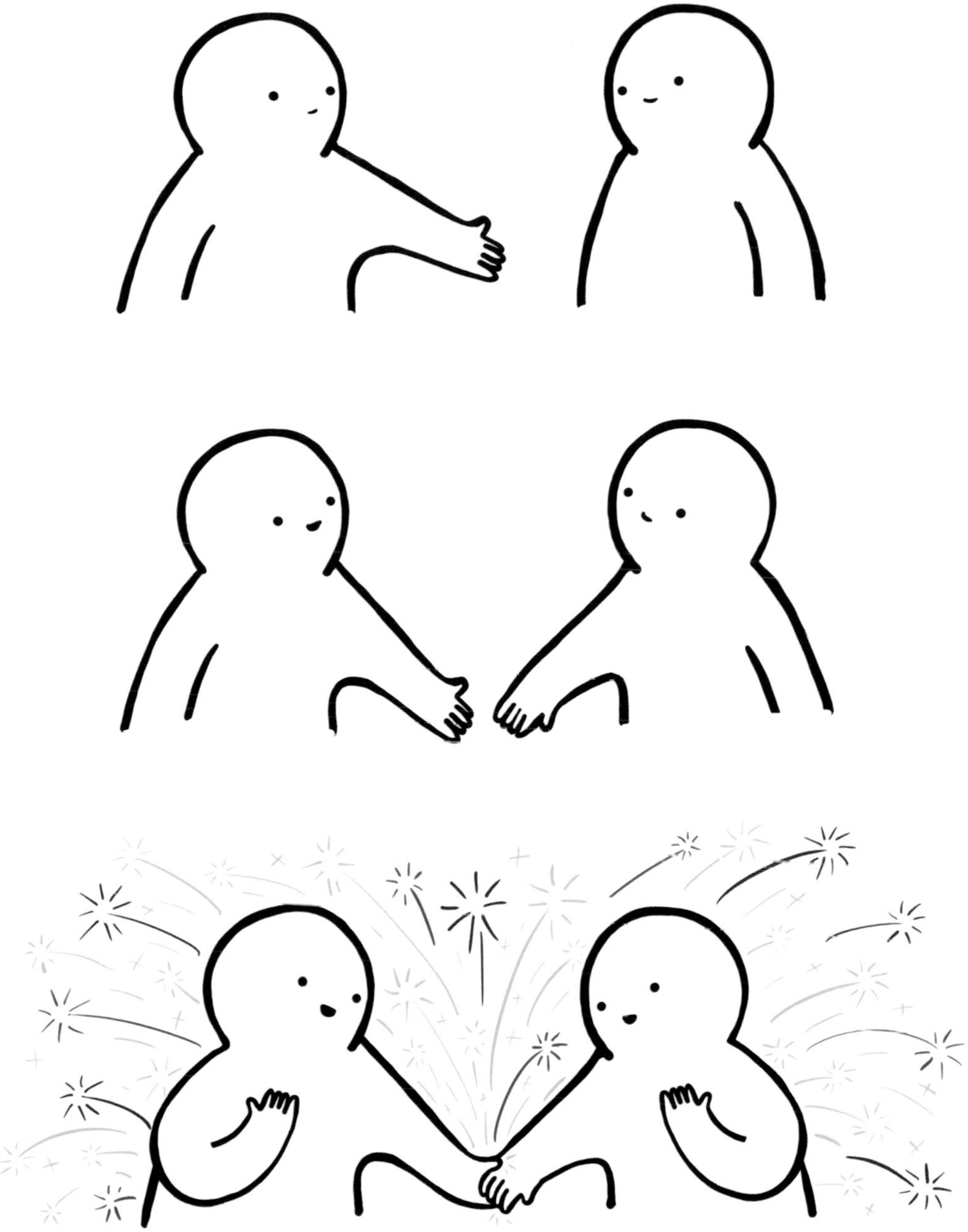

OUT OF OFFICE

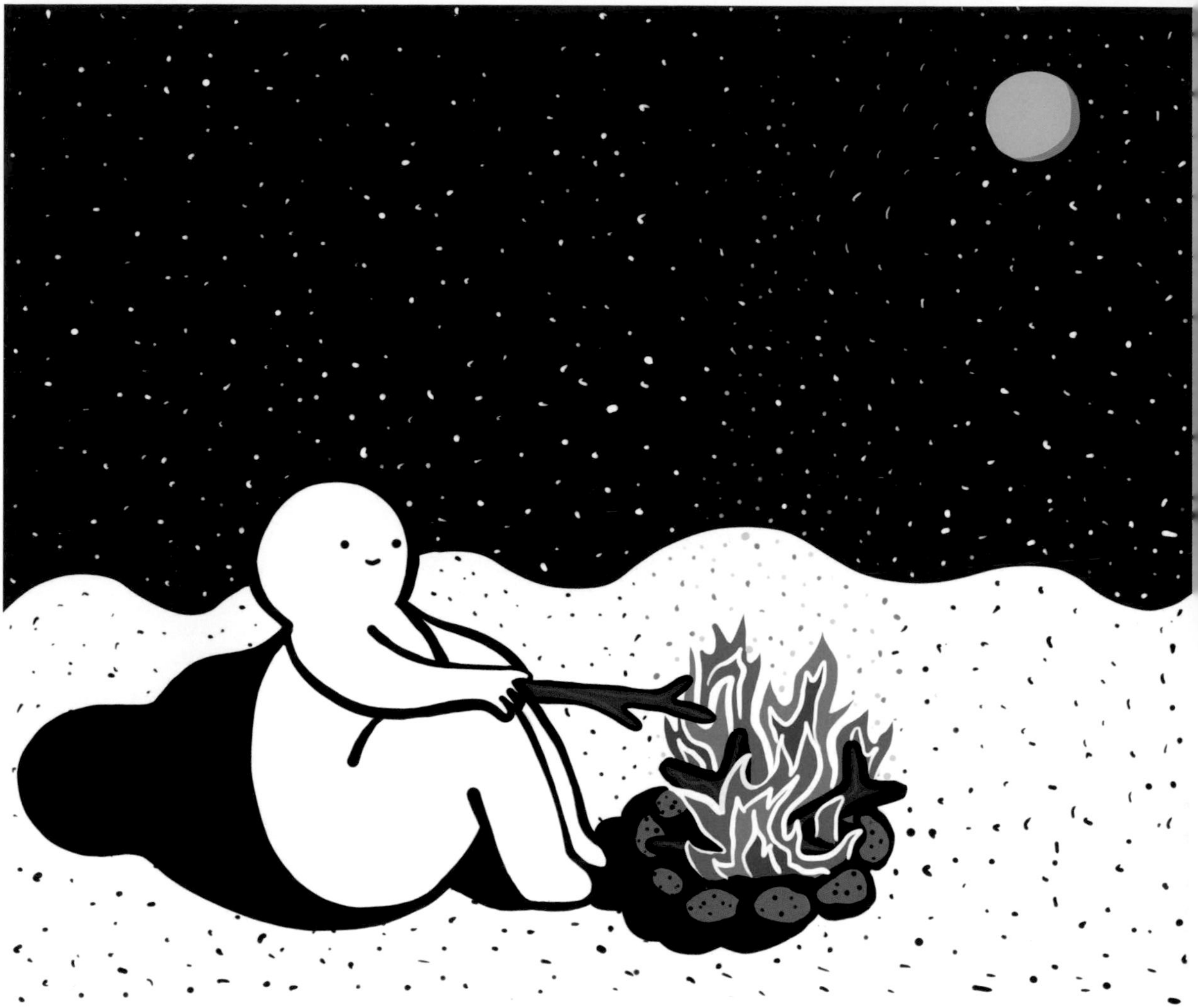

THANKS FOR YOUR EMAIL.

I AM CURRENTLY
OUT OF THE OFFICE.

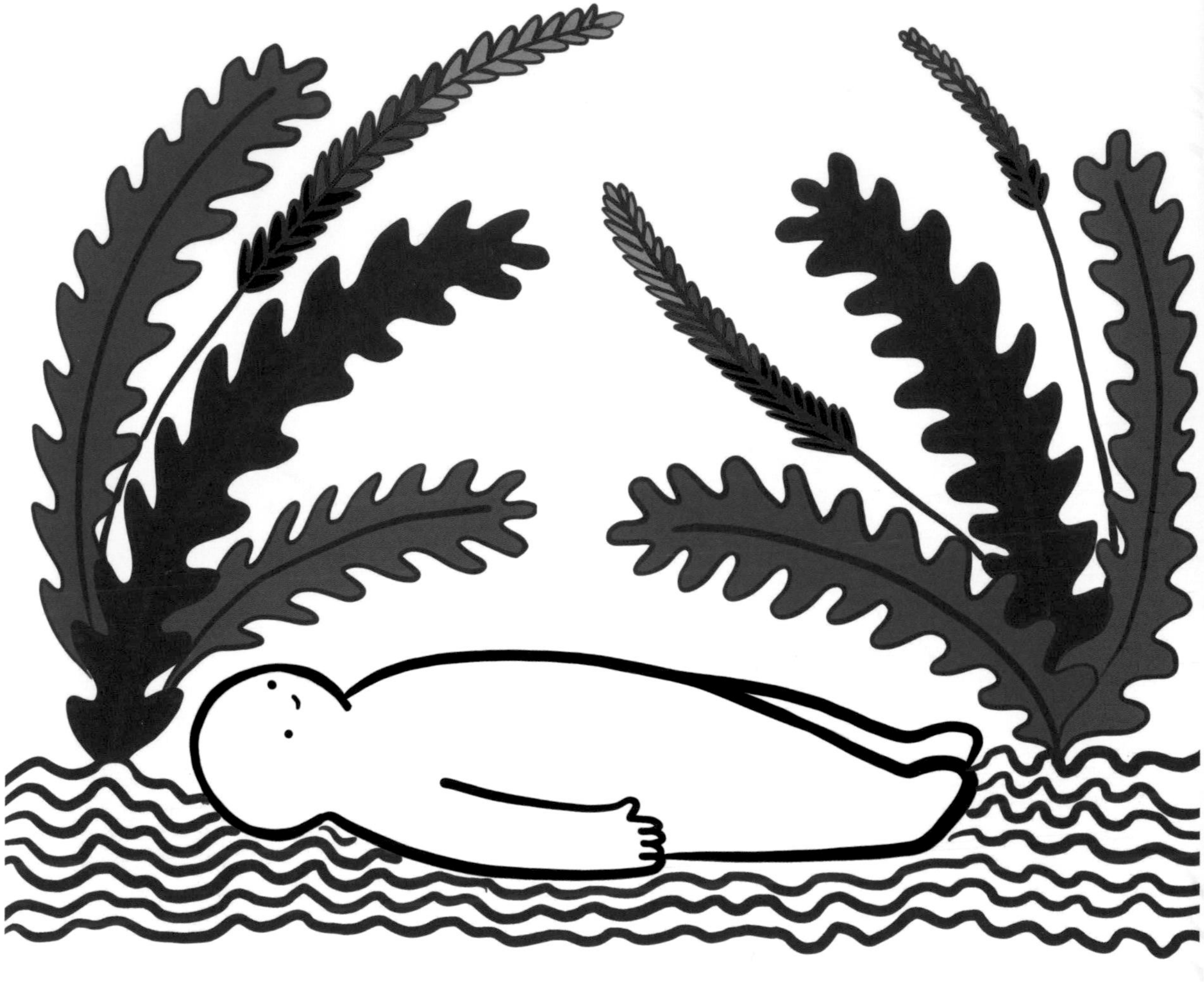

I HAVE DECIDED TO RUN AWAY AND LIVE WITH THE PLANTS.

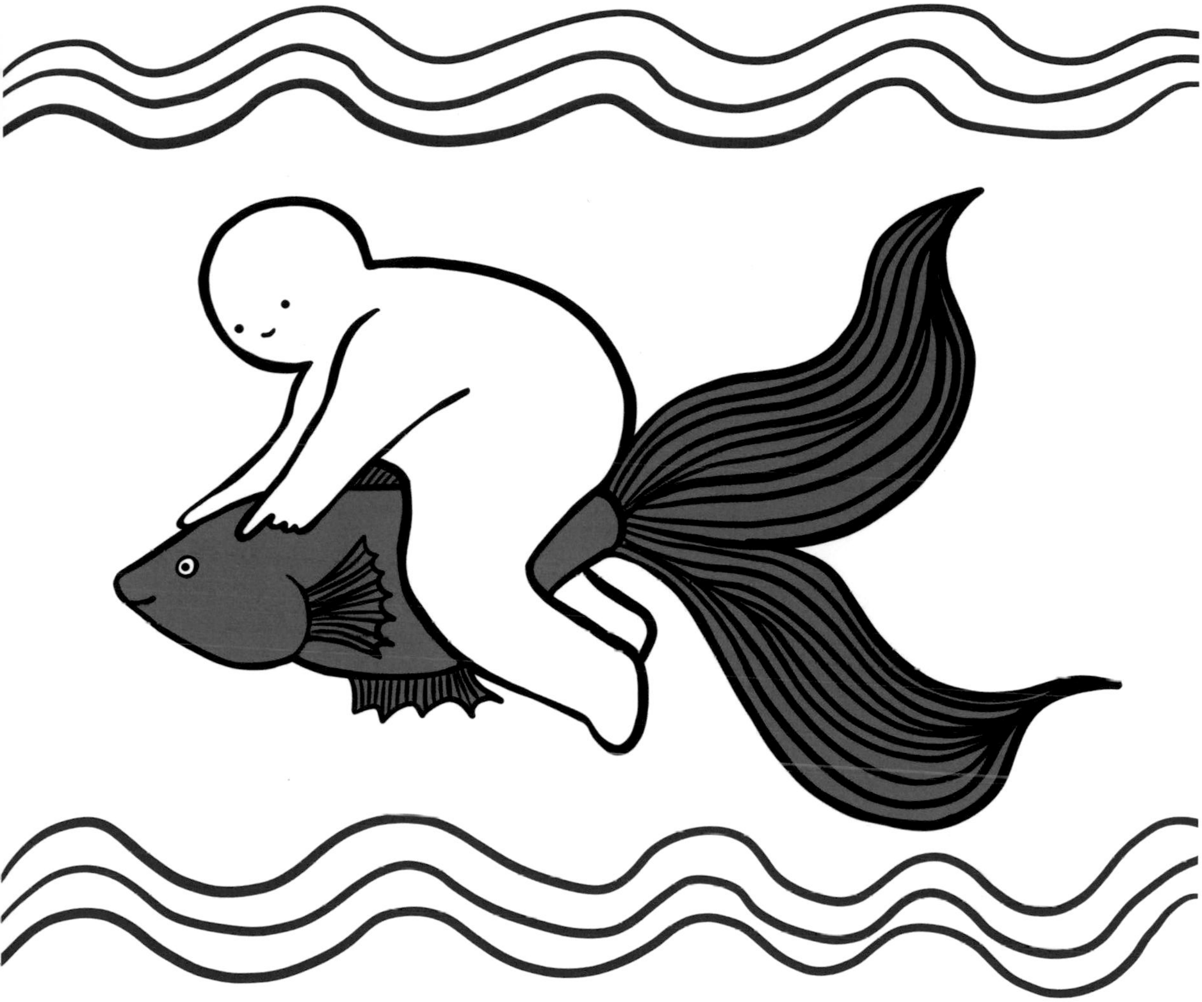

OR PERHAPS THE FISH,

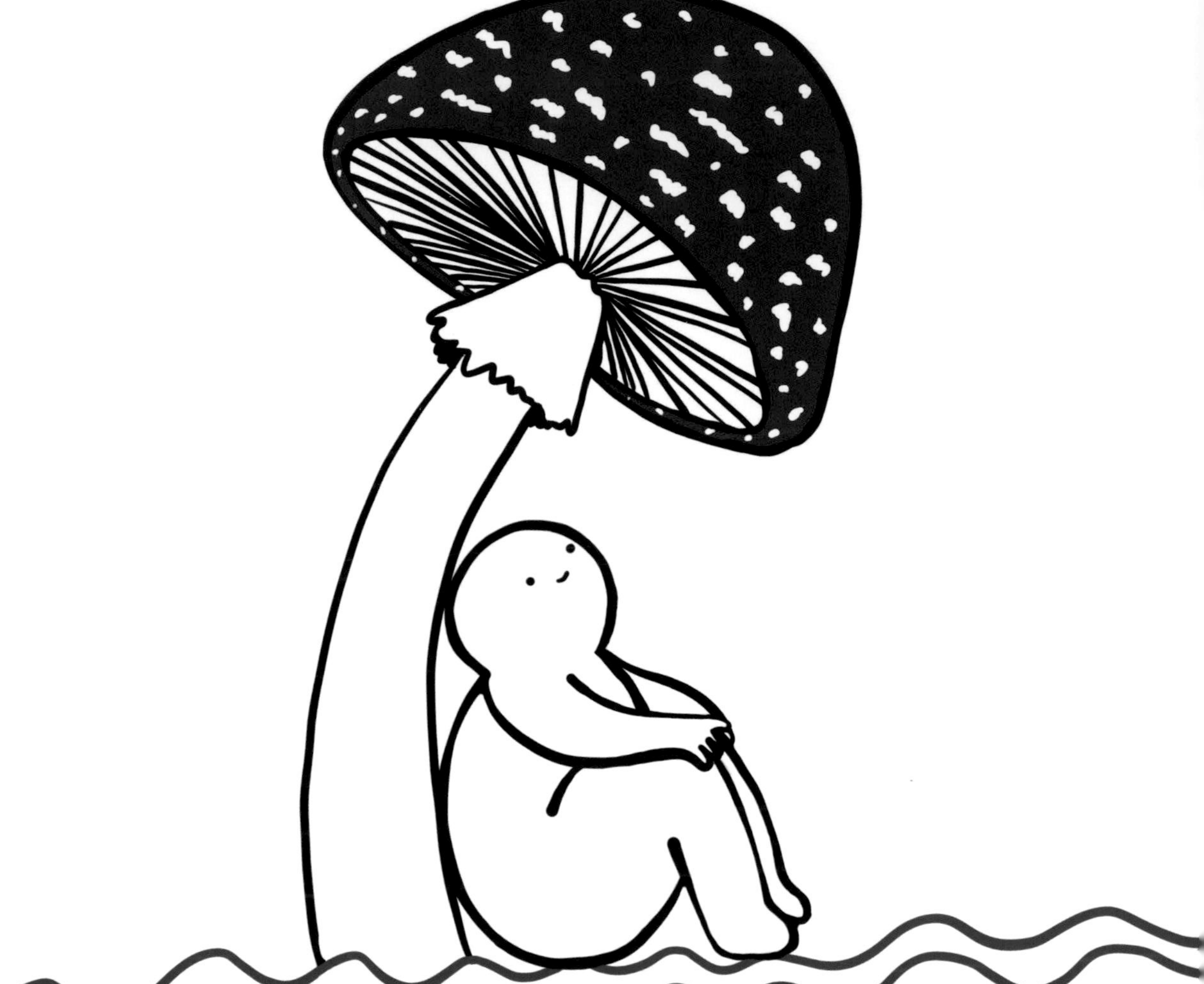

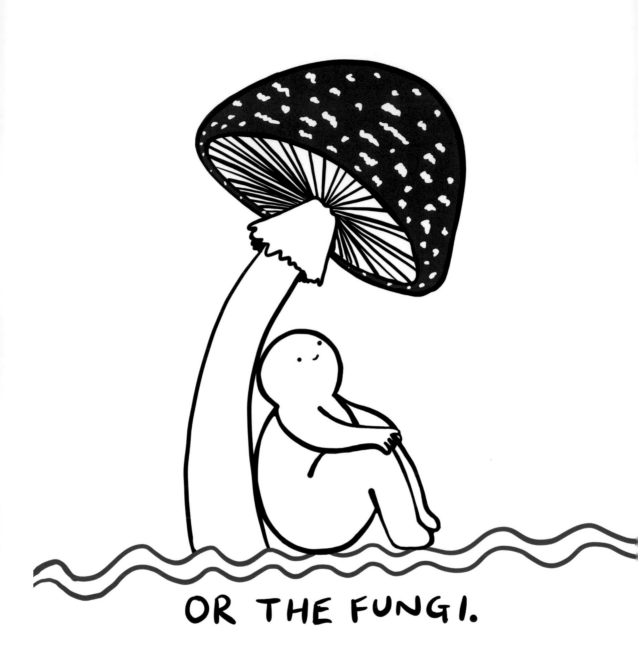

OR THE FUNGI.

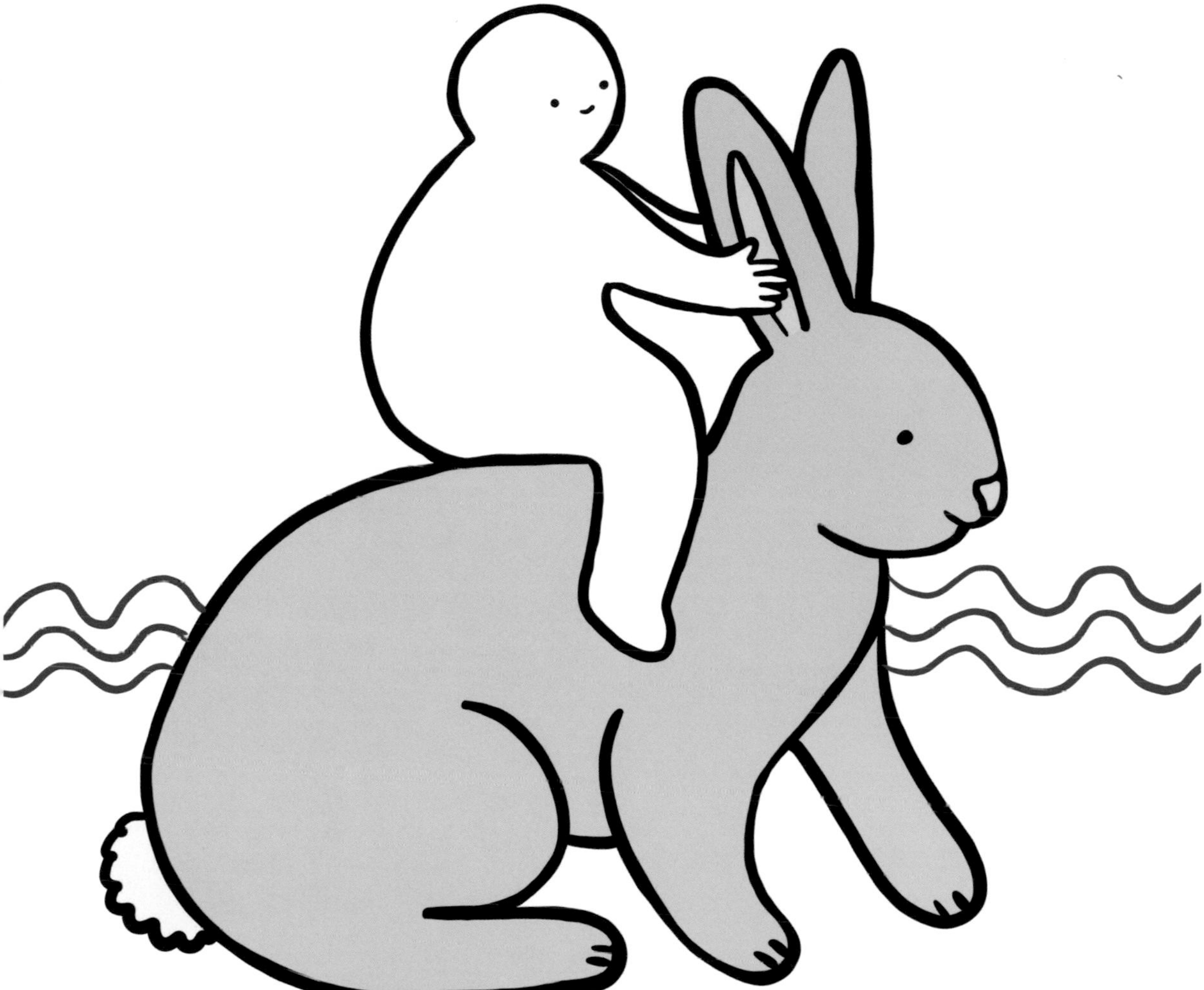

SINCERE APOLOGIES FOR
ANY INCONVENIENCE CAUSED.

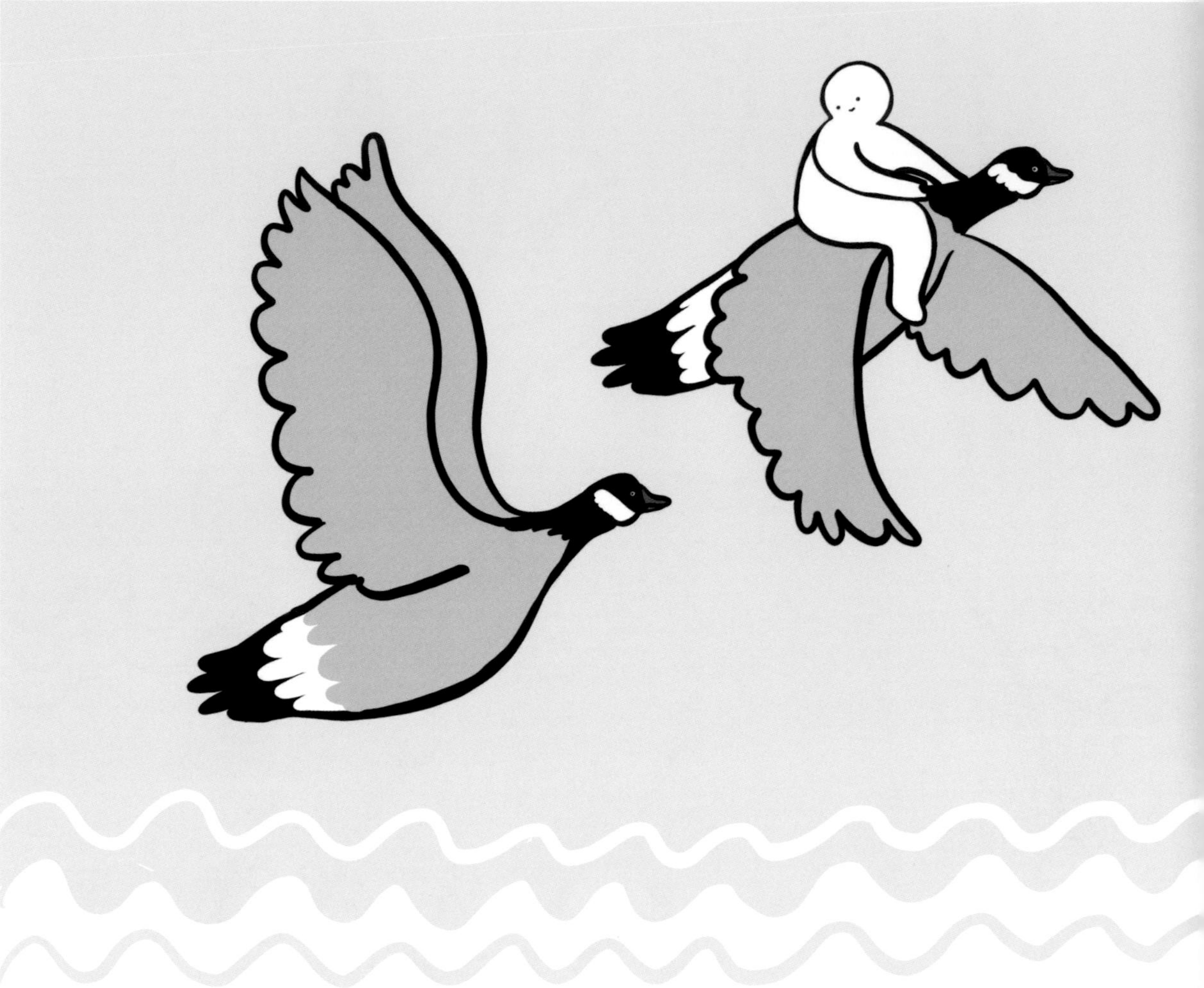

IF THE MATTER IS URGENT,

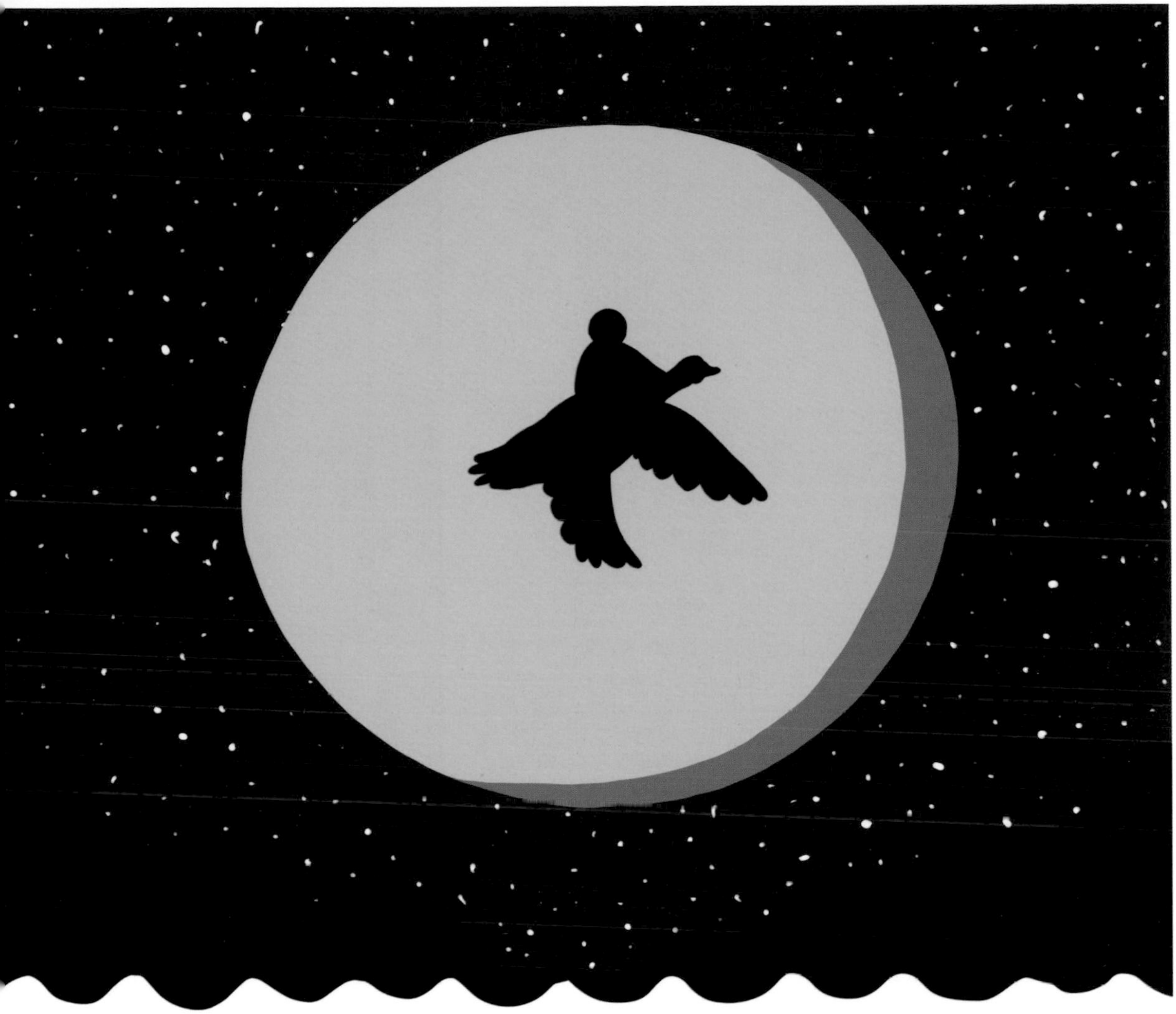

PLEASE CONTACT RECEPTION.

PUTTING THE SIGH IN HINDSIGHT

I PUT THE FUN
IN DYSFUNCTIONAL,

THE RAD IN
SPORADIC,

THE ZING IN
CATASTROPHIZING,

AND THE SIGH
IN HINDSIGHT.

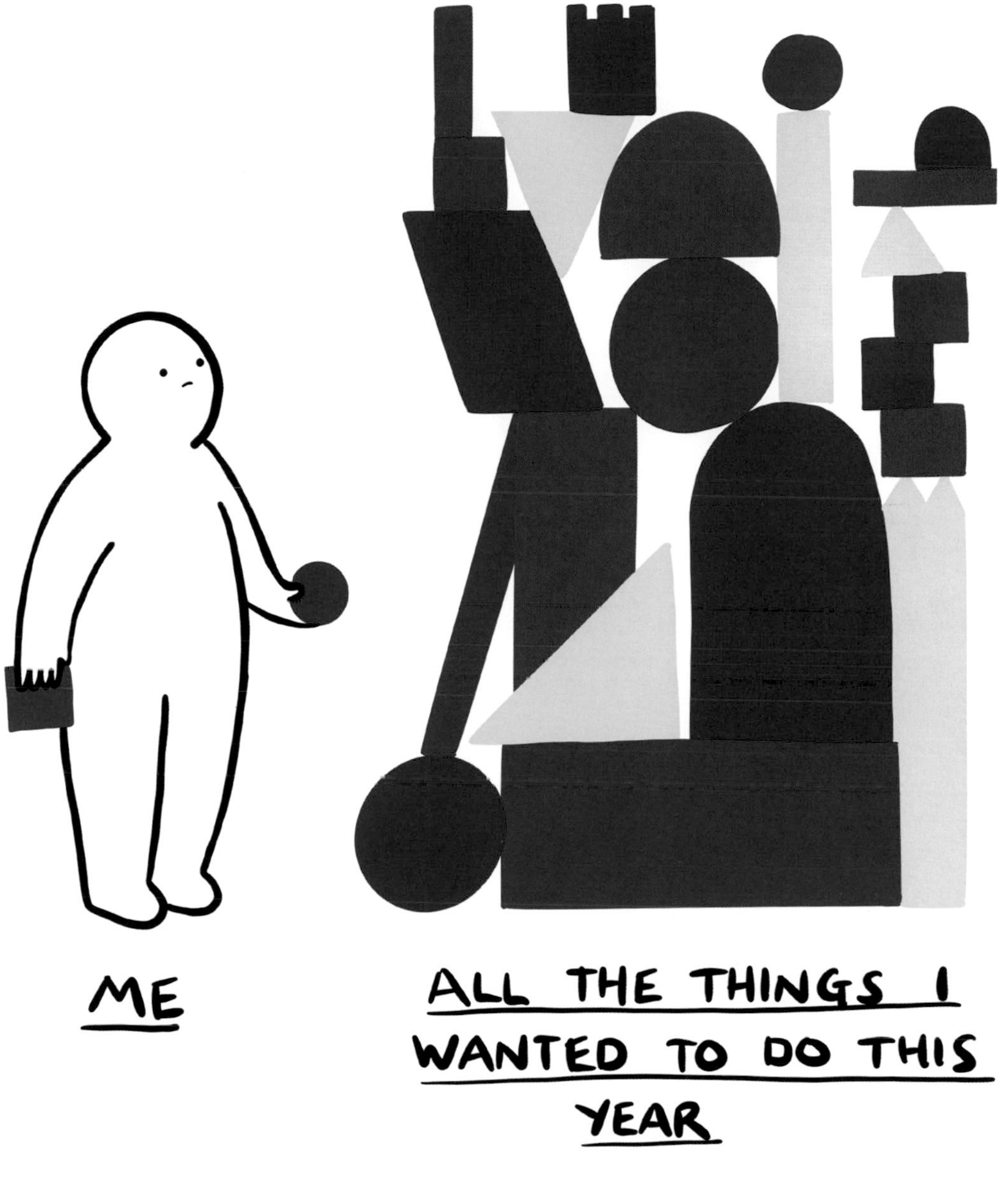
ME
ALL THE THINGS I WANTED TO DO THIS YEAR

THERE IS NO PAST,

THERE IS NO FUTURE,

THERE IS ONLY NOW.

MIGHT AS WELL TRY TO GET COMFORTABLE, MAYBE TAKE A NAP.

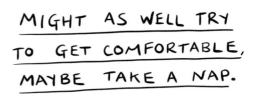

LIFE, LIKE A SAUSAGE DOG, IS

VERY LONG AND VERY SHORT,

COMPLETELY WONDERFUL
AND ABSOLUTELY RIDICULOUS.

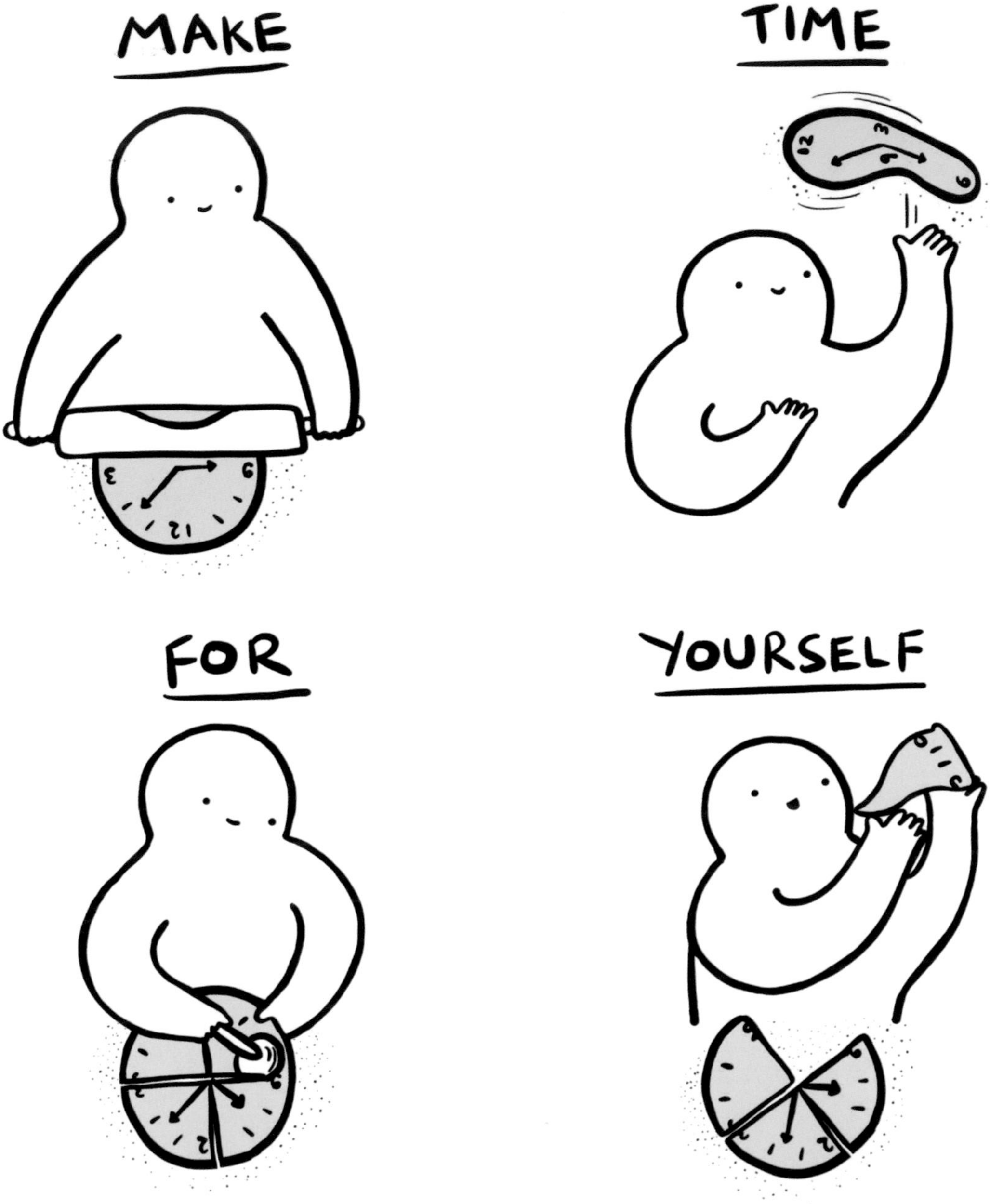
MAKE
TIME
FOR
YOURSELF

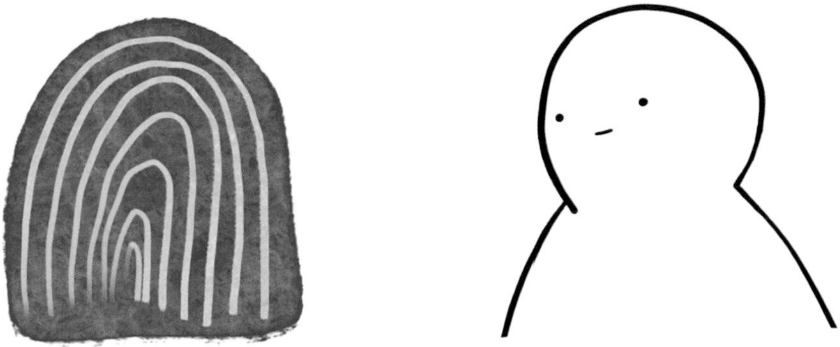

I THOUGHT MY PAST
WAS BEHIND ME,

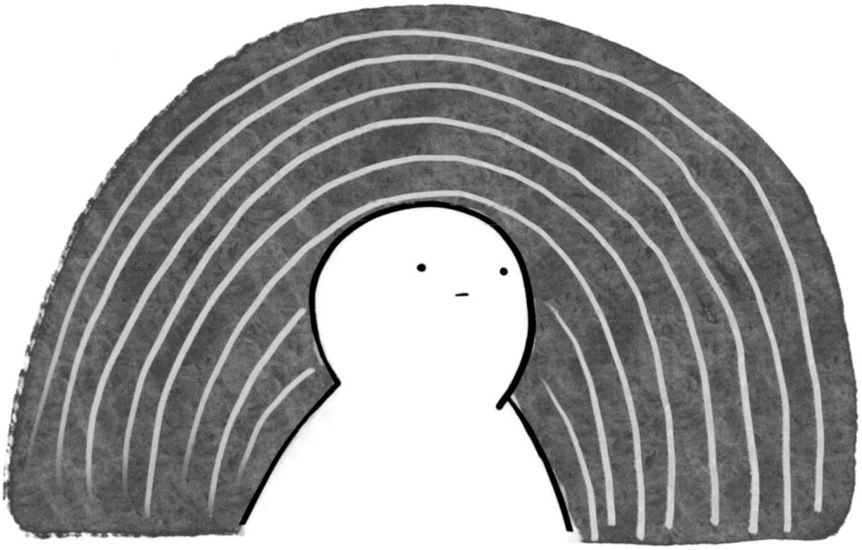

BUT IT TURNS OUT
MY PAST'S ALL AROUND ME.

I'M A

WORK

IN

PROGRESS

I WILL AGE
GRACEFULLY

LIKE A POTATO,

THE OLDER
I GET,

THE MORE
I'LL GROW.

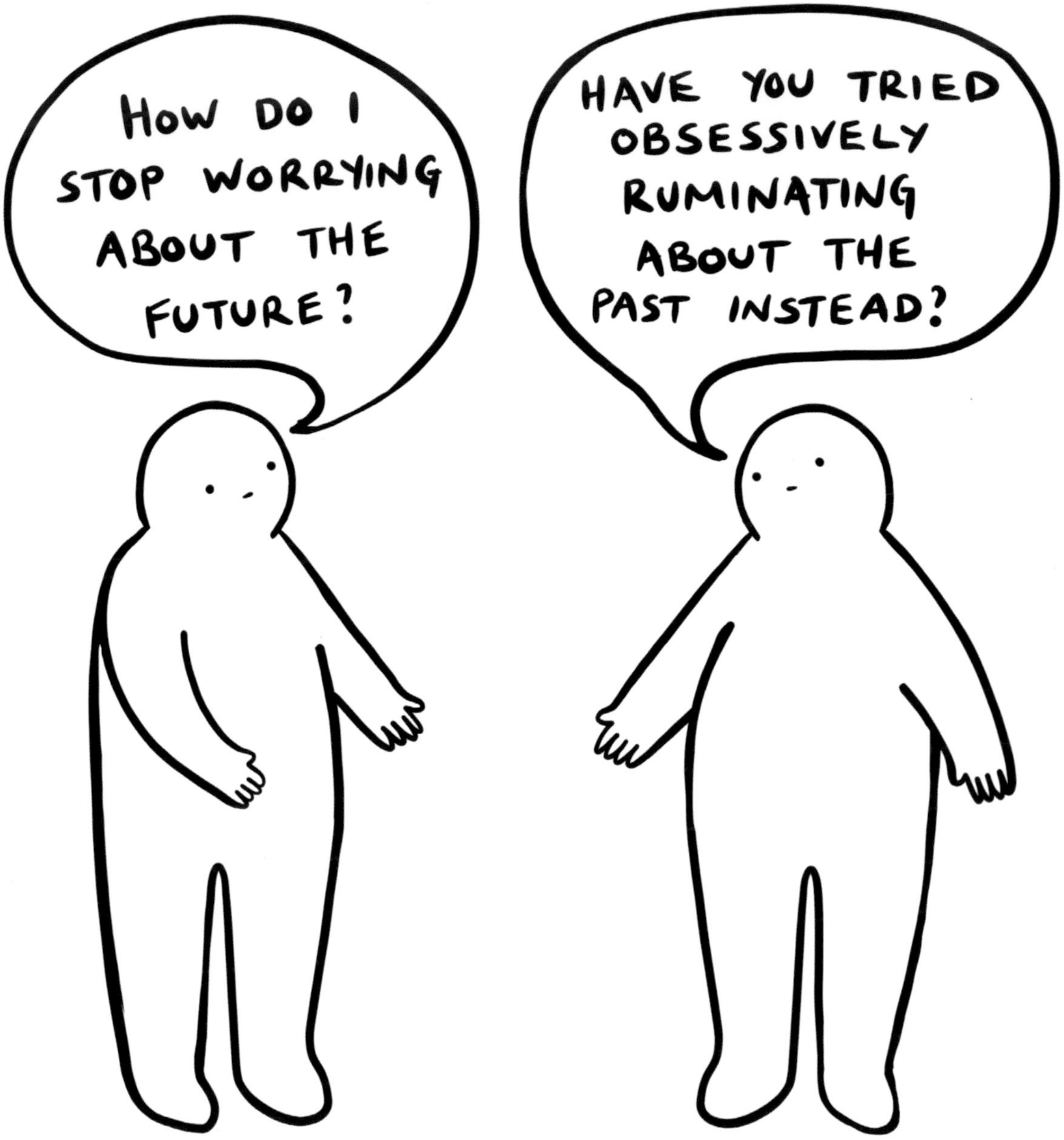
HOW DO I STOP WORRYING ABOUT THE FUTURE?
HAVE YOU TRIED OBSESSIVELY RUMINATING ABOUT THE PAST INSTEAD?

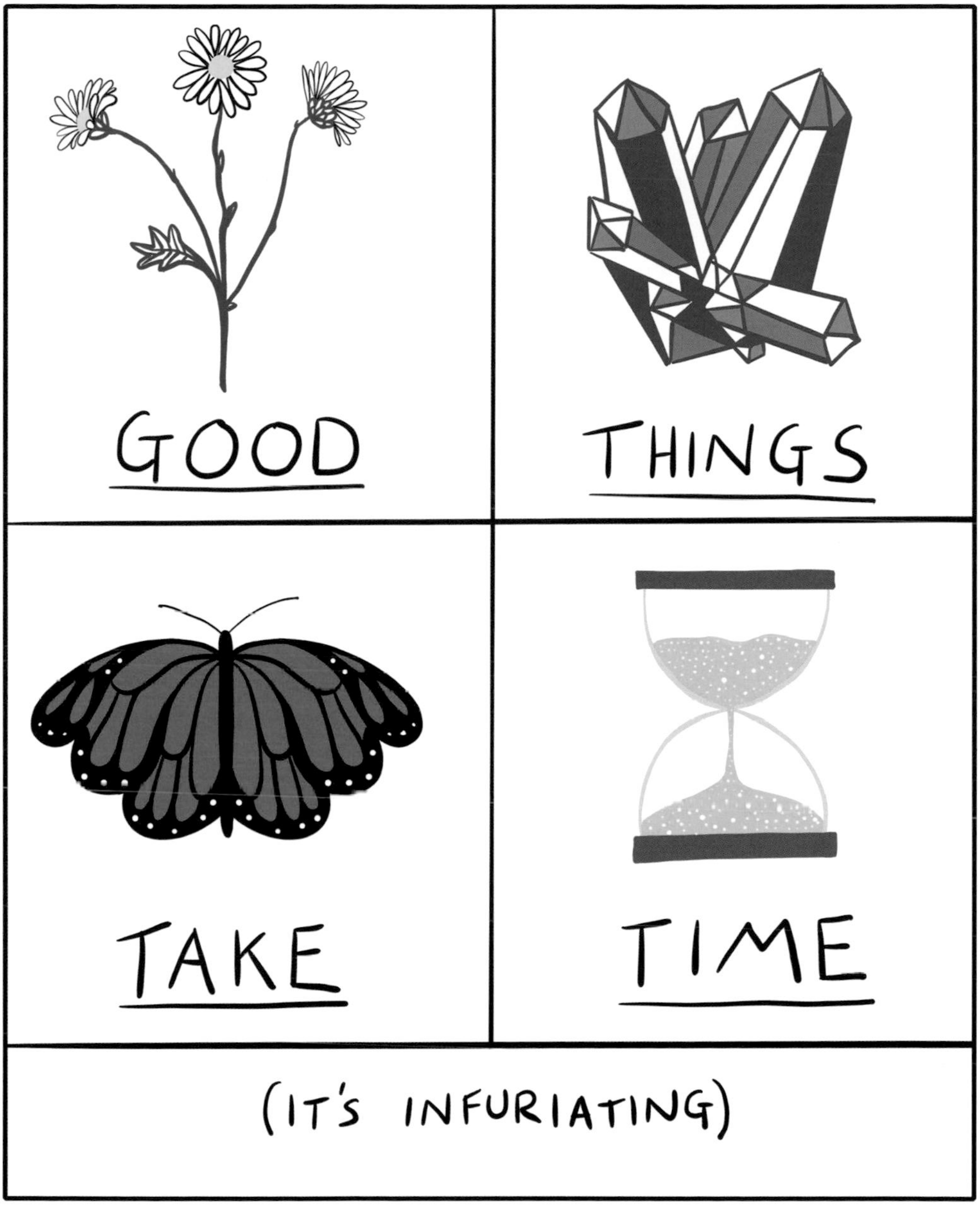
GOOD
THINGS
TAKE
TIME
(IT'S INFURIATING)

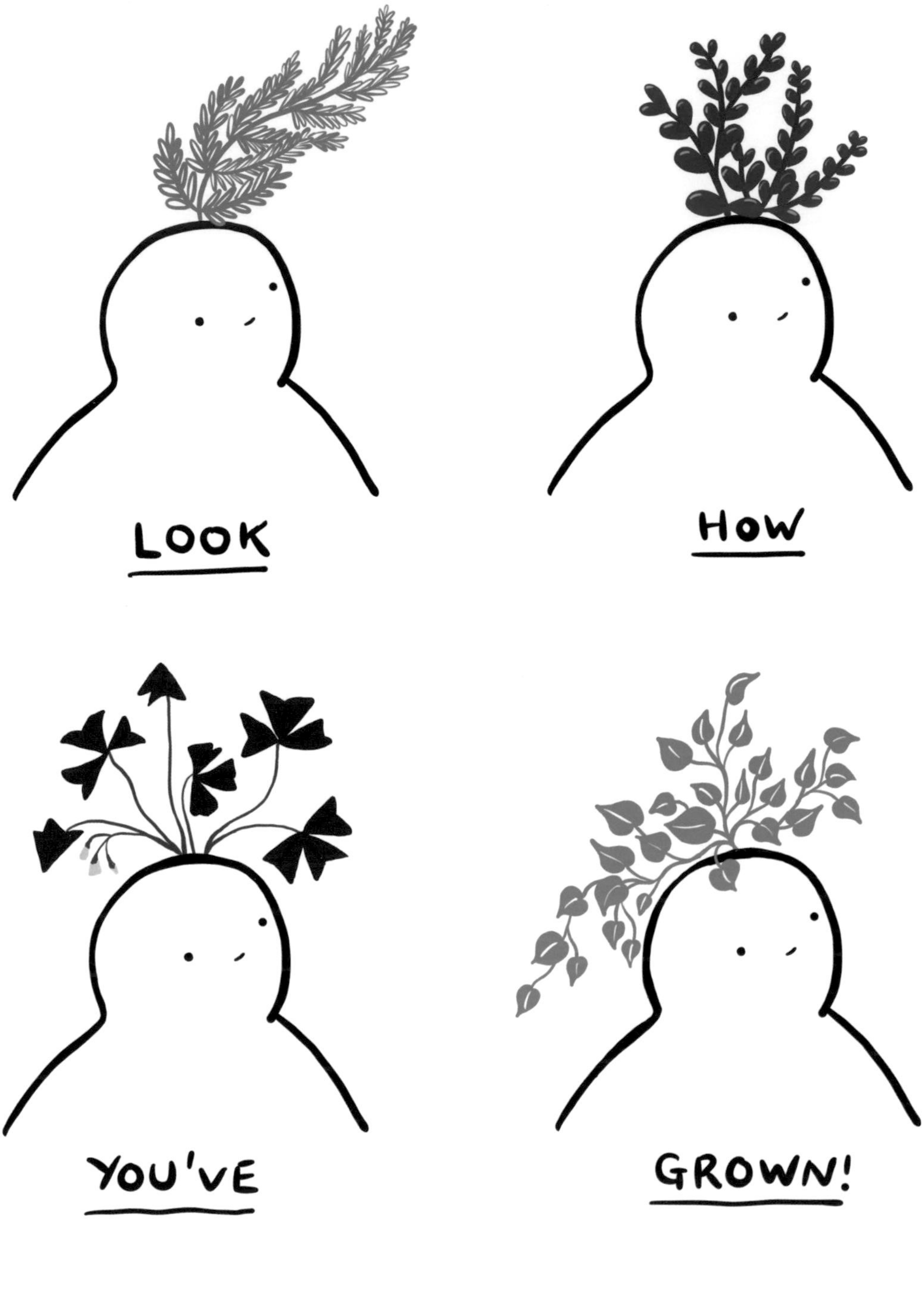
LOOK
HOW
YOU'VE
GROWN!

I FEEL OK
TODAY.

YESTERDAY
WAS ROUGH,

AND TOMORROW
MIGHT BE TOUGH,

BUT I FEEL
OK TODAY.

ME, CURRENTLY ON DAY 768
OF WAITING FOR THINGS TO
CALM DOWN A BIT:

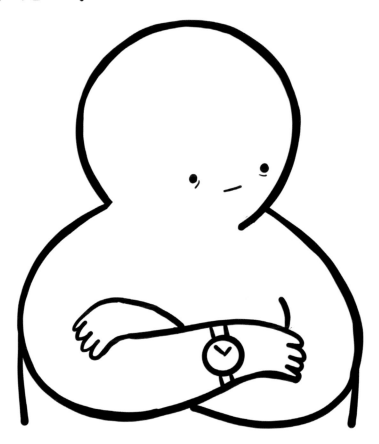

THERE WILL BE
TIMES OF GROWTH

THERE WILL BE
TIMES OF CHANGE

THERE WILL BE
HARD TIMES

THERE WILL
BE TIMES
OF REST

THERE WILL
BE TIMES OF
REGENERATION

AND THERE
WILL BE TIMES
OF GROWTH

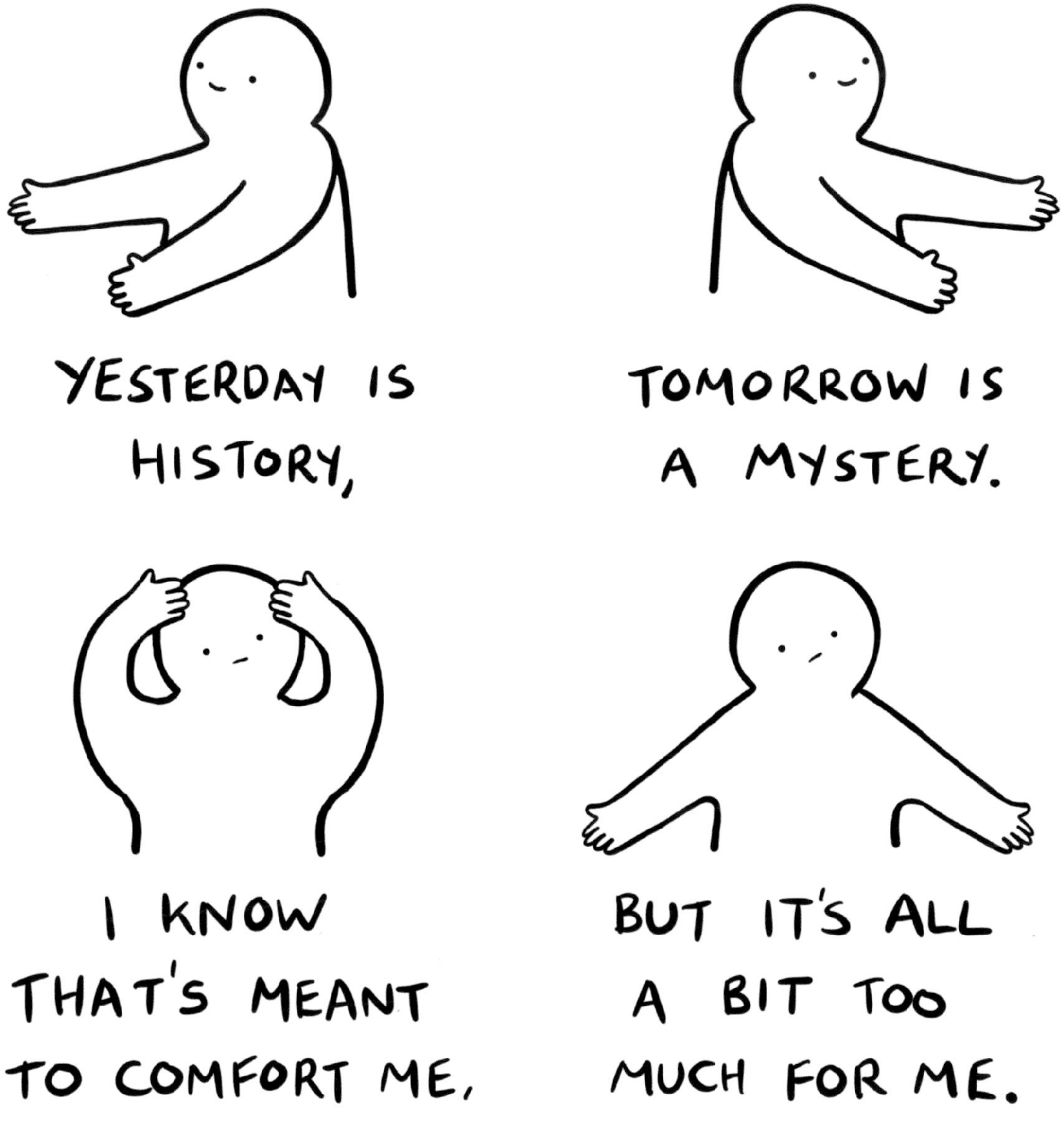
YESTERDAY IS HISTORY,
TOMORROW IS A MYSTERY.
I KNOW THAT'S MEANT TO COMFORT ME,
BUT IT'S ALL A BIT TOO MUCH FOR ME.

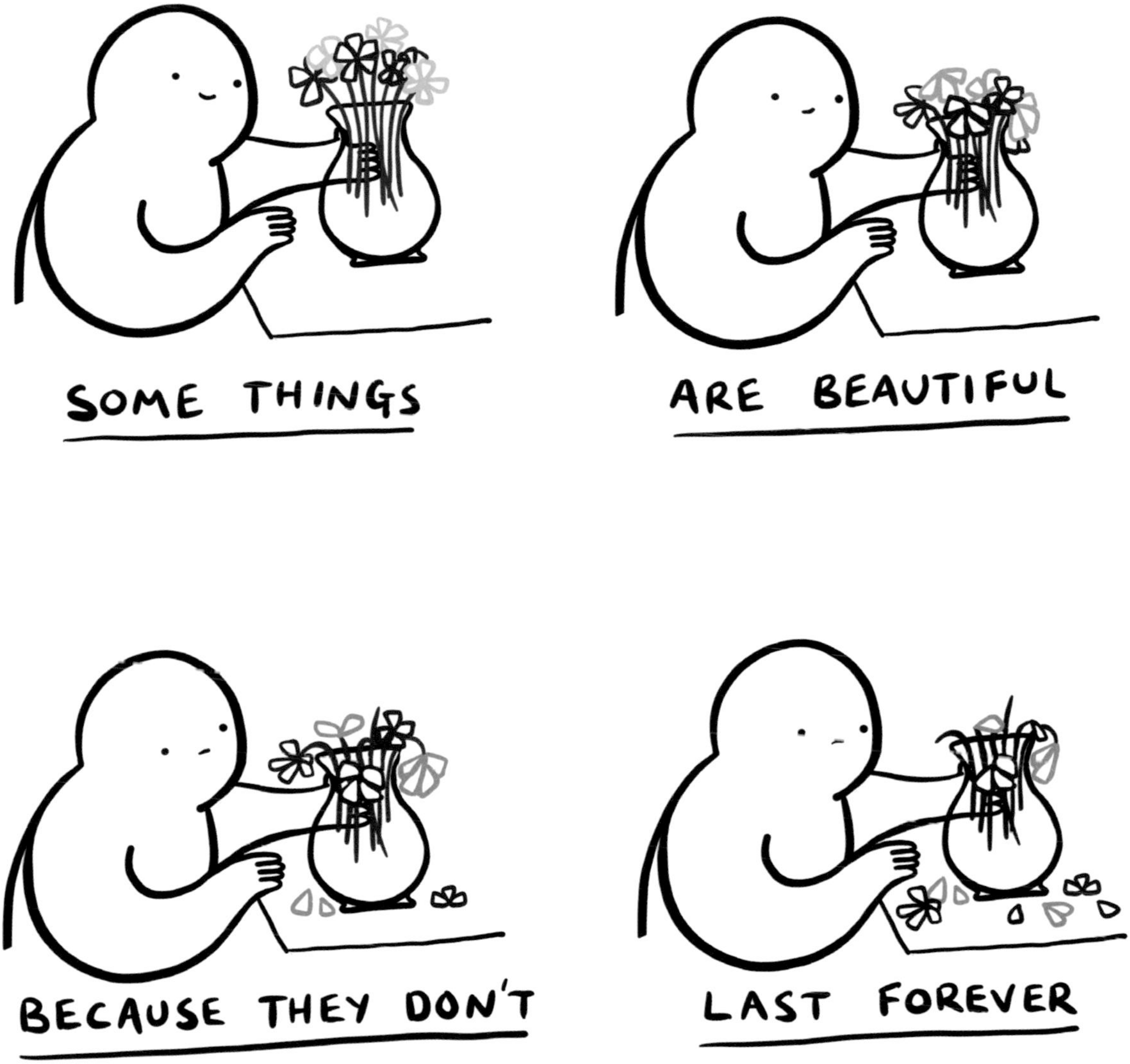
SOME THINGS
ARE BEAUTIFUL
BECAUSE THEY DON'T
LAST FOREVER

SOMETIMES I
FEEL LIKE IT'S JUST
ONE THING AFTER
ANOTHER, IN THIS LIFE.

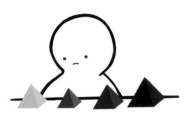

THAT TIME IS A
CONVEYOR BELT - A
GRINDINGLY LINEAR
SEQUENCE OF THINGS
TO DEAL WITH.

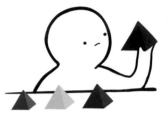

BUT WHAT WOULD
I PREFER?

THAT ALL THINGS
HAPPENED COMPLETELY
RANDOMLY?

OR ALL HAPPENED
SIMULTANEOUSLY?

OR THAT NOTHING
HAPPENED AT ALL?

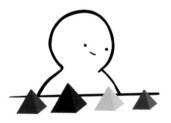

I GUESS ON REFLECTION
I DON'T HAVE A PROBLEM
WITH THE ORDER,

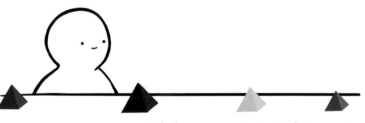

BUT I WOULD LIKE TO HAVE A WORD WITH
SOMEONE ABOUT THE FREQUENCY.

LOOKING FORWARD TO HAVING MORE THINGS TO LOOK FORWARD TO.

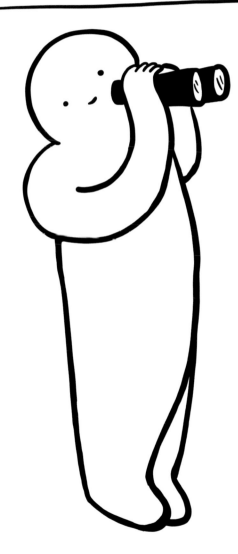

TRYING TO BE NORMAL IS WEIRD

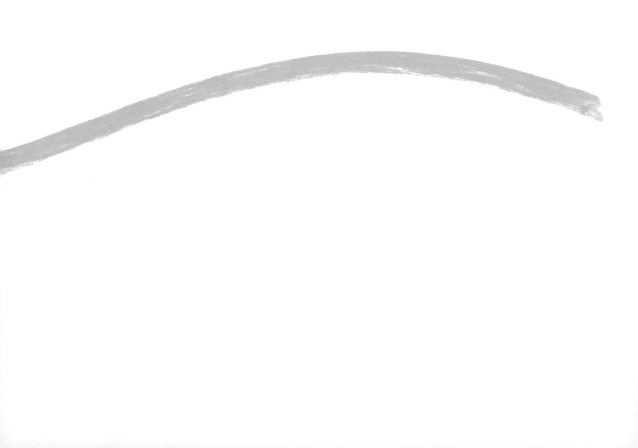

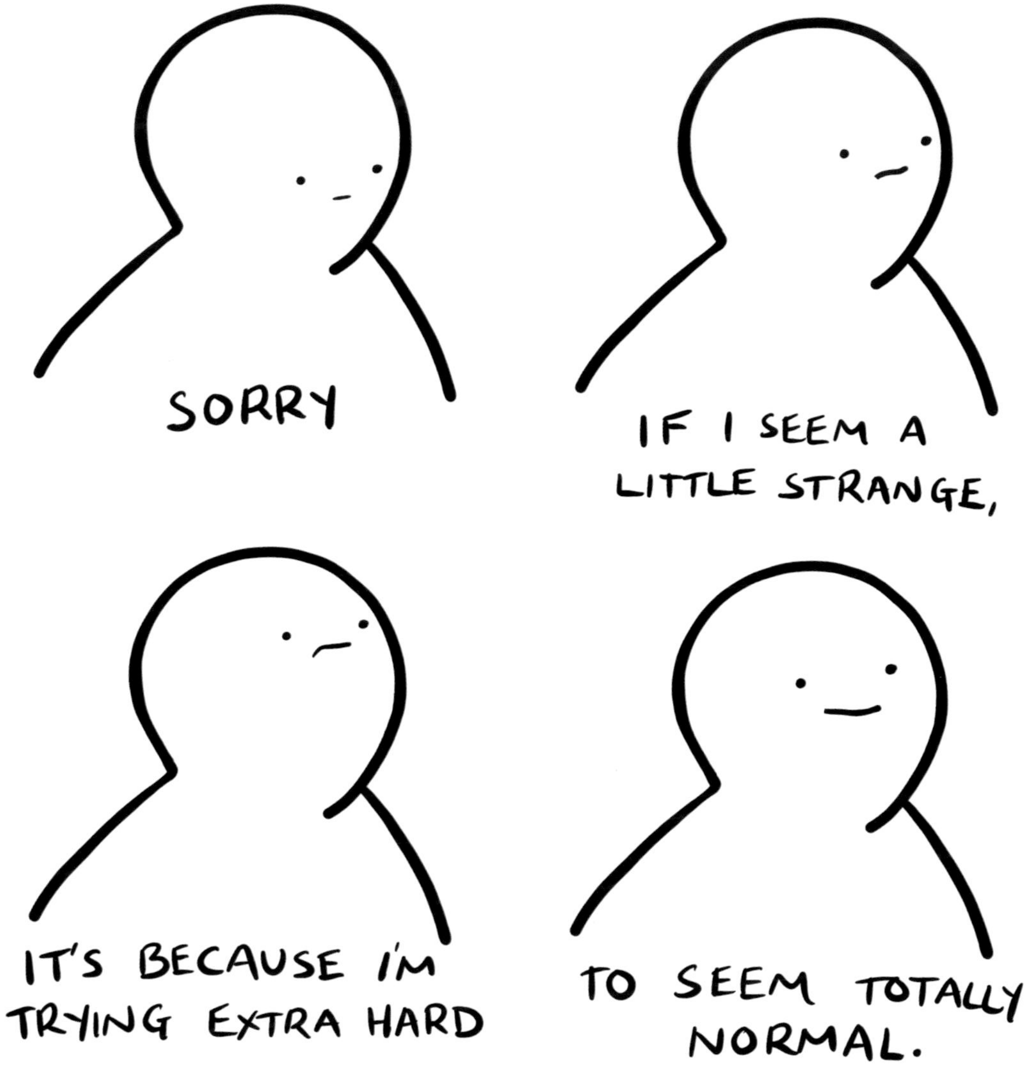
SORRY
IF I SEEM A LITTLE STRANGE,
IT'S BECAUSE I'M TRYING EXTRA HARD
TO SEEM TOTALLY NORMAL.

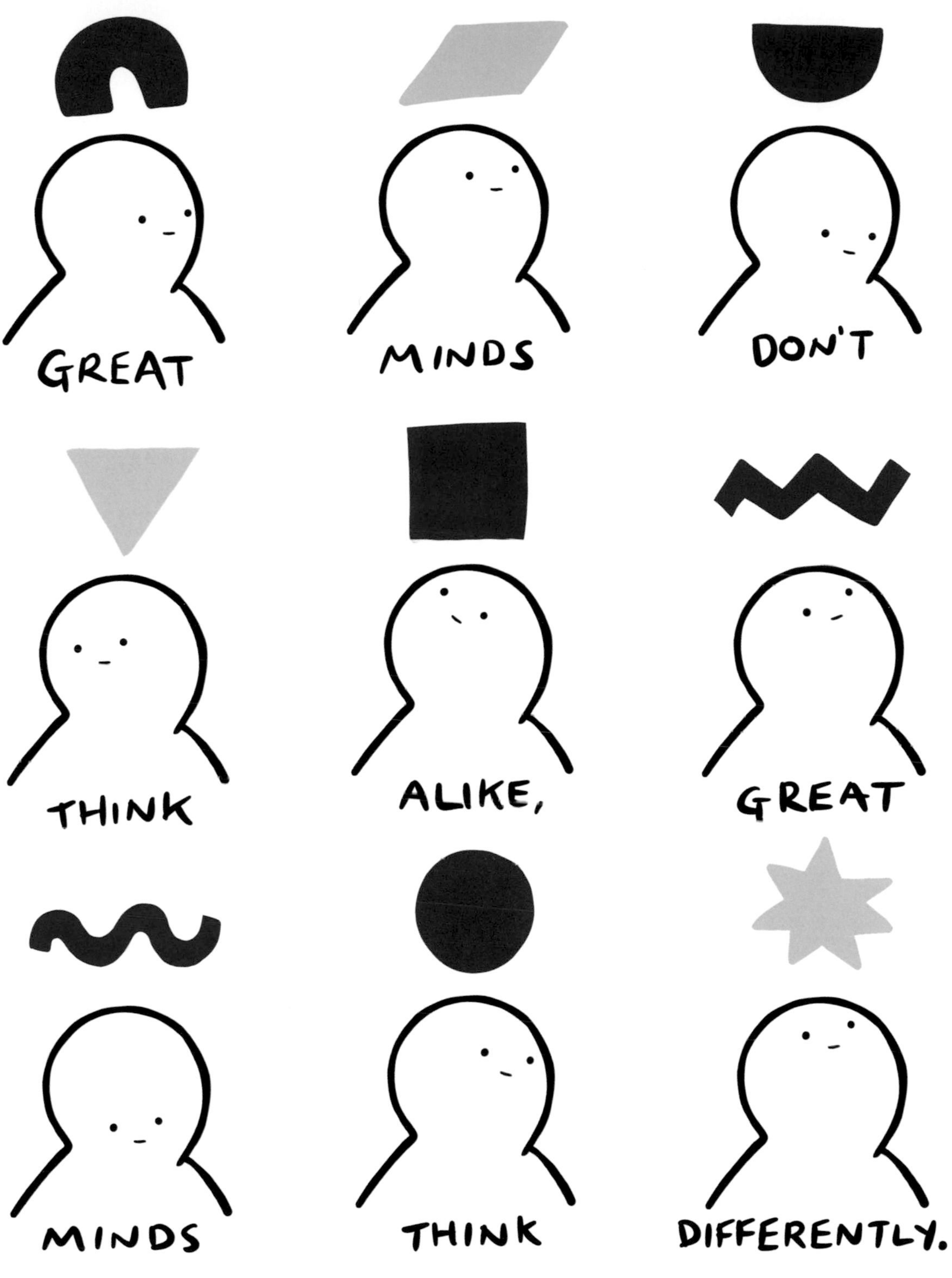
GREAT
MINDS
DON'T
THINK
ALIKE,
GREAT
MINDS
THINK
DIFFERENTLY.

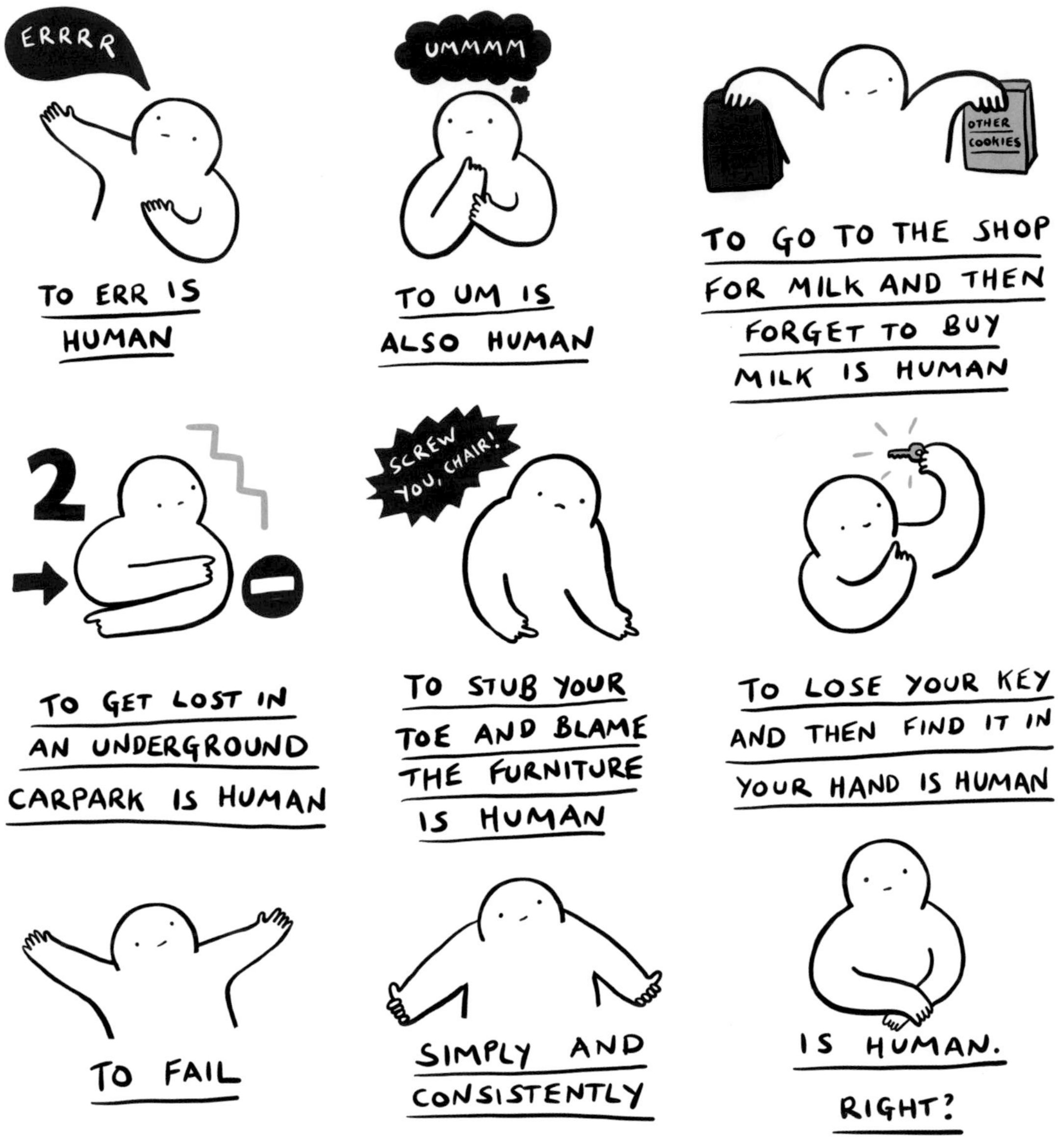

ERRRR
TO ERR IS HUMAN
UMMMM
TO UM IS ALSO HUMAN
OTHER COOKIES
TO GO TO THE SHOP FOR MILK AND THEN FORGET TO BUY MILK IS HUMAN
2
TO GET LOST IN AN UNDERGROUND CARPARK IS HUMAN
SCREW YOU, CHAIR!
TO STUB YOUR TOE AND BLAME THE FURNITURE IS HUMAN
TO LOSE YOUR KEY AND THEN FIND IT IN YOUR HAND IS HUMAN
TO FAIL
SIMPLY AND CONSISTENTLY
IS HUMAN.
RIGHT?

I WAS FOCUSING SO HARD ON LOOKING LIKE I WAS LISTENING

THAT I DIDN'T HEAR WHAT YOU WERE SAYING.

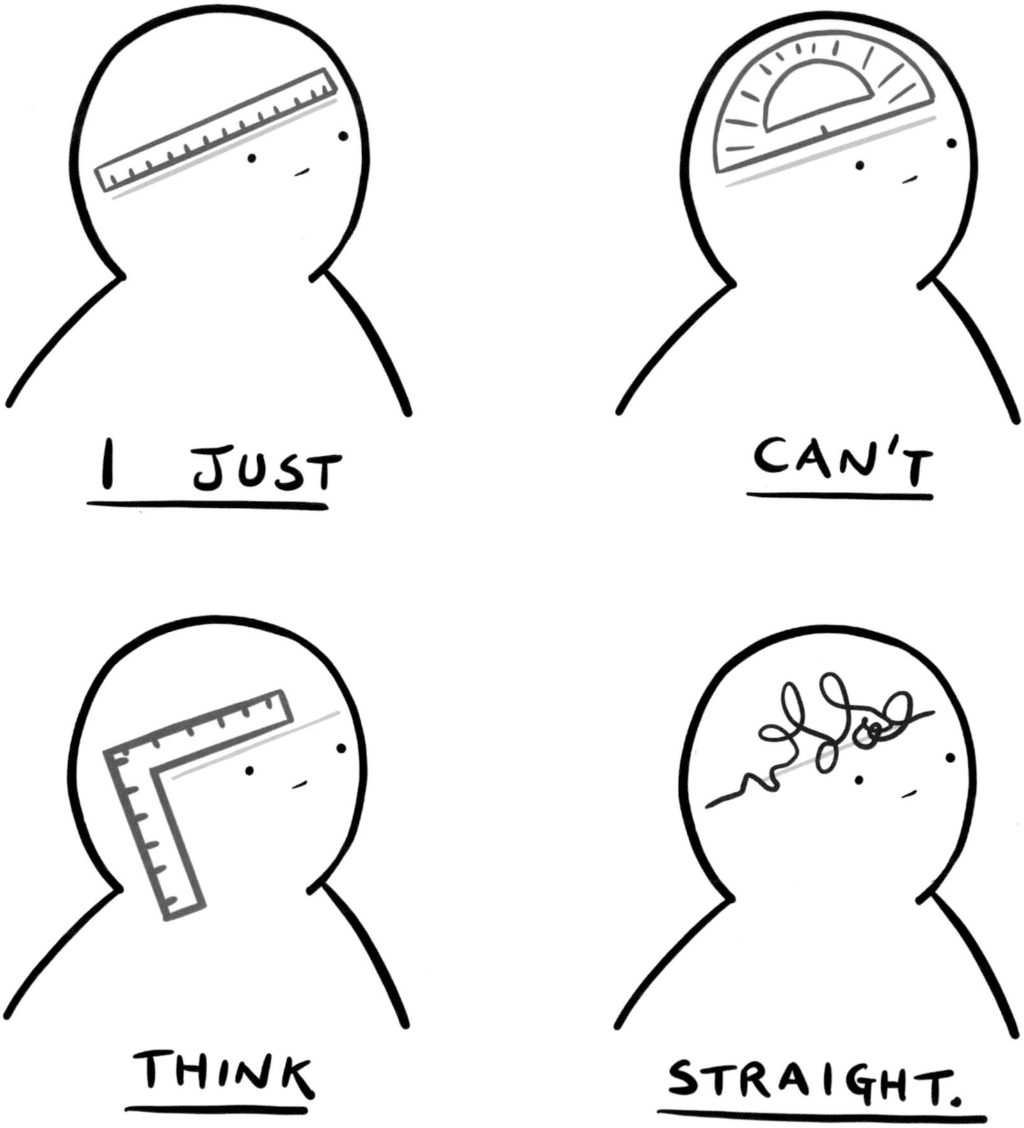
I JUST
CAN'T
THINK
STRAIGHT.

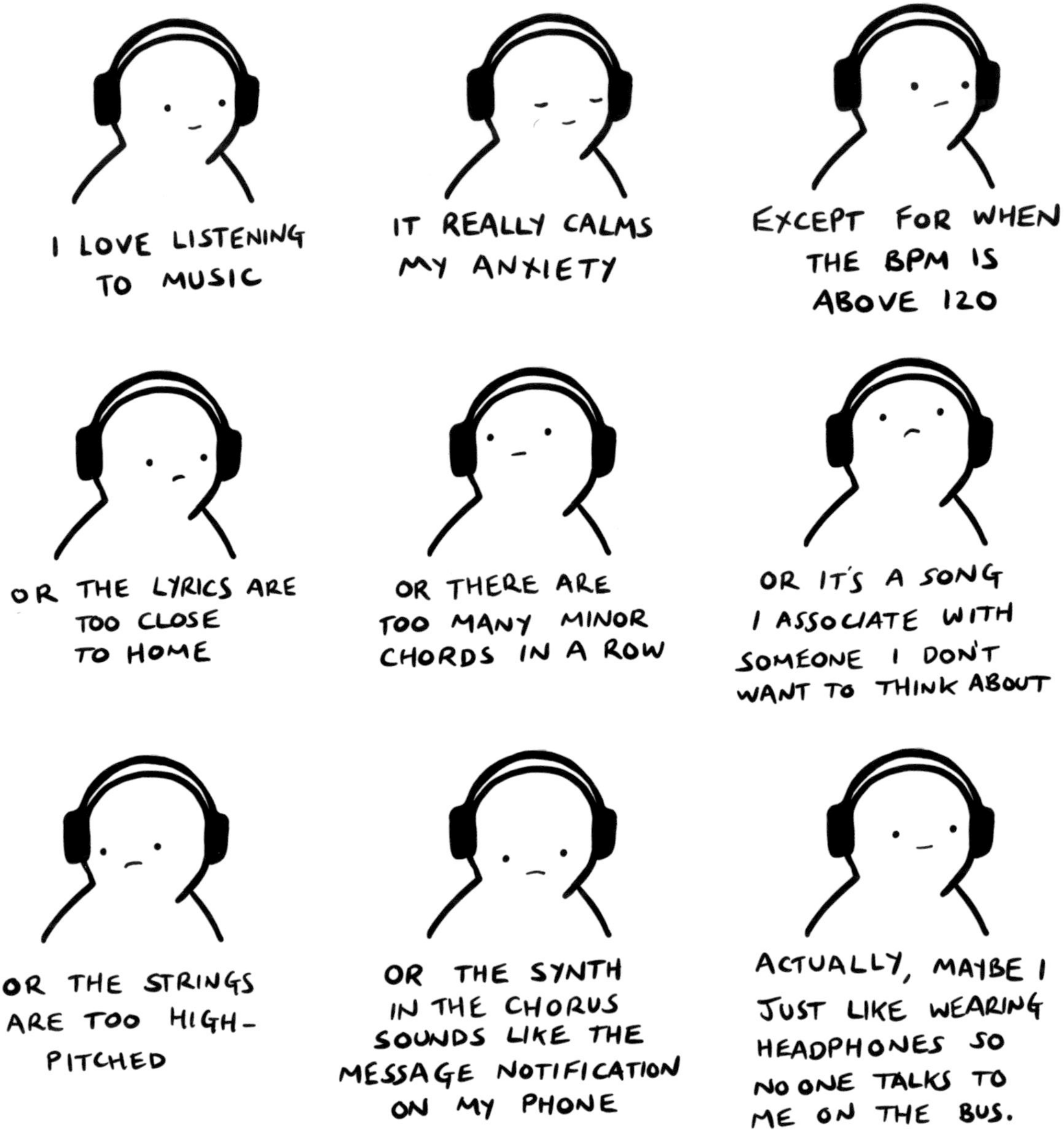
I LOVE LISTENING TO MUSIC
IT REALLY CALMS MY ANXIETY
EXCEPT FOR WHEN THE BPM IS ABOVE 120
OR THE LYRICS ARE TOO CLOSE TO HOME
OR THERE ARE TOO MANY MINOR CHORDS IN A ROW
OR IT'S A SONG I ASSOCIATE WITH SOMEONE I DON'T WANT TO THINK ABOUT
OR THE STRINGS ARE TOO HIGH-PITCHED
OR THE SYNTH IN THE CHORUS SOUNDS LIKE THE MESSAGE NOTIFICATION ON MY PHONE
ACTUALLY, MAYBE I JUST LIKE WEARING HEADPHONES SO NO ONE TALKS TO ME ON THE BUS.

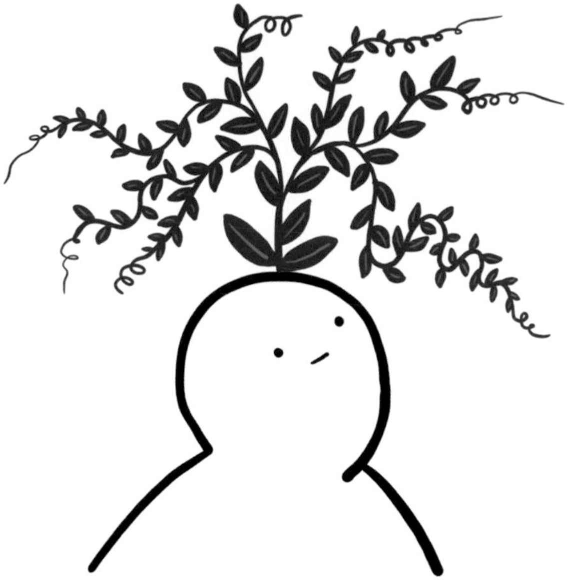

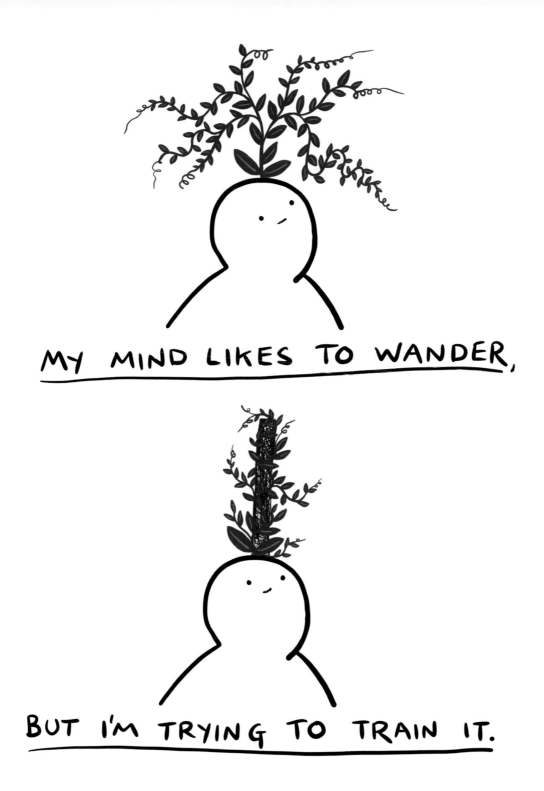

MY MIND LIKES TO WANDER,

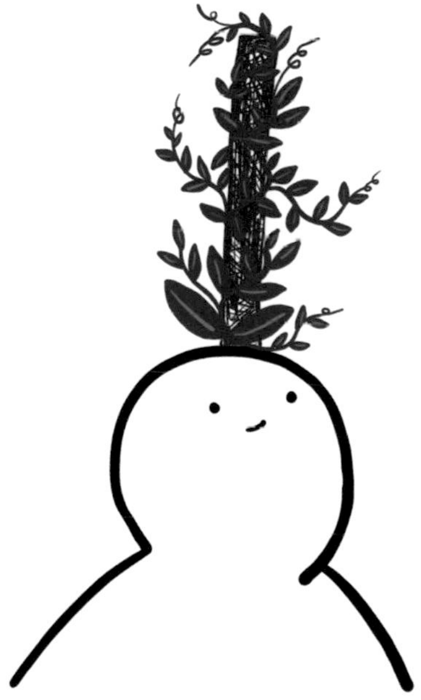

BUT I'M TRYING TO TRAIN IT.

PLEASE

TAKE ME AWAY

FROM THE SOCIAL SITUATION

MAYBE I SHARED
TOO MUCH?

OR MAYBE I DIDN'T
SHARE ENOUGH?

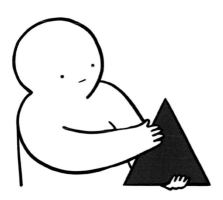

OR MAYBE I SHARED THE
WRONG KIND OF THING

IN THE WRONG
KIND OF WAY?

FEELING SAD,
ACTING SAD.

FEELING SAD,
ACTING HAPPY.

FEELING HAPPY,
ACTING SAD.

FEELING HAPPY,
ACTING HAPPY.

FEELING WEIRD,
ACTING NORMAL.

FEELING WEIRD,
ACTING WEIRD.

SOMETIMES ANTISOCIAL

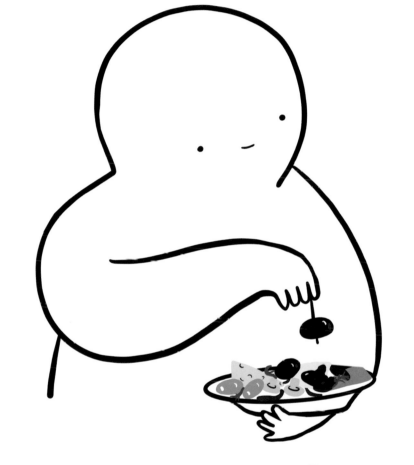

ALWAYS ANTIPASTO

OTHER PEOPLE ABSORBING INFORMATION:

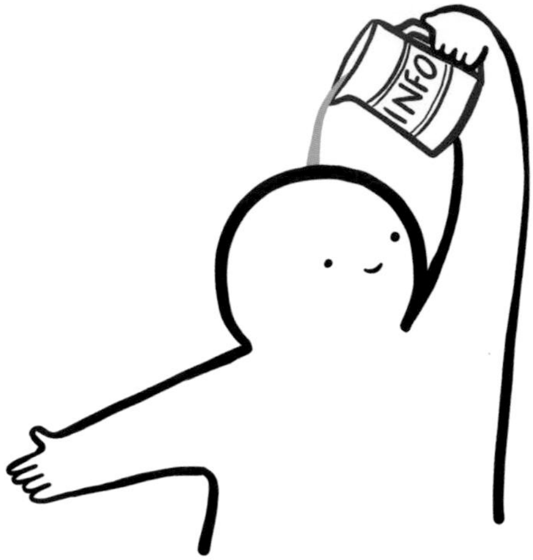
INFO

ME TRYING TO ABSORB INFORMATION:

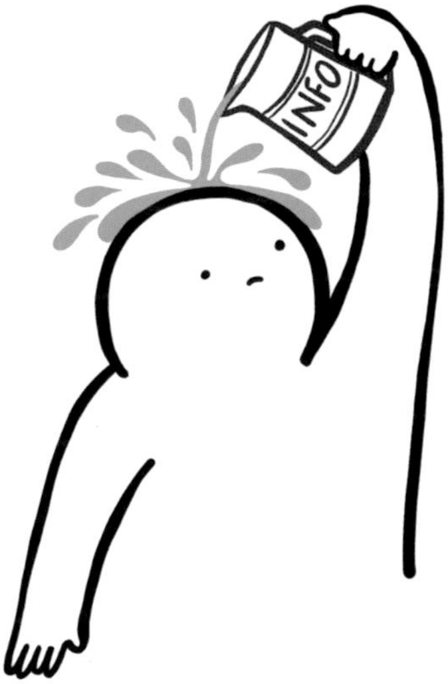
INFO

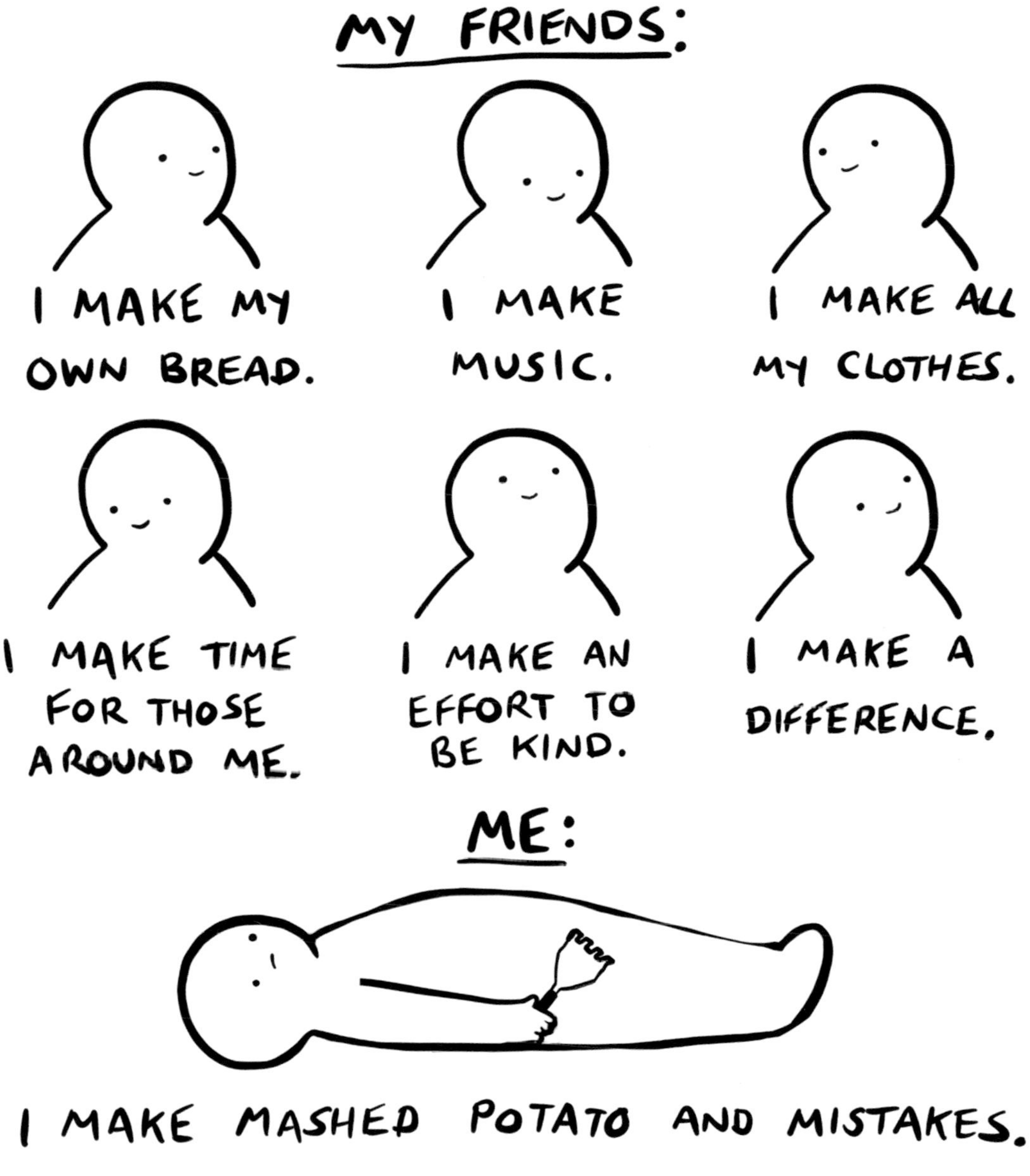
MY FRIENDS:
I MAKE MY OWN BREAD.
I MAKE MUSIC.
I MAKE ALL MY CLOTHES.
I MAKE TIME FOR THOSE AROUND ME.
I MAKE AN EFFORT TO BE KIND.
I MAKE A DIFFERENCE.
ME:
I MAKE MASHED POTATO AND MISTAKES.

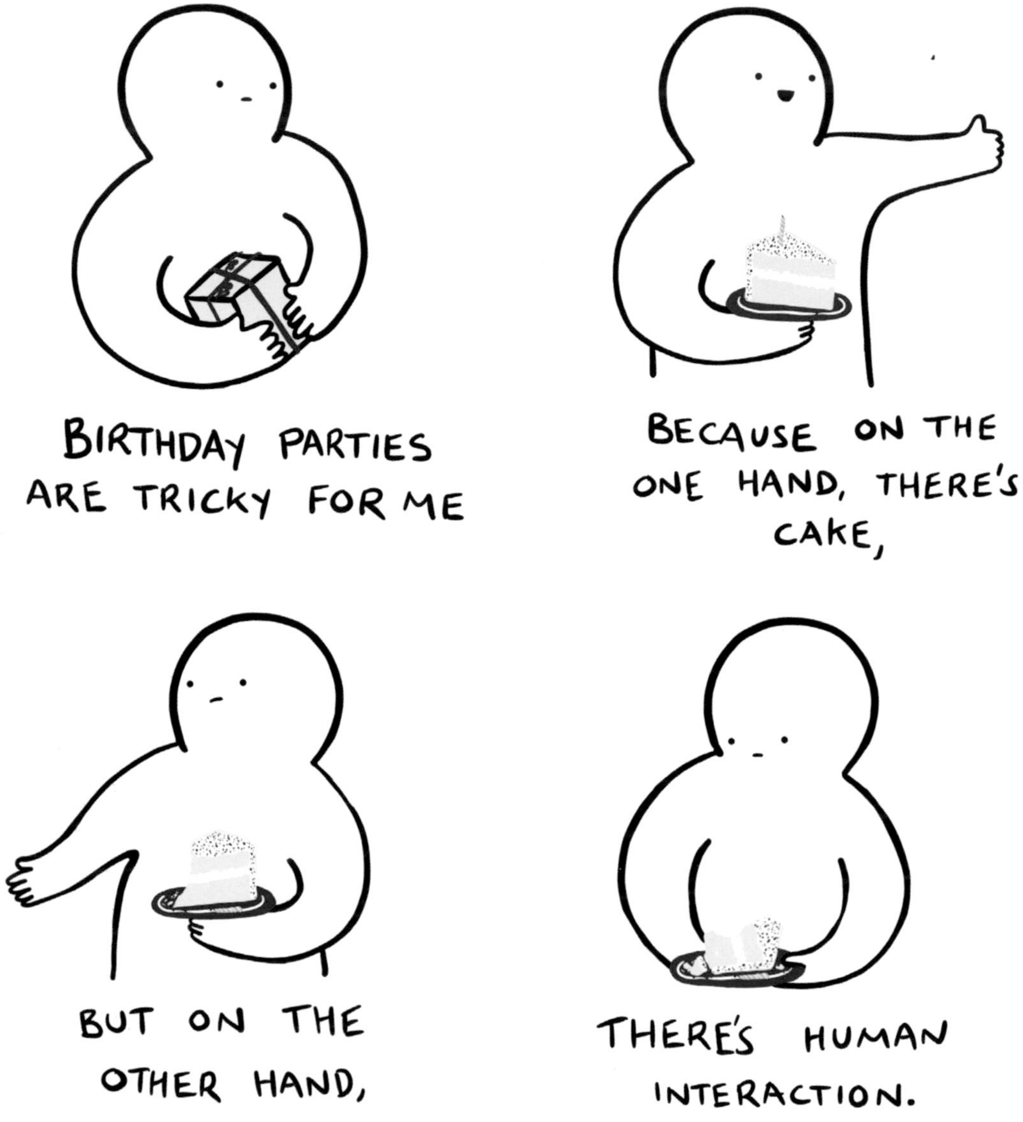
BIRTHDAY PARTIES ARE TRICKY FOR ME
BECAUSE ON THE ONE HAND, THERE'S CAKE,
BUT ON THE OTHER HAND,
THERE'S HUMAN INTERACTION.

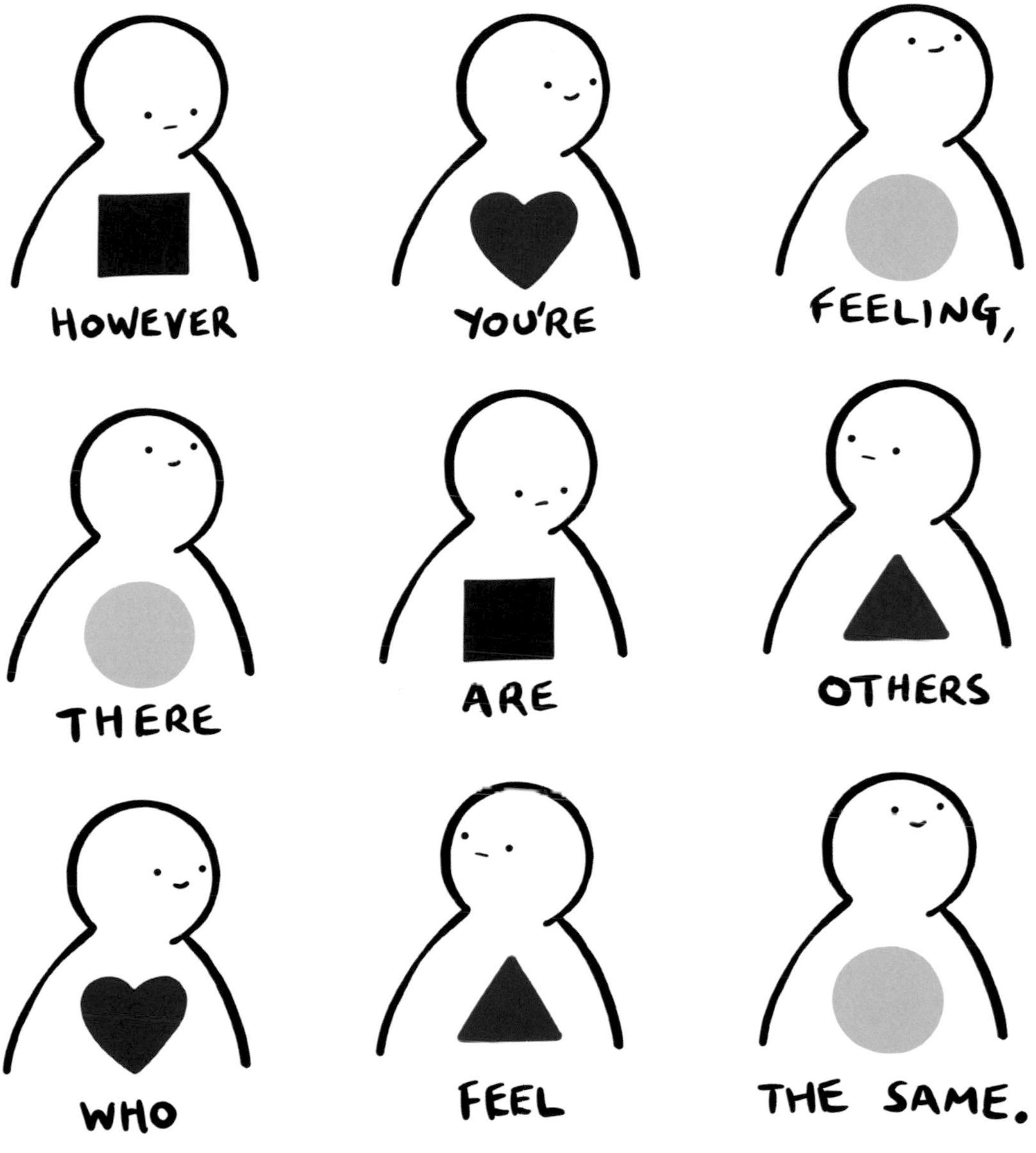
HOWEVER
YOU'RE
FEELING,
THERE
ARE
OTHERS
WHO
FEEL
THE SAME.

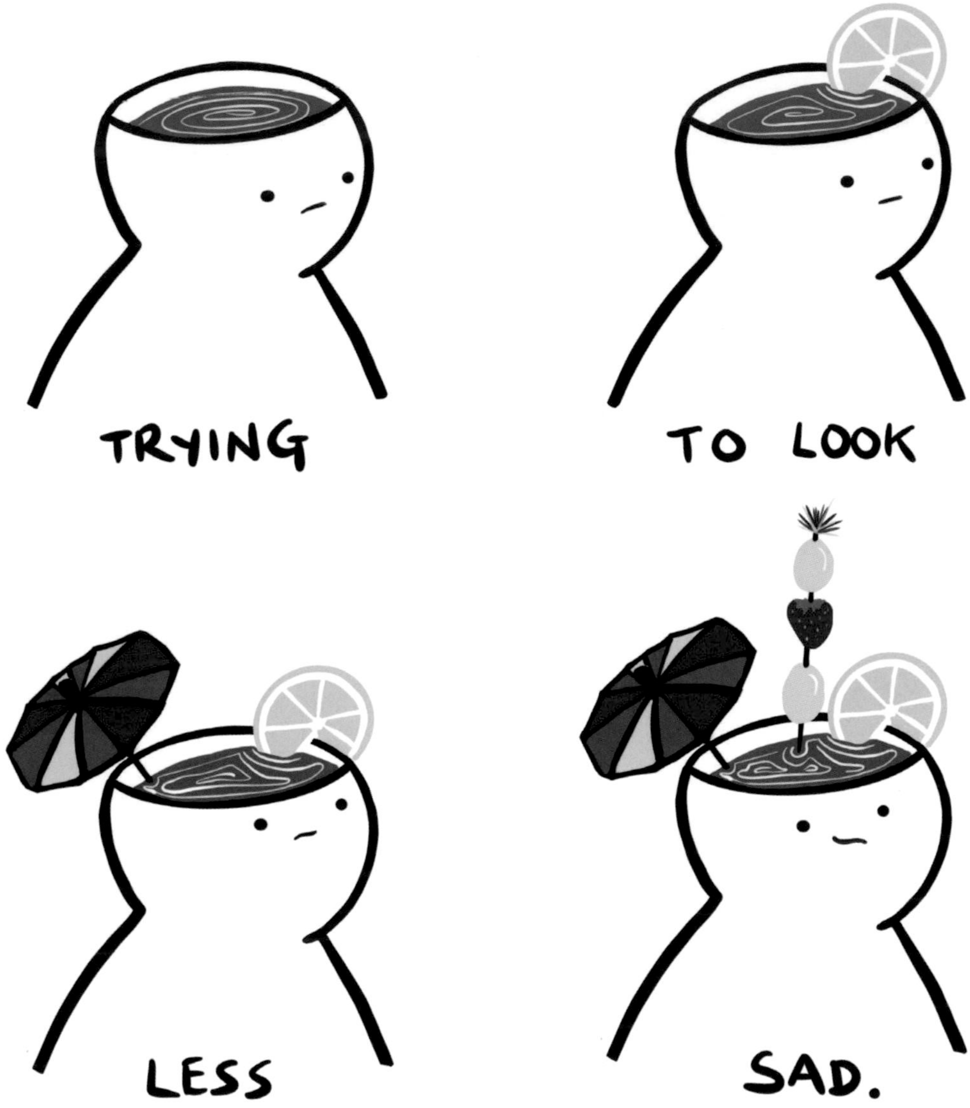
TRYING
TO LOOK
LESS
SAD.

SORRY IF I SEEM ODD,

IT'S JUST BECAUSE I CAN'T EVEN.

IT'S NOT OVER TIL
I'M OVERTHINKING IT

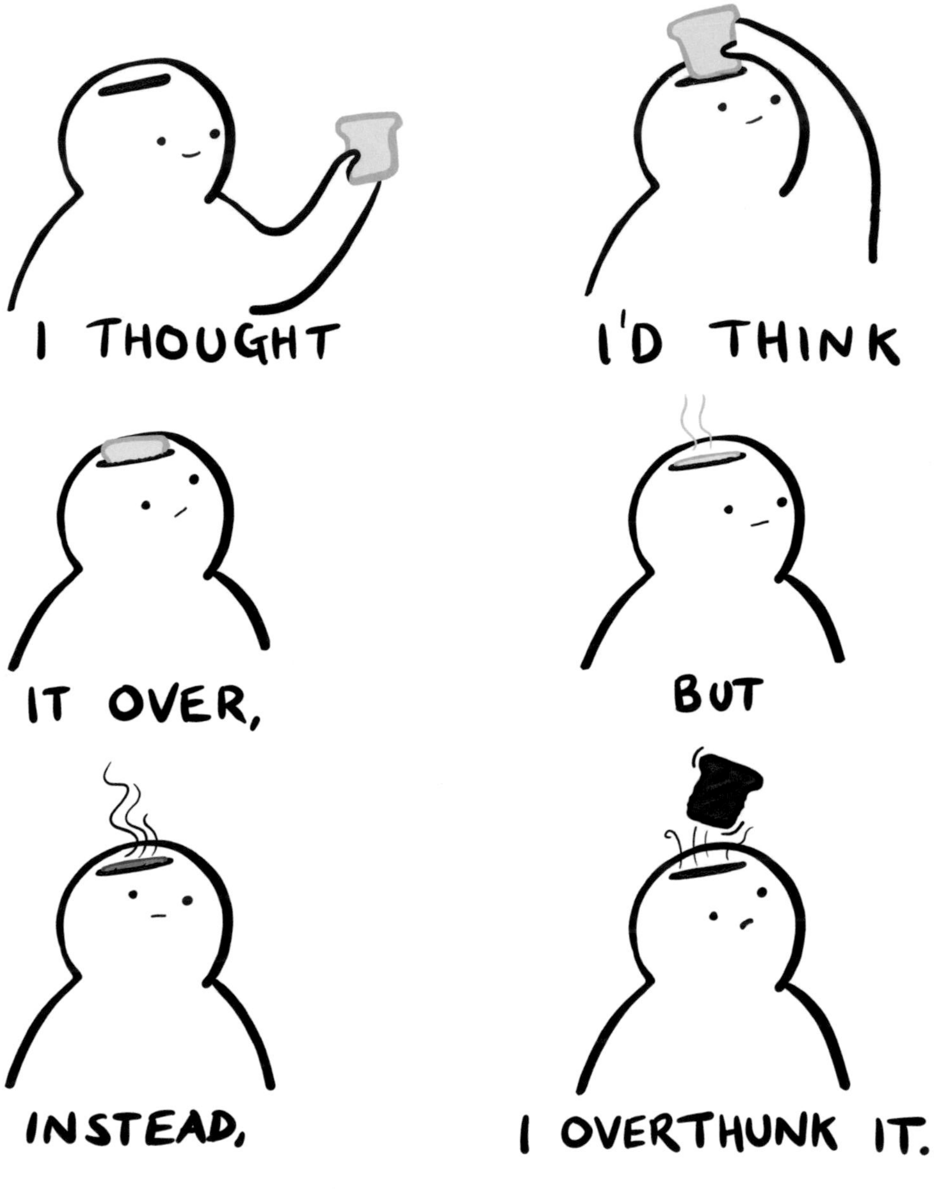
I THOUGHT
I'D THINK
IT OVER,
BUT
INSTEAD,
I OVERTHUNK IT.

I'M ALWAYS GETTING
STUCK IN MY HEAD,
SO I'M TRYING TO MAKE IT
A NICE PLACE TO BE.

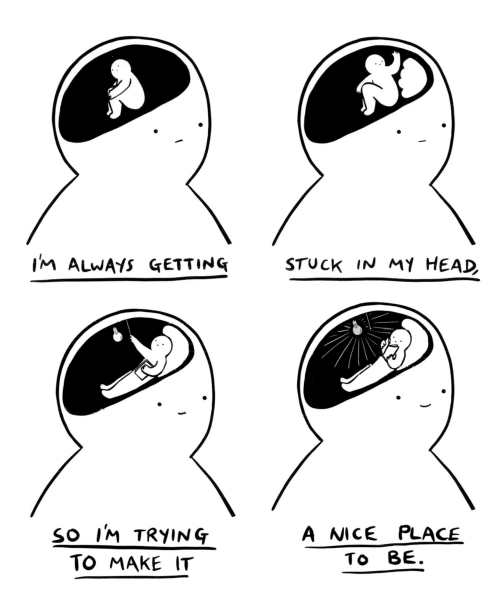

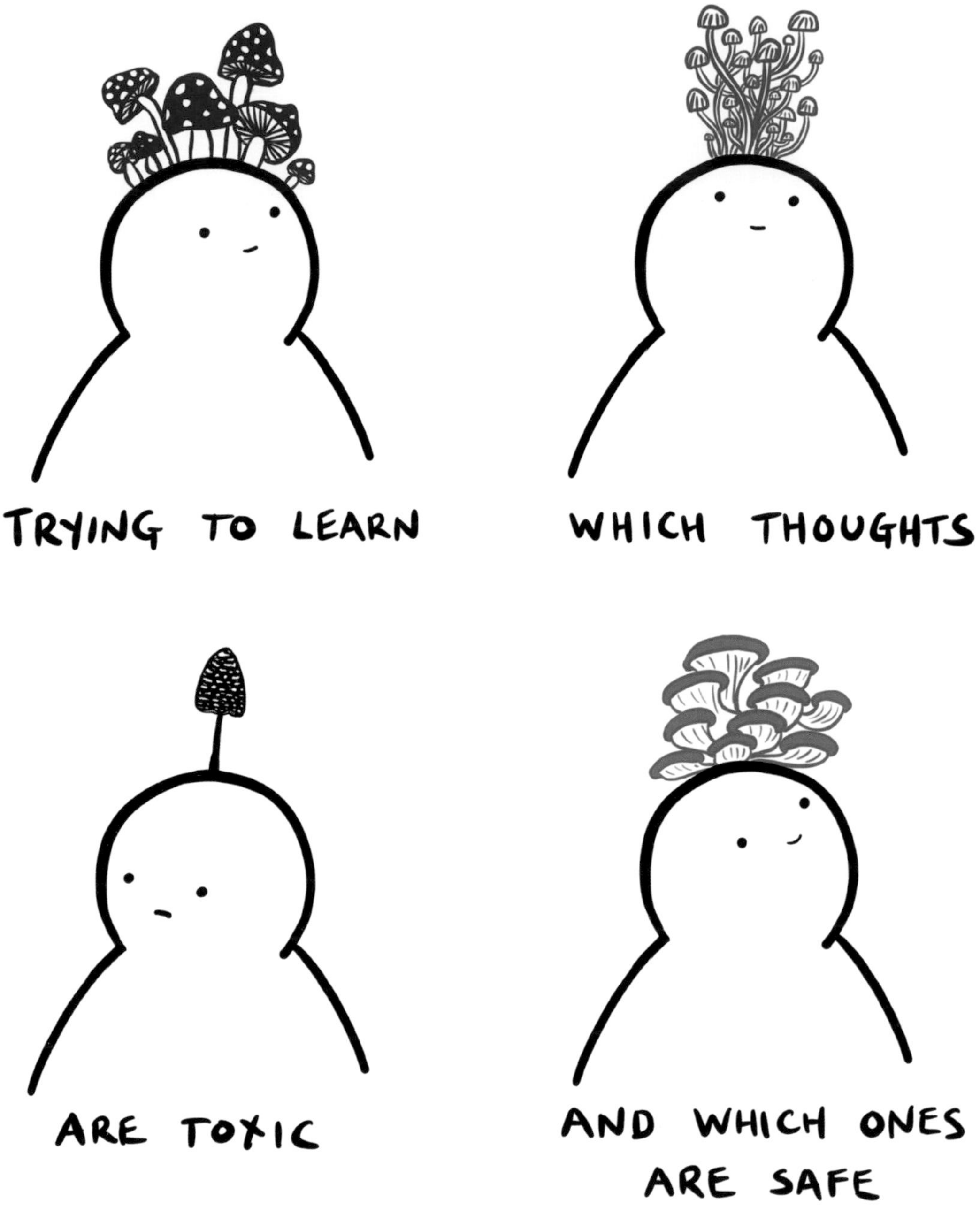
TRYING TO LEARN
WHICH THOUGHTS
ARE TOXIC
AND WHICH ONES ARE SAFE

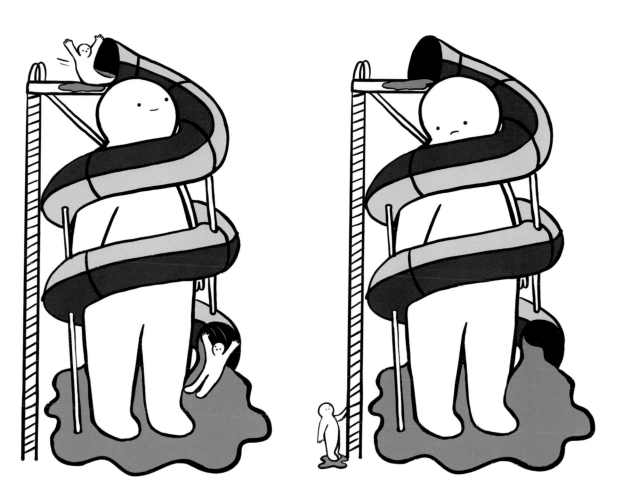

HOW EASY IT IS
TO SPIRAL
DOWNWARDS

HOW HARD IT IS
TO CLIMB BACK
UPWARDS

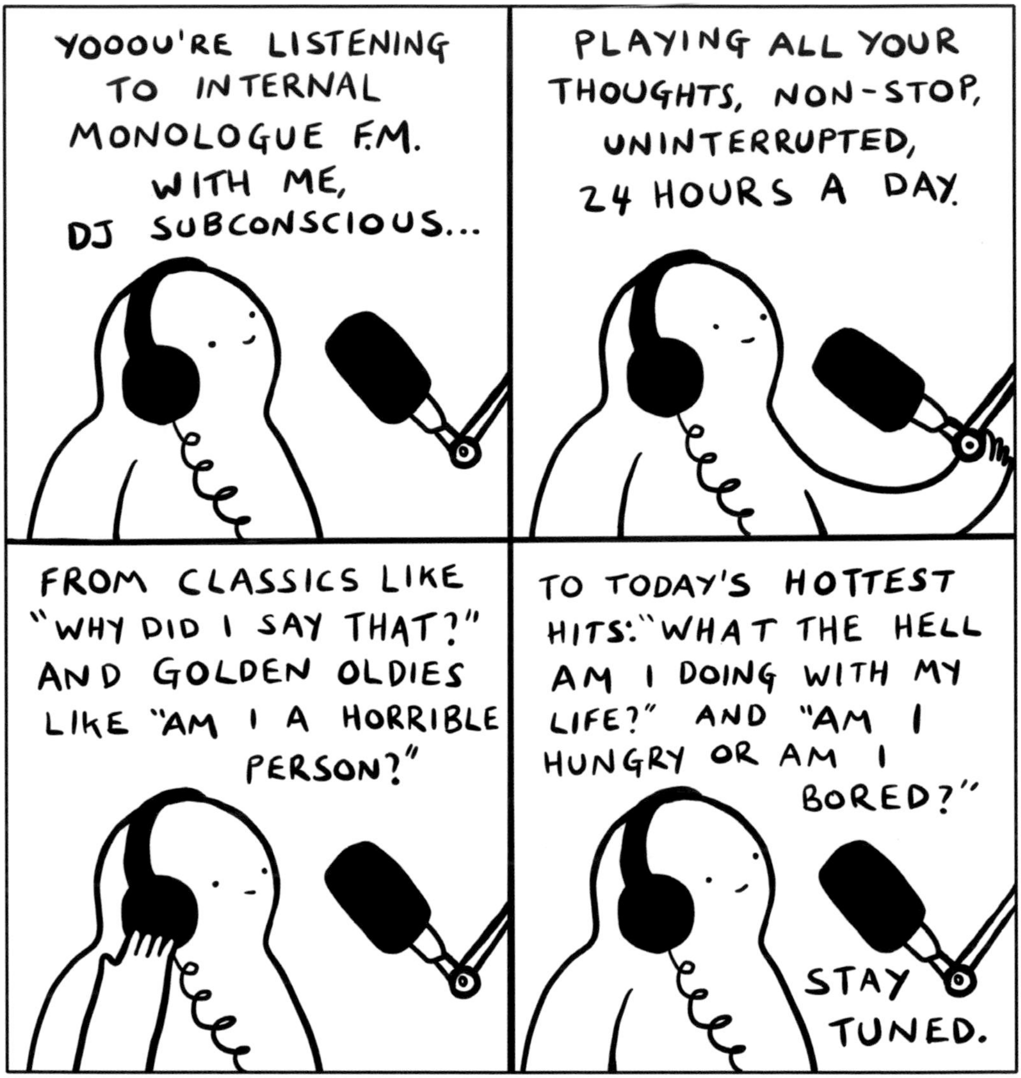
YOOOU'RE LISTENING TO INTERNAL MONOLOGUE F.M. WITH ME, DJ SUBCONSCIOUS...
PLAYING ALL YOUR THOUGHTS, NON-STOP, UNINTERRUPTED, 24 HOURS A DAY.
FROM CLASSICS LIKE "WHY DID I SAY THAT?" AND GOLDEN OLDIES LIKE "AM I A HORRIBLE PERSON?"
TO TODAY'S HOTTEST HITS: "WHAT THE HELL AM I DOING WITH MY LIFE?" AND "AM I HUNGRY OR AM I BORED?"
STAY TUNED.

THE MIND IS A PRISM

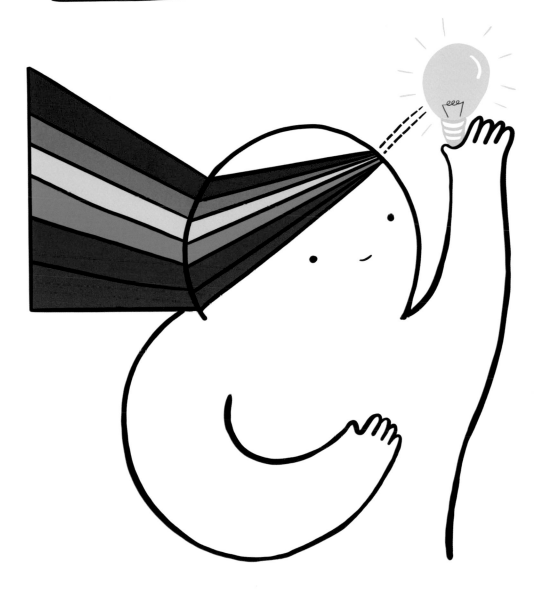

HERE TO GROW,
NOT TO KNOW.

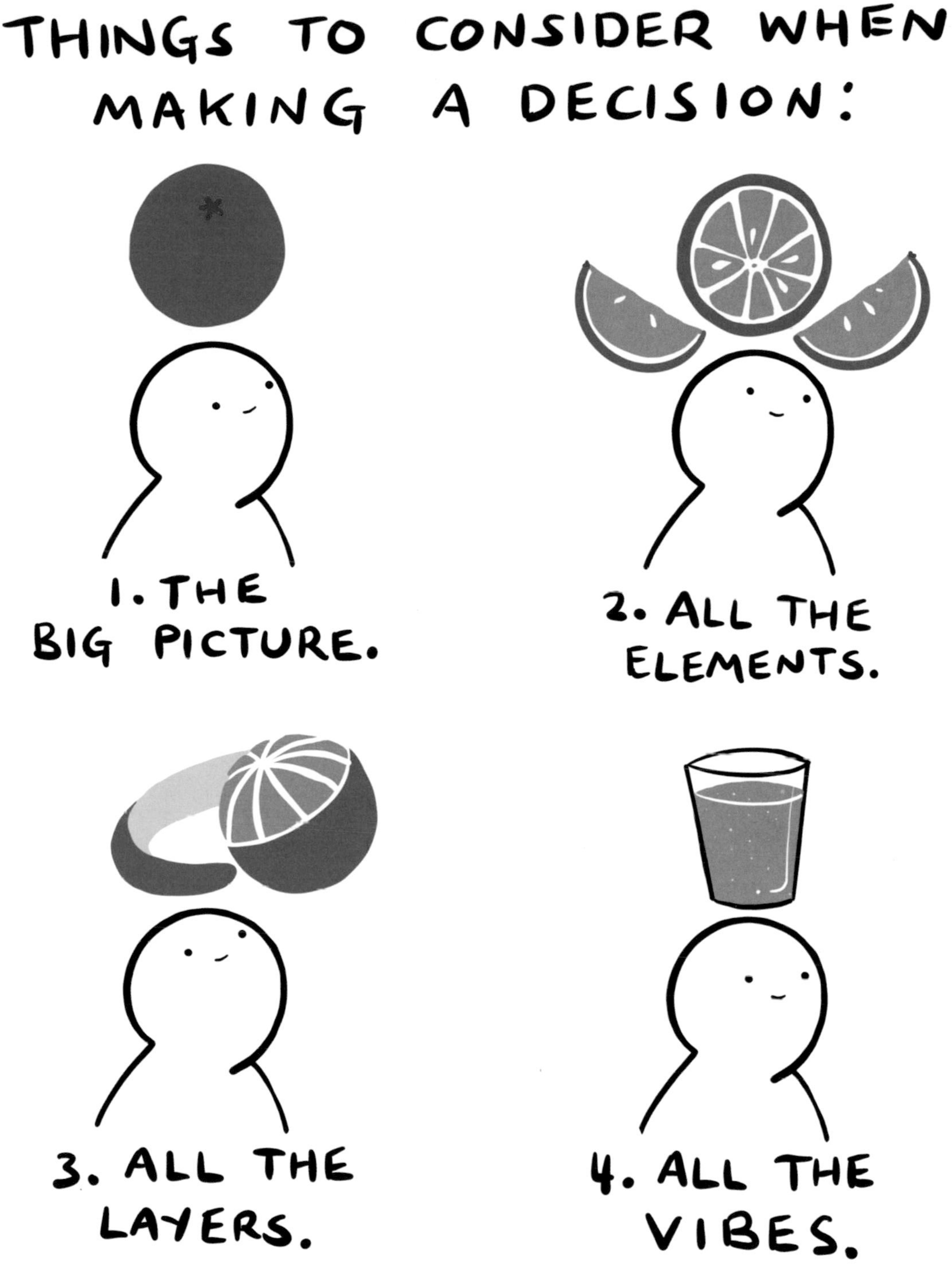
THINGS TO CONSIDER WHEN MAKING A DECISION:
1. THE BIG PICTURE.
2. ALL THE ELEMENTS.
3. ALL THE LAYERS.
4. ALL THE VIBES.

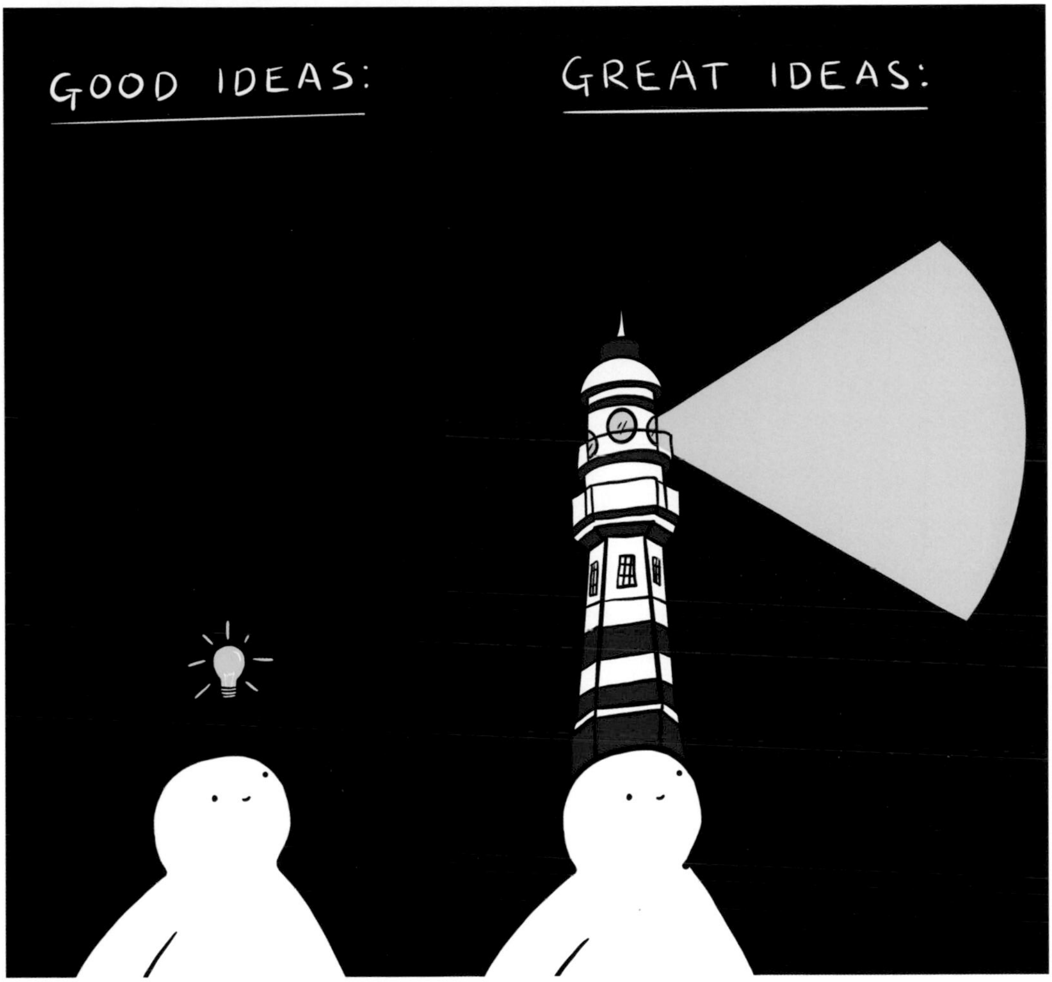
GOOD IDEAS:
GREAT IDEAS:

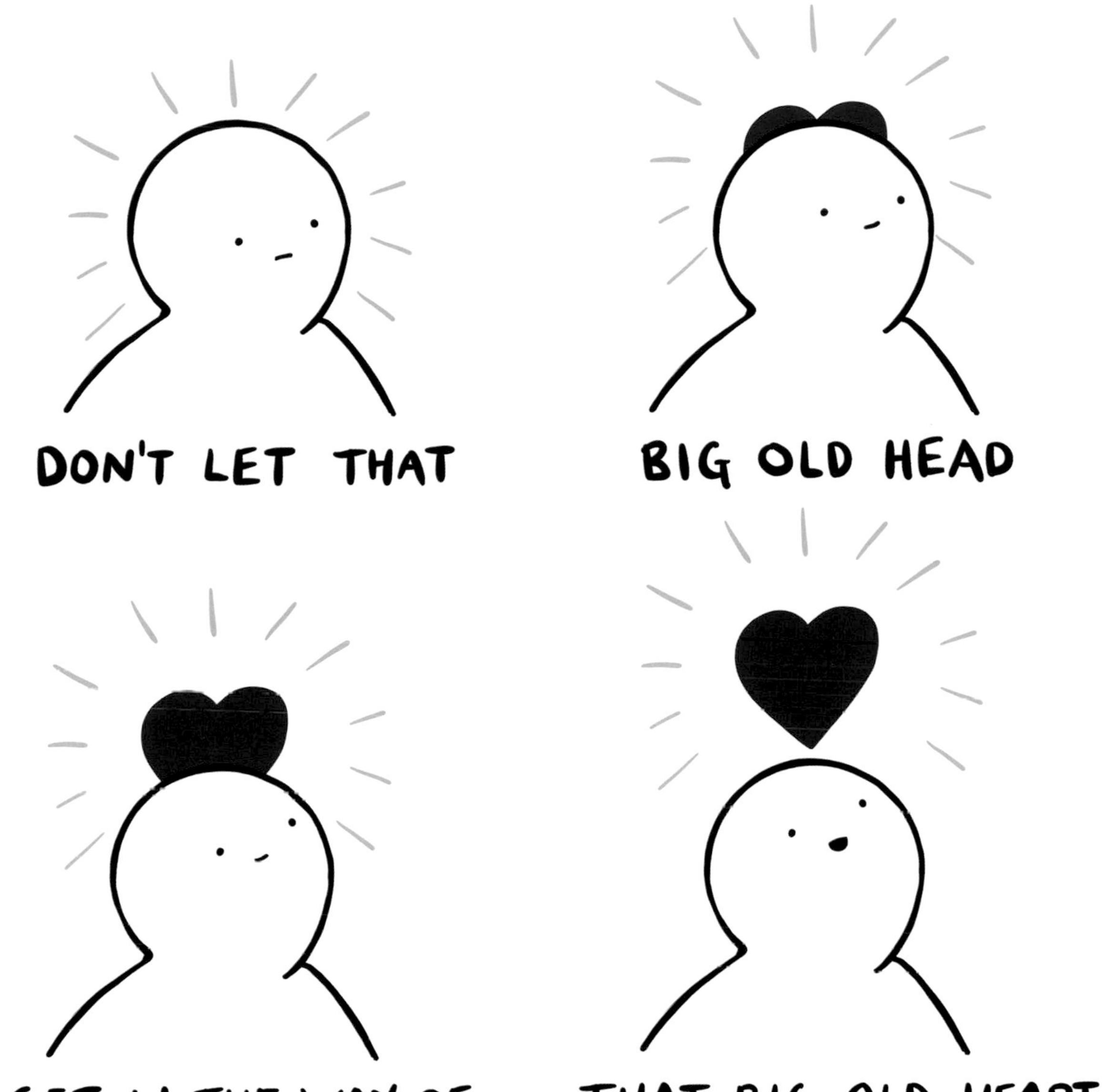
DON'T LET THAT
BIG OLD HEAD
GET IN THE WAY OF
THAT BIG OLD HEART

IF IDEAS ARE FLOWERS,
WORDS ARE POLLINATORS.

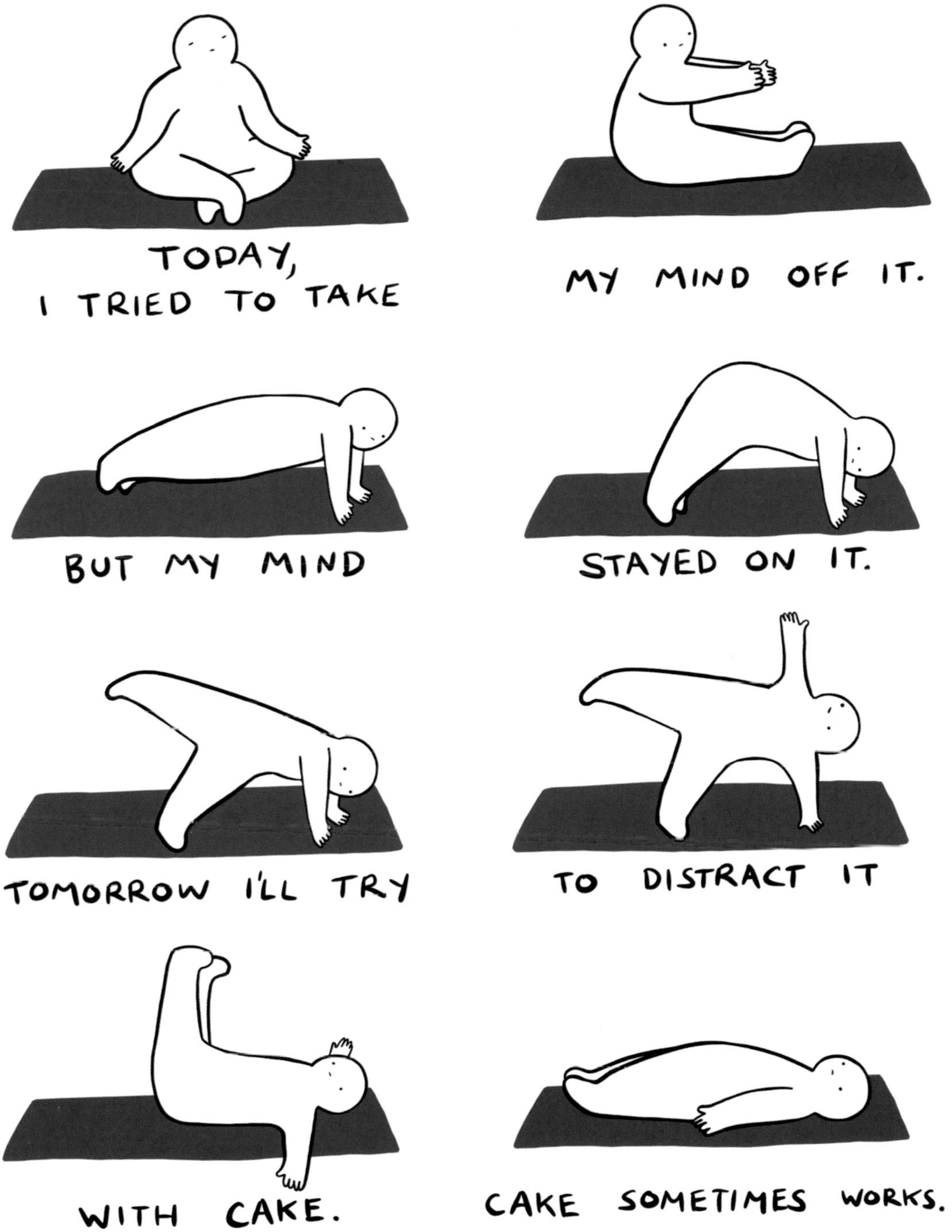
TODAY, I TRIED TO TAKE
MY MIND OFF IT.
BUT MY MIND
STAYED ON IT.
TOMORROW I'LL TRY
TO DISTRACT IT
WITH CAKE.
CAKE SOMETIMES WORKS.

FOCUS POCUS

I DRESS FOR THE
JOB I WANT.

ME TRYING TO GET MYSELF TO JUST
SIT DOWN AND FOCUS FOR FIVE MINUTES.

I DON'T LACK VISION...

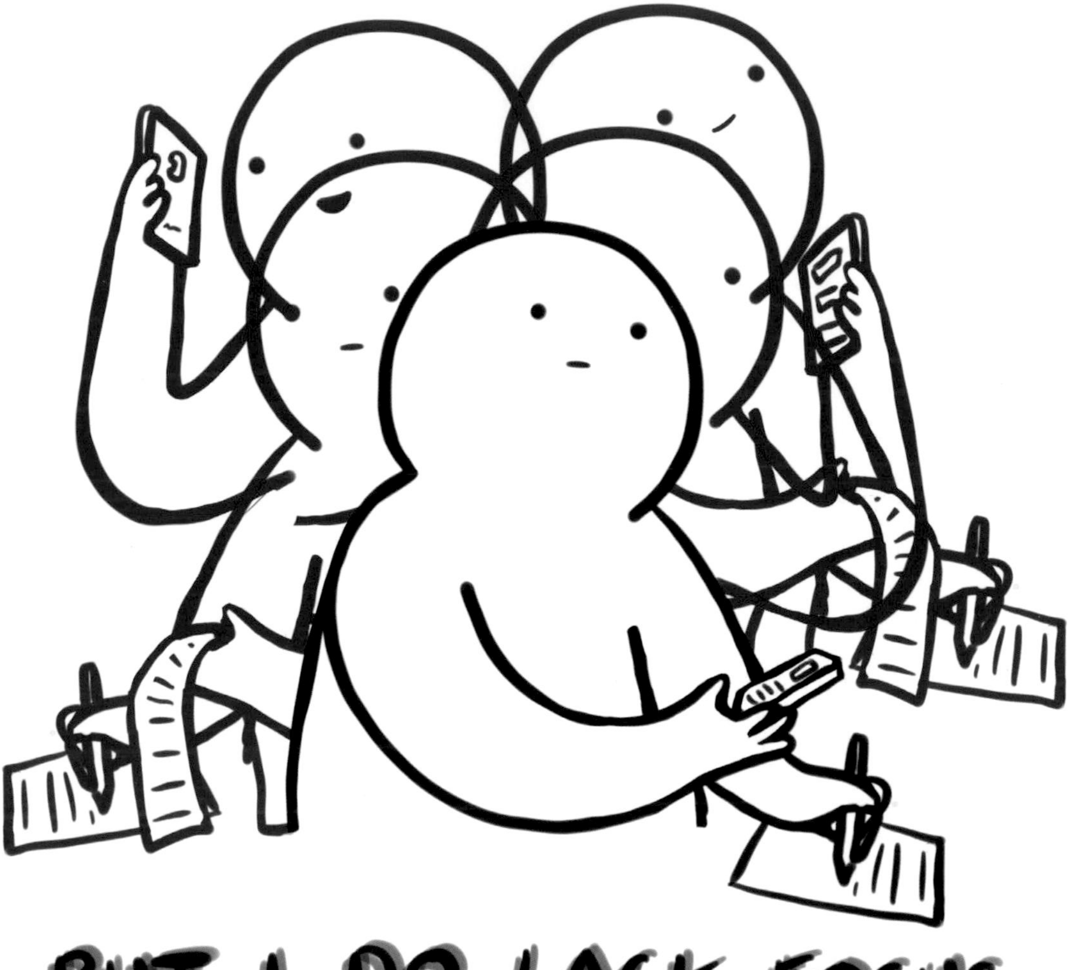

BUT I DO LACK FOCUS.

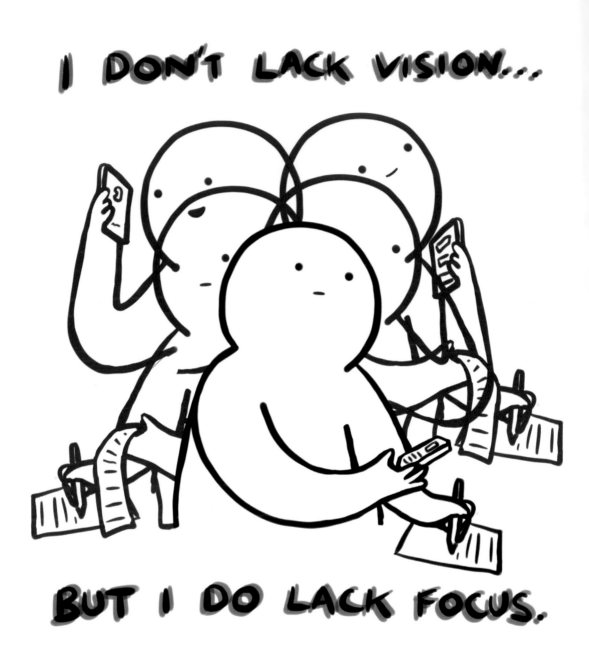

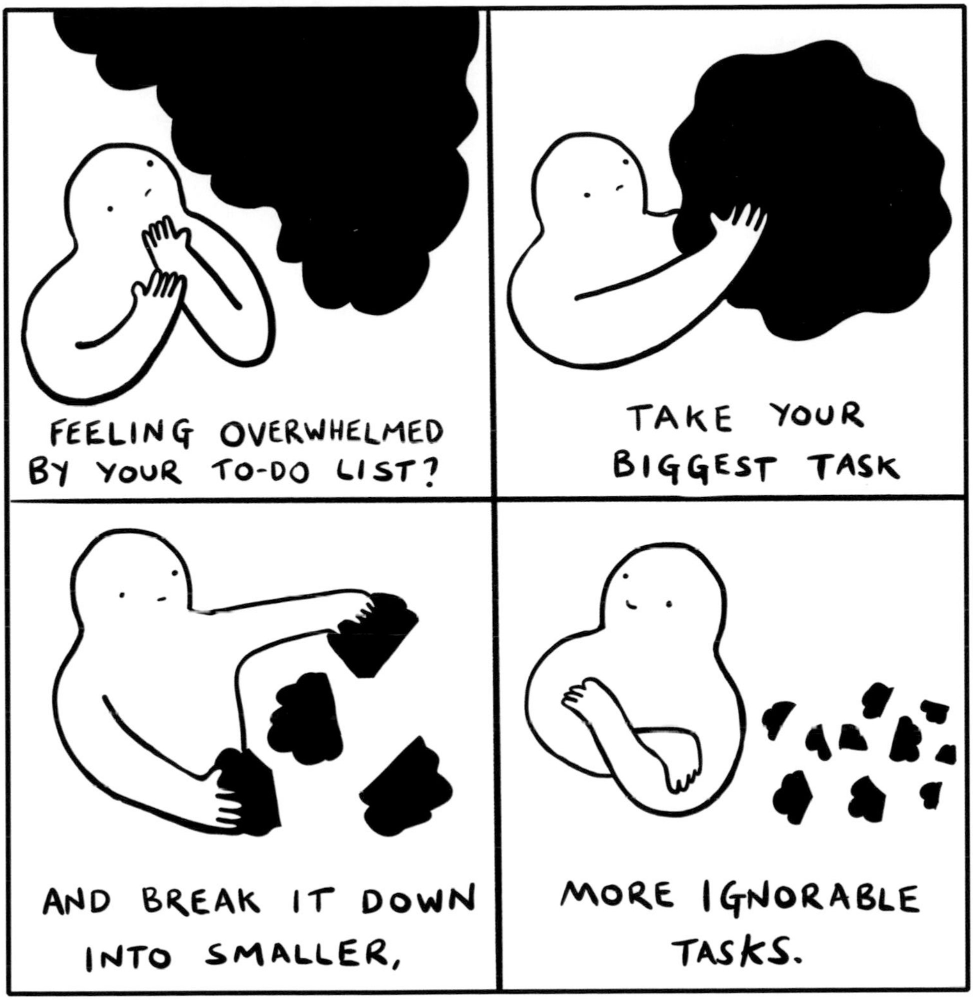
FEELING OVERWHELMED BY YOUR TO-DO LIST?
TAKE YOUR BIGGEST TASK
AND BREAK IT DOWN INTO SMALLER,
MORE IGNORABLE TASKS.

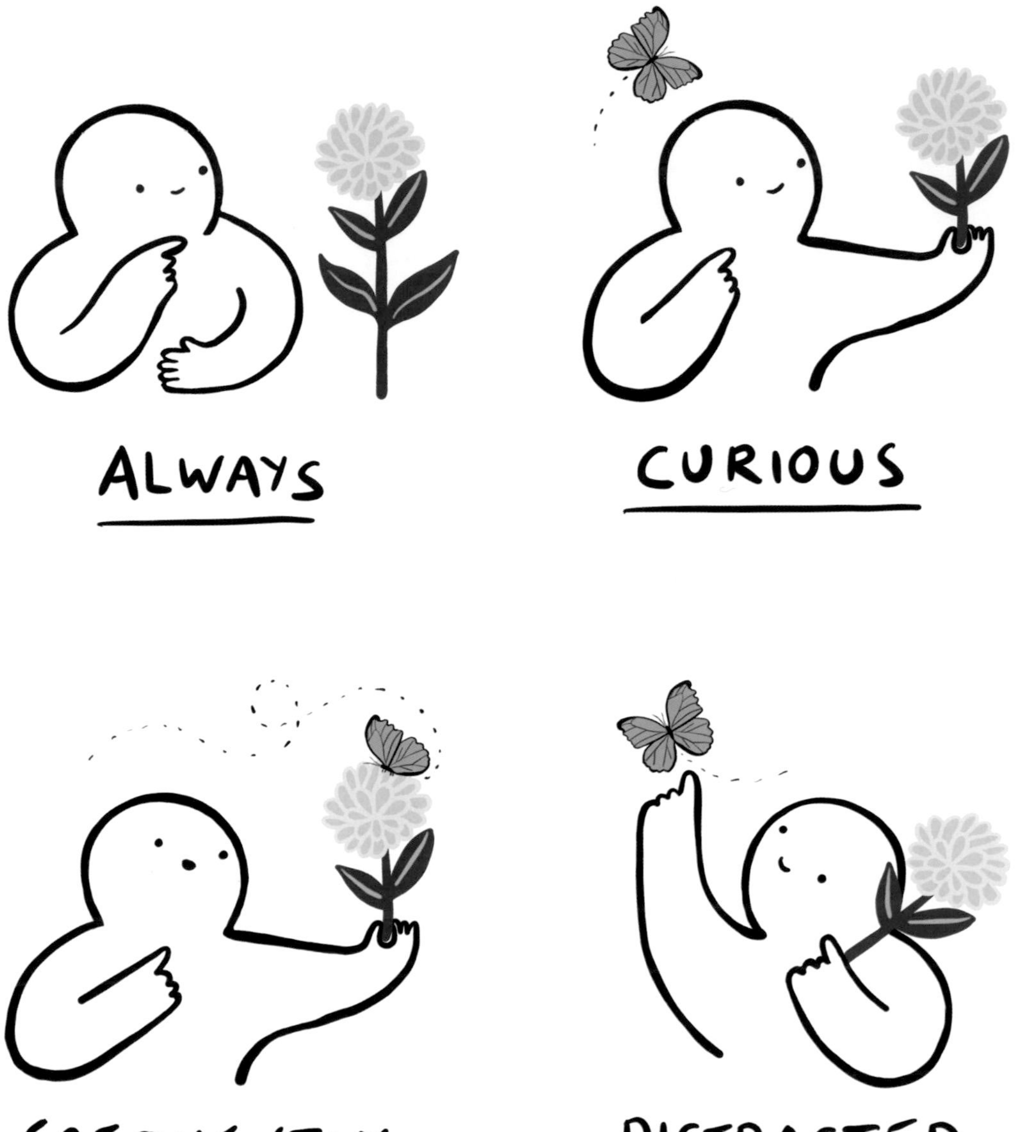
ALWAYS
CURIOUS
FREQUENTLY
DISTRACTED

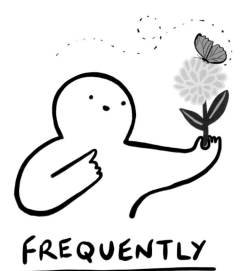

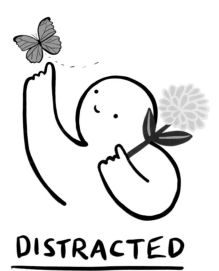

I'M PRETTY GOOD AT
STARTING PROJECTS

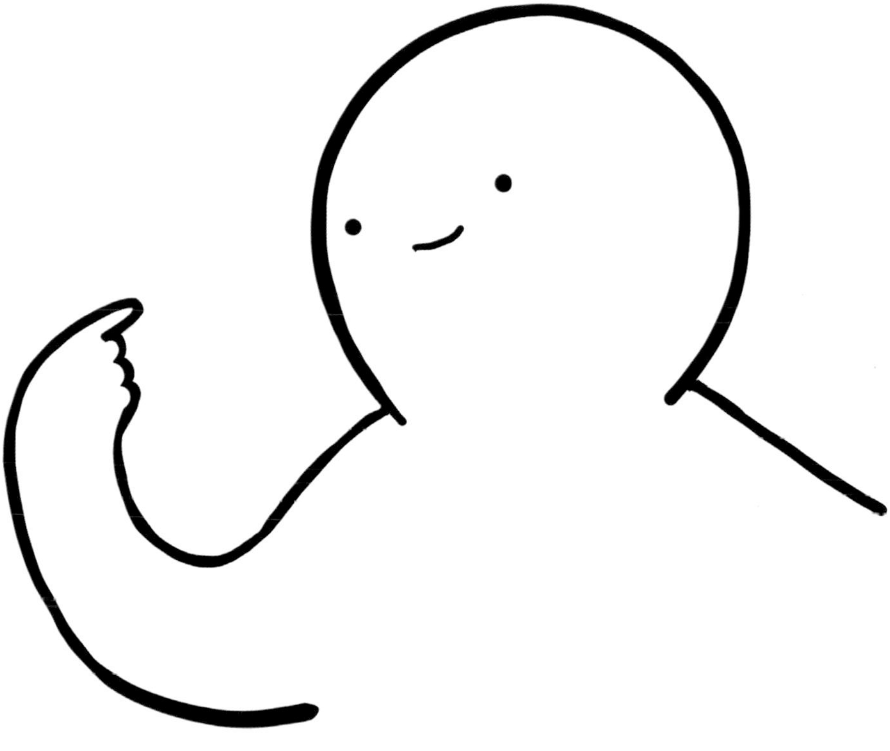

BUT I'M NOT
SO GOOD AT

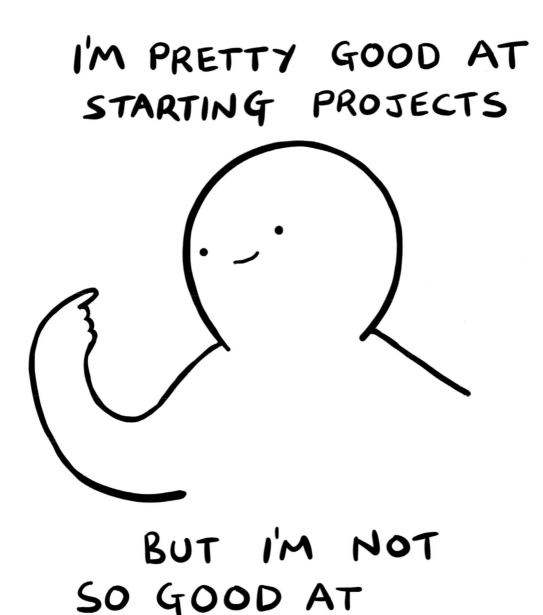

OK. I CAN
DO THIS.

ALL I HAVE TO
DO IS STAY
FOCUSED.

JUST FOCUS.

WOAH! HANDS
ARE SO WEIRD!

I TAKE THE STRUGGLE BUS TO WORK

AND GO HOME ON THE HOT MESS EXPRESS

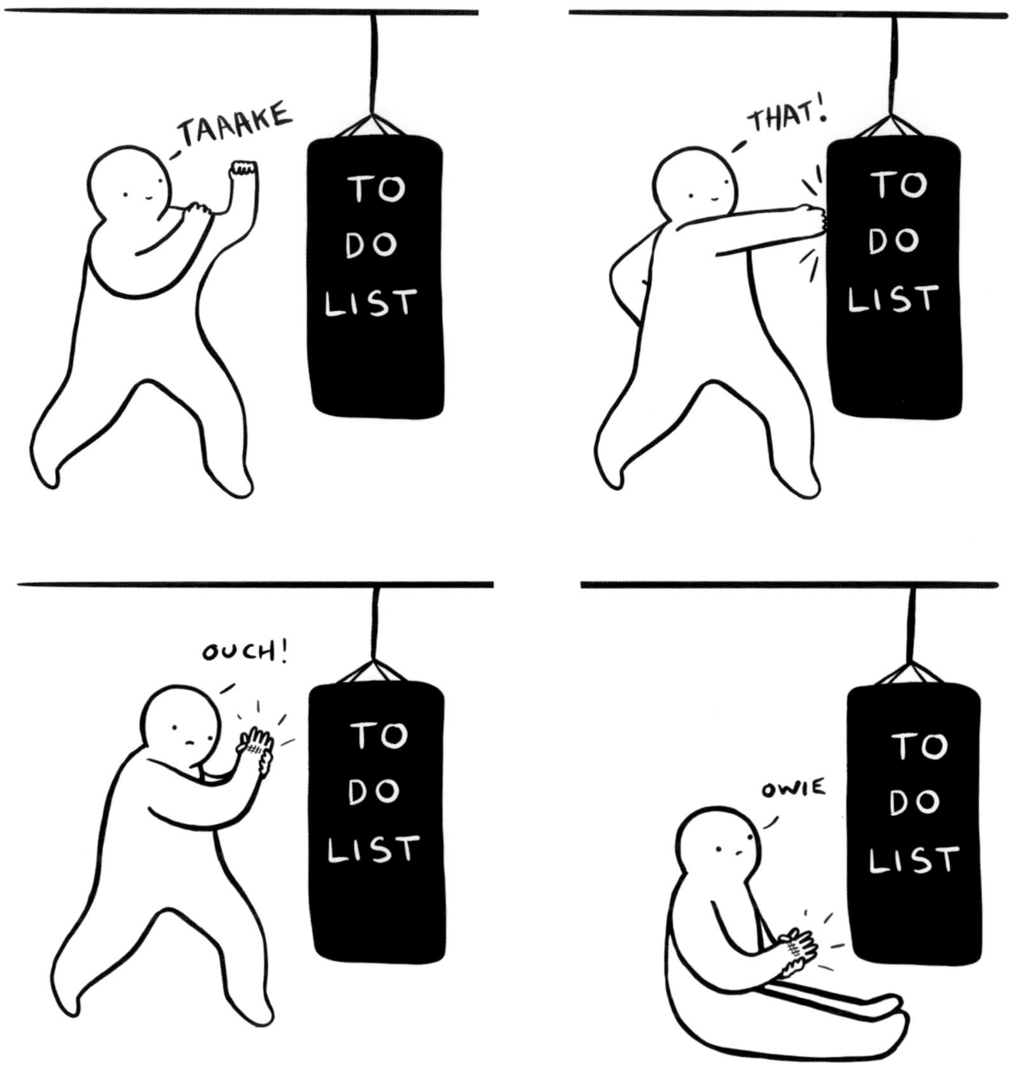
TAAAKE
TO DO LIST
THAT!
TO DO LIST
OUCH!
TO DO LIST
OWIE
TO DO LIST

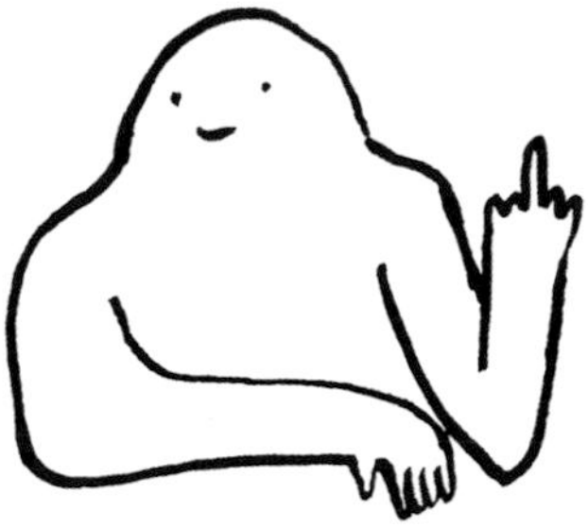

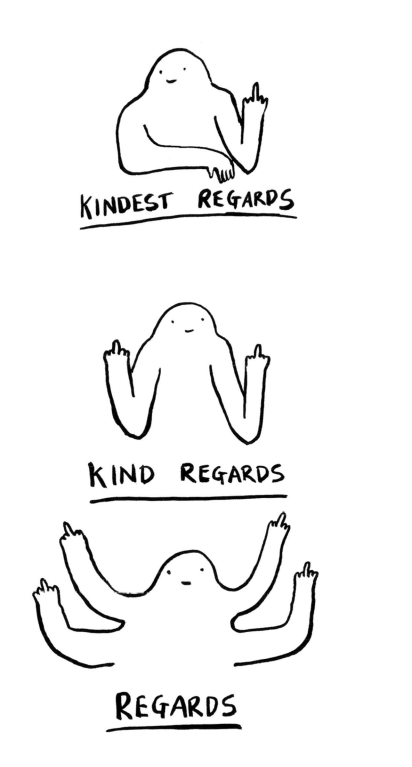

KINDEST REGARDS

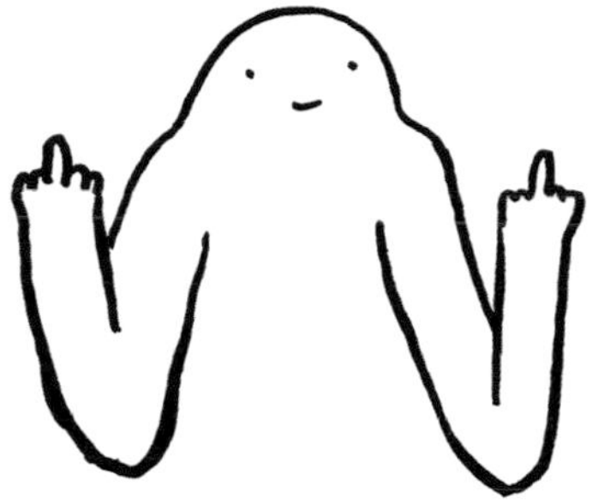

KIND REGARDS

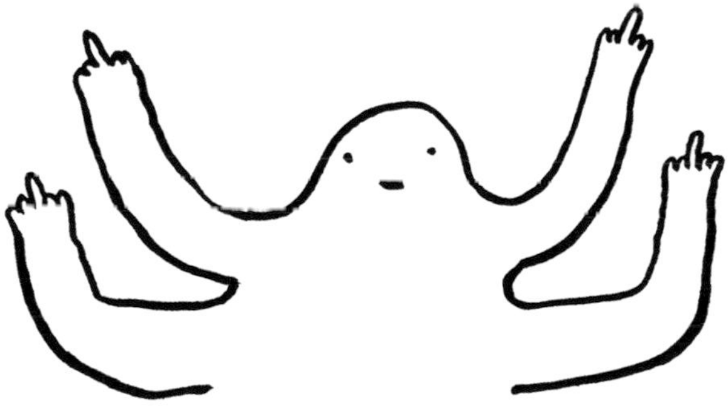

REGARDS

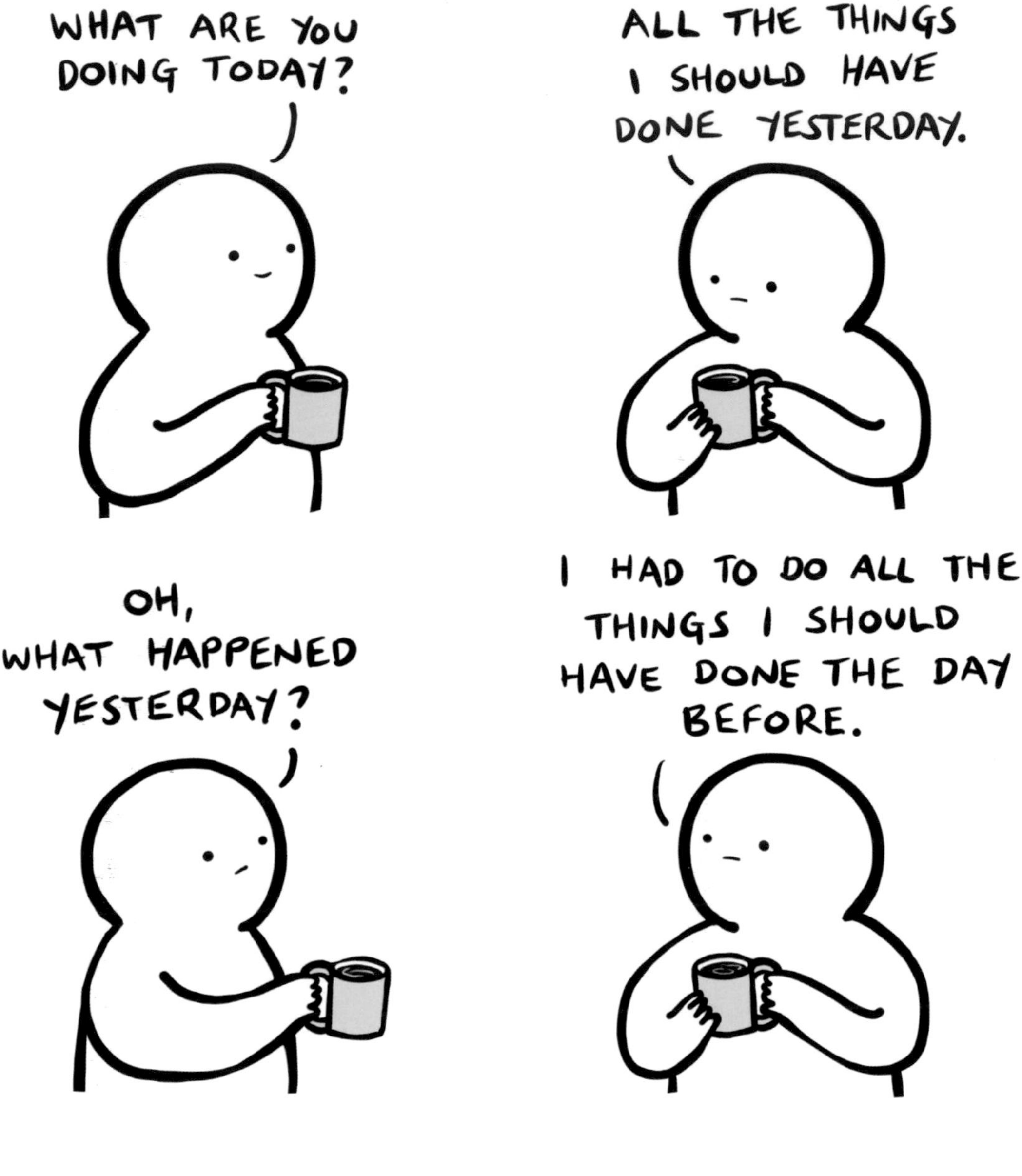
WHAT ARE YOU DOING TODAY?
ALL THE THINGS I SHOULD HAVE DONE YESTERDAY.
OH, WHAT HAPPENED YESTERDAY?
I HAD TO DO ALL THE THINGS I SHOULD HAVE DONE THE DAY BEFORE.

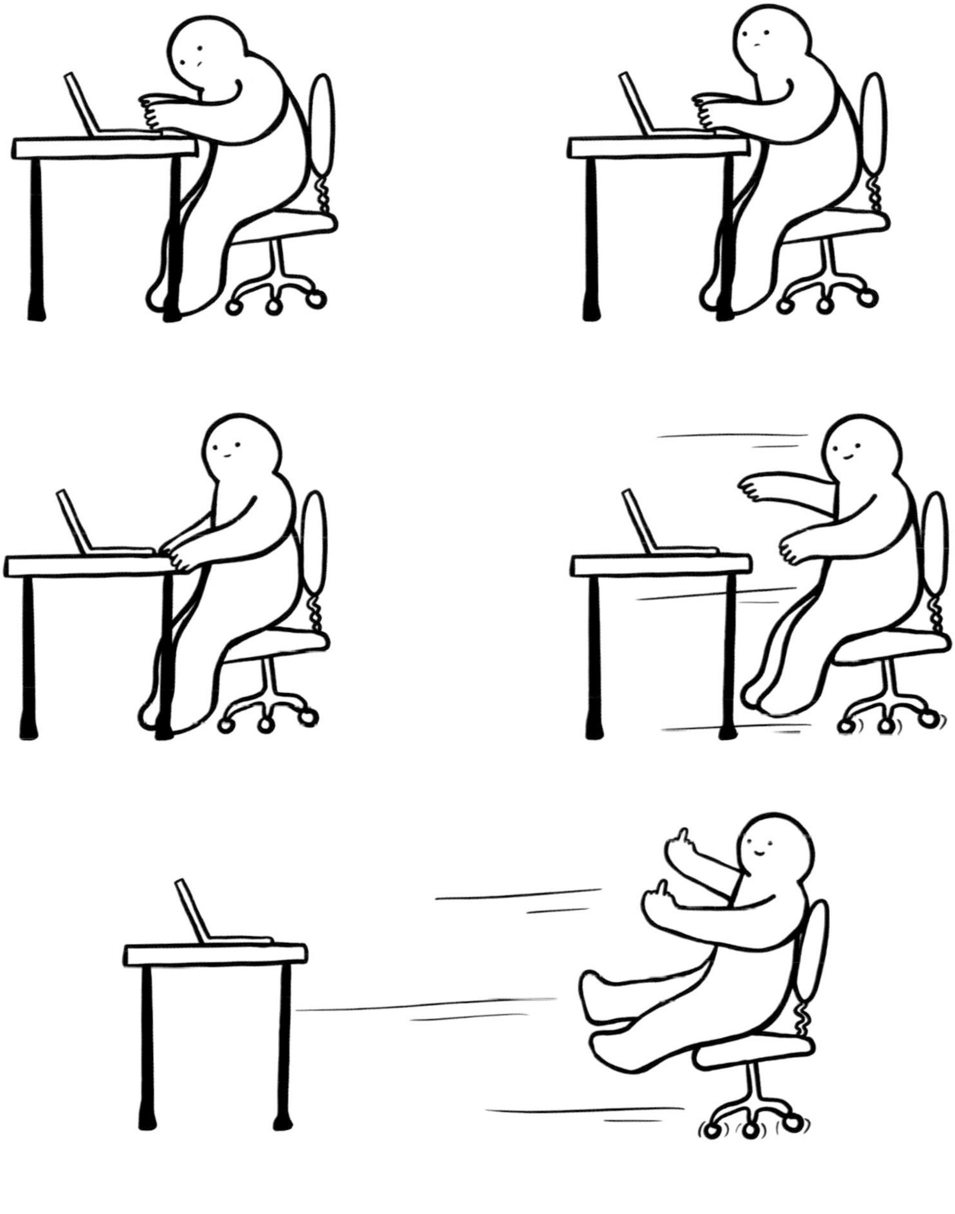

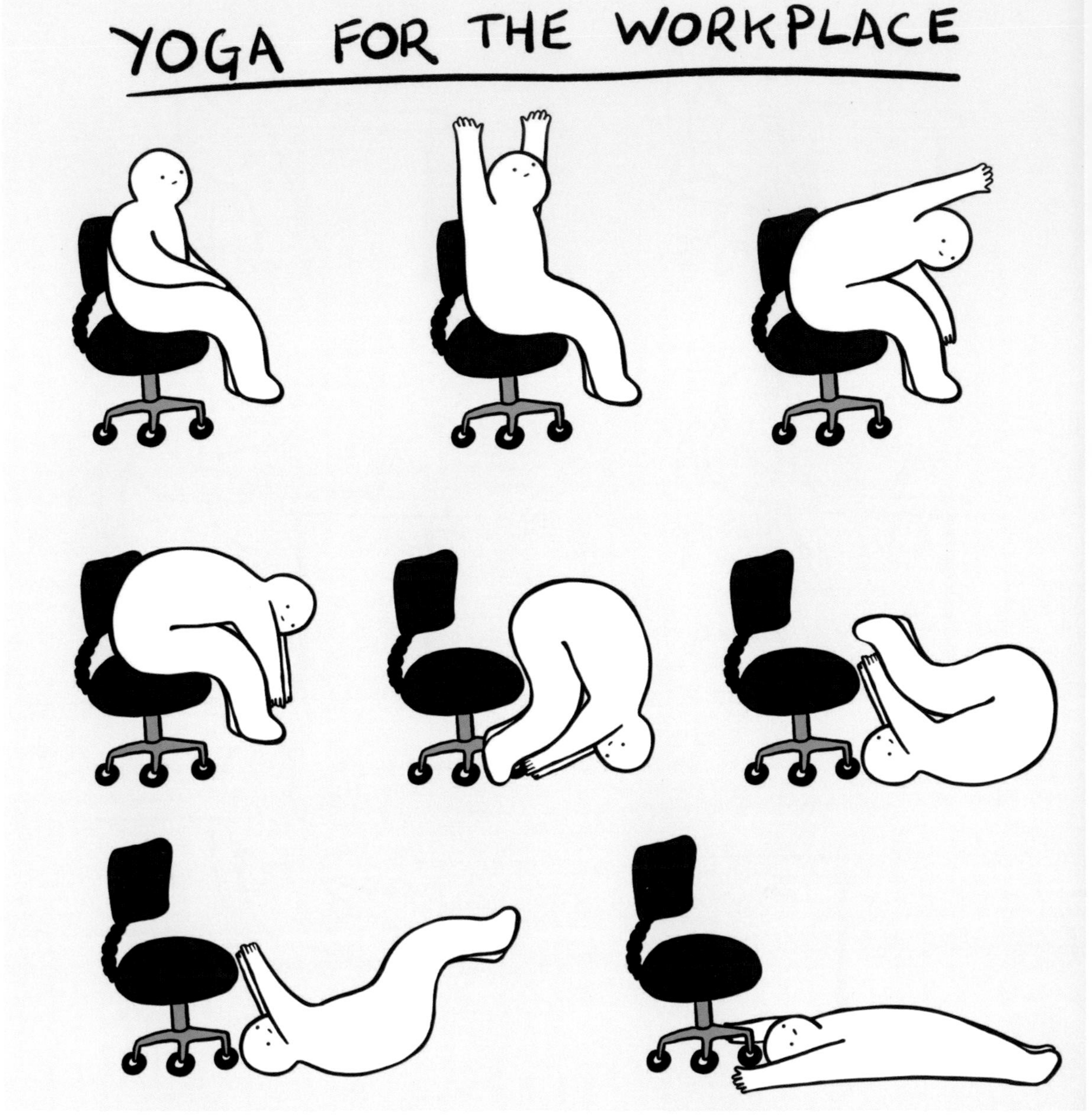
YOGA FOR THE WORKPLACE

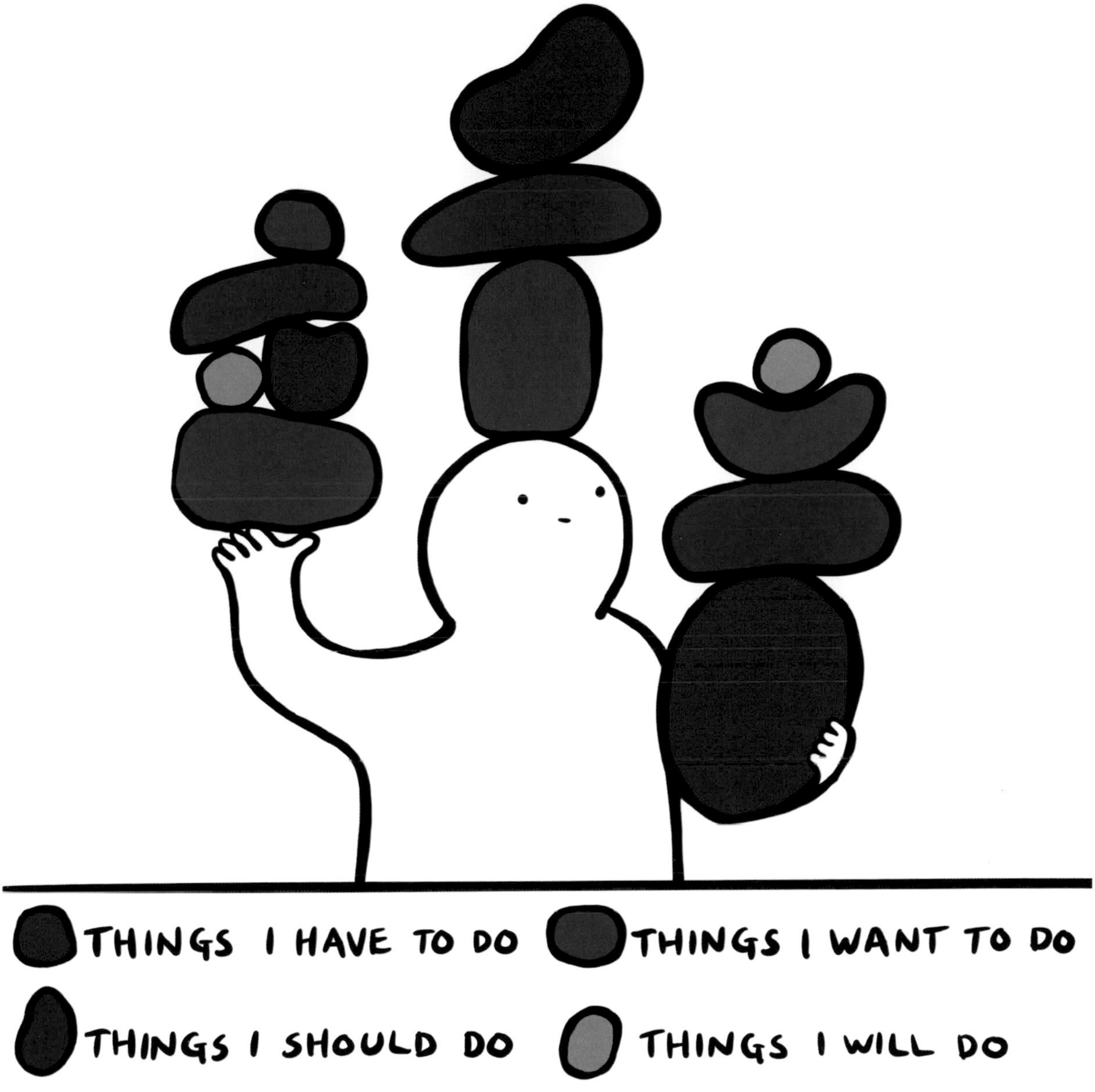
THINGS I HAVE TO DO
THINGS I WANT TO DO
THINGS I SHOULD DO
THINGS I WILL DO

I KNEW I MIGHT
BE STRESSED,

AND I KNEW I
MIGHT BE BORED,

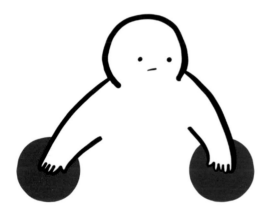

BUT I DIDN'T KNOW
IT WAS POSSIBLE

TO BE
BOTH AT THE
SAME TIME.

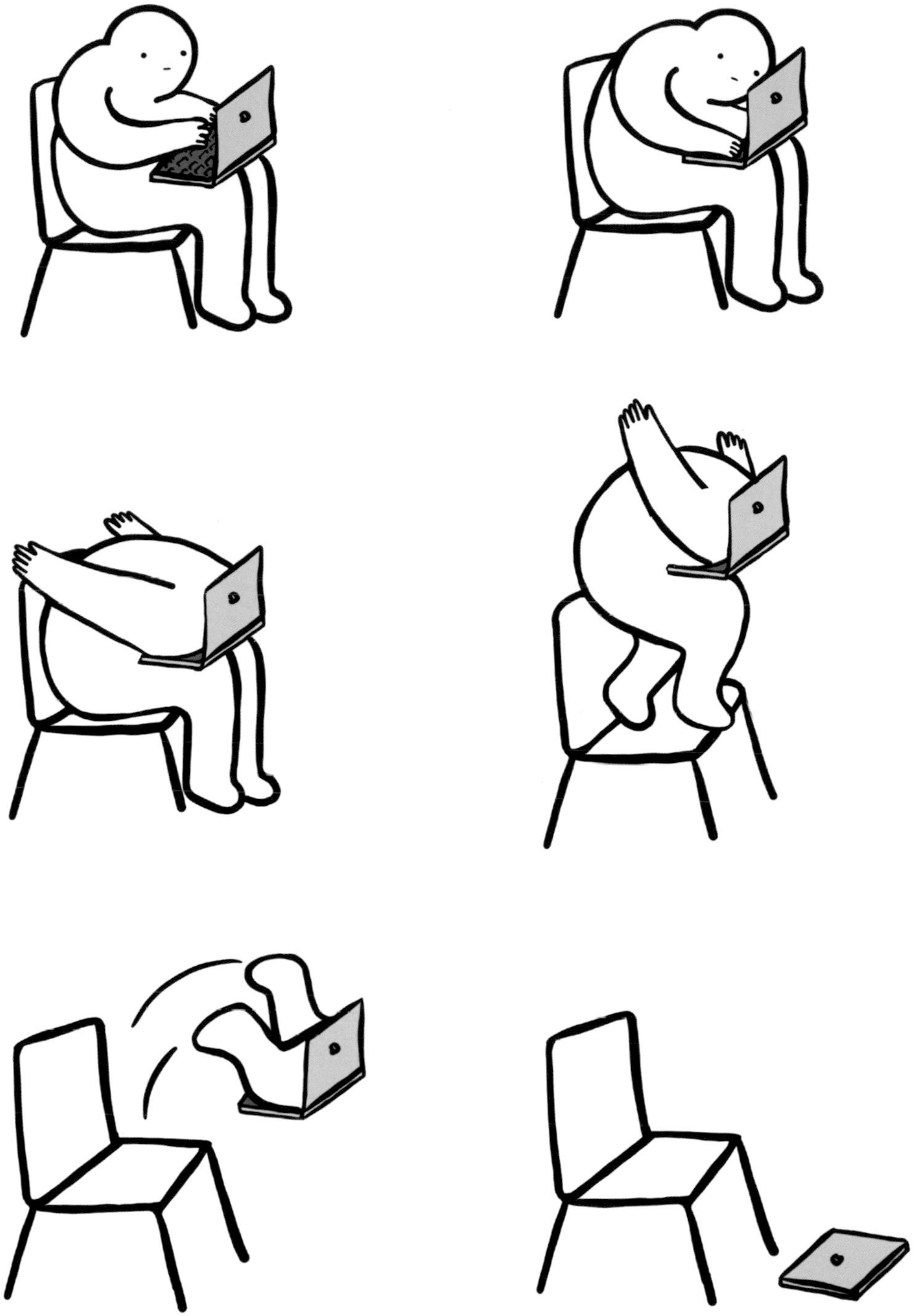

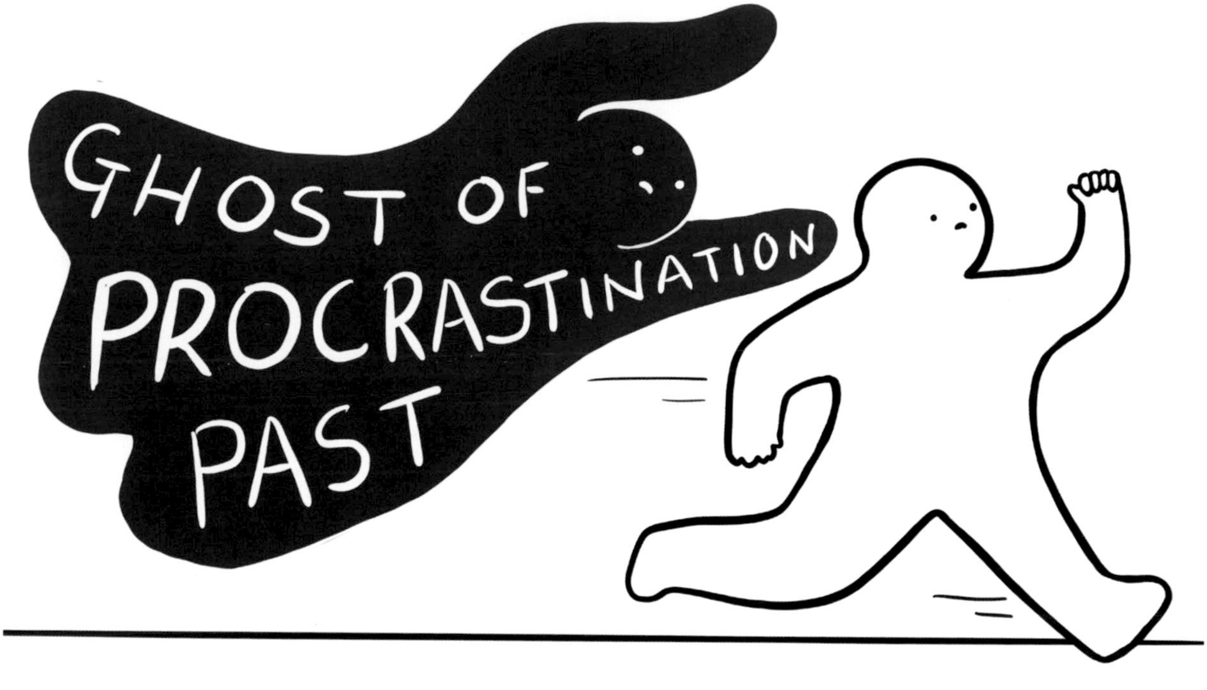
GHOST OF
PROCRASTINATION
PAST

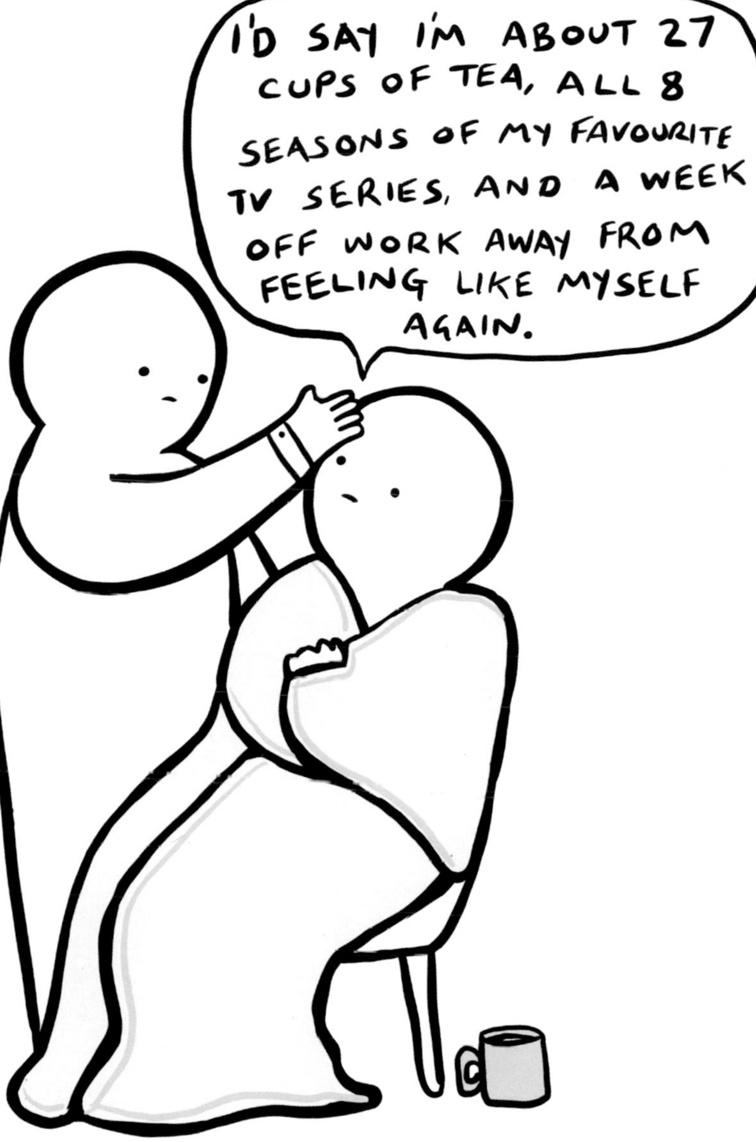
I'D SAY I'M ABOUT 27 CUPS OF TEA, ALL 8 SEASONS OF MY FAVOURITE TV SERIES, AND A WEEK OFF WORK AWAY FROM FEELING LIKE MYSELF AGAIN.

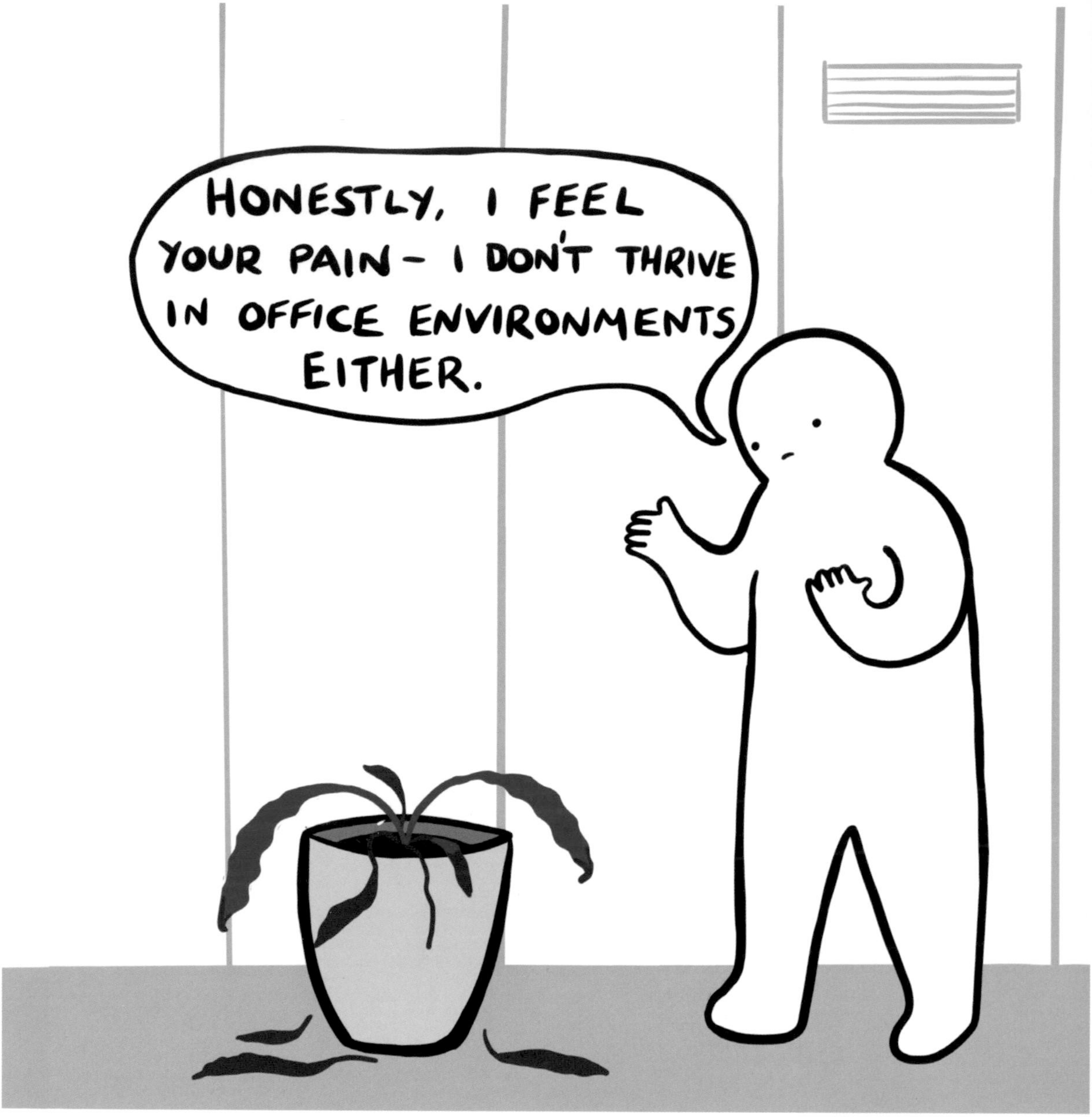
HONESTLY, I FEEL YOUR PAIN – I DON'T THRIVE IN OFFICE ENVIRONMENTS EITHER.

I THINK

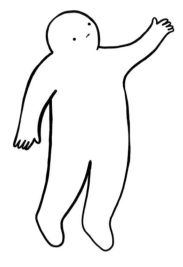

I'M HAVING A

MID-WEEK

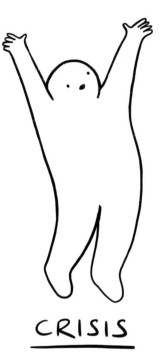

CRISIS

CAKE IT TIL YOU MAKE IT

EMOTIONALLY UNSTABLE

AND IN NEED OF A BAGEL

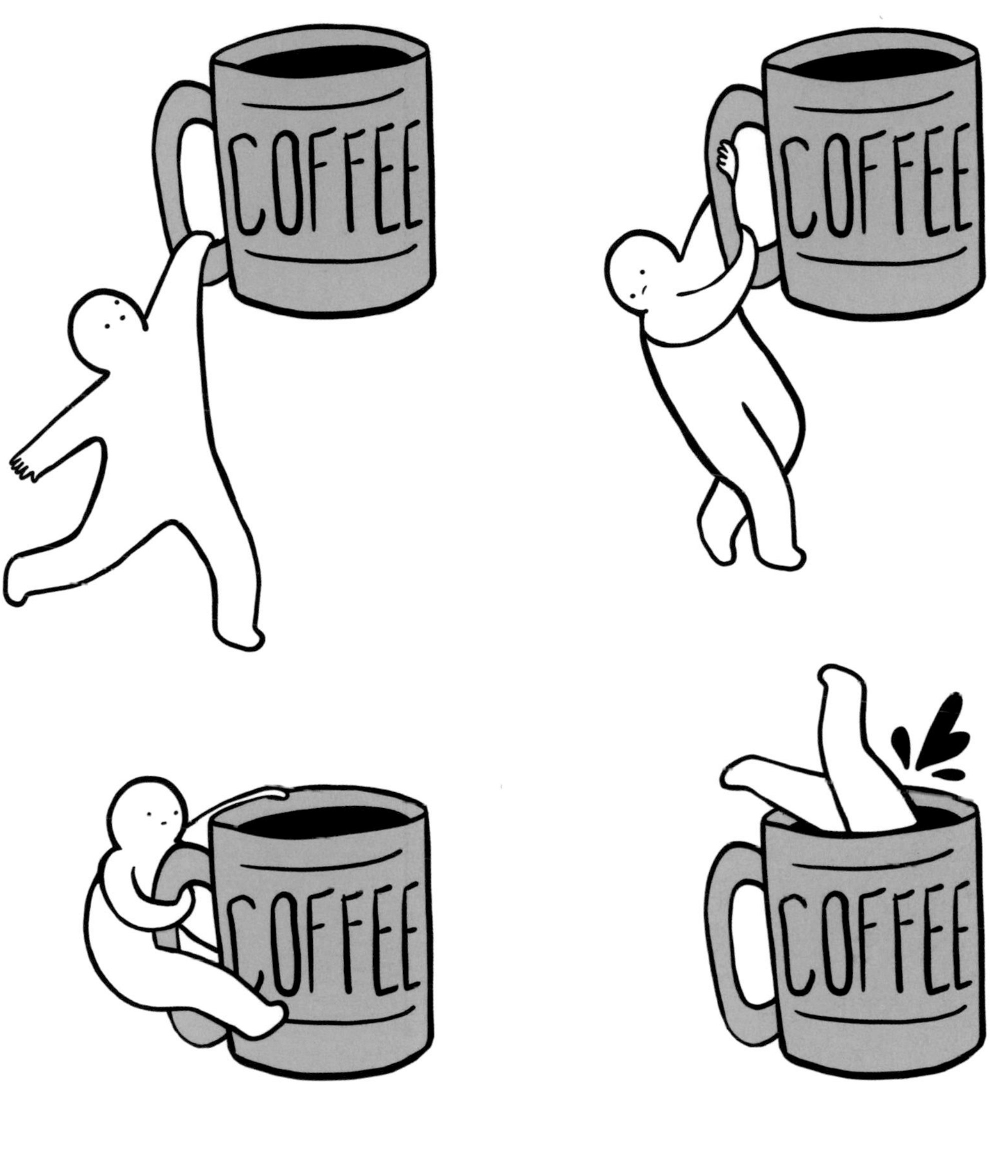
COFFEE
COFFEE
COFFEE
COFFEE

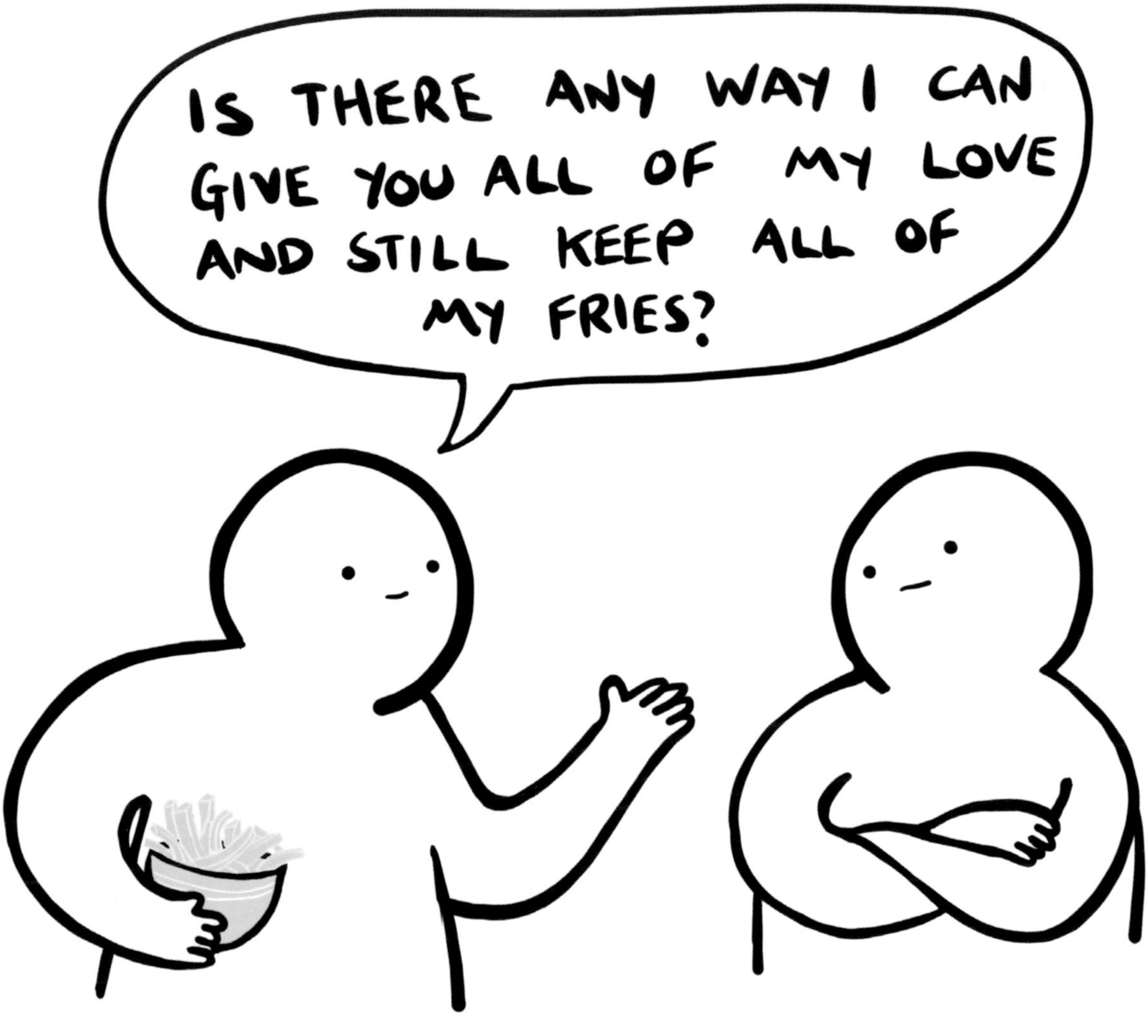
IS THERE ANY WAY I CAN GIVE YOU ALL OF MY LOVE AND STILL KEEP ALL OF MY FRIES?

TODAY IS THE
FIRST DAY

OF THE REST
OF MY LIFE.

AND SO, LIKE WITH
FIRST PANCAKES,

IT'S PROBABLY GOING
TO BE A BIT WEIRD.

HEAD FULL OF NONSENSE
HEART FULL OF LOVE
BELLY FULL OF POTATO

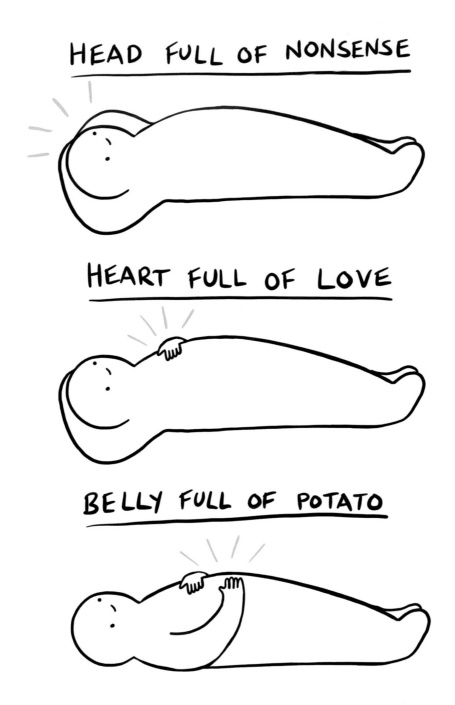

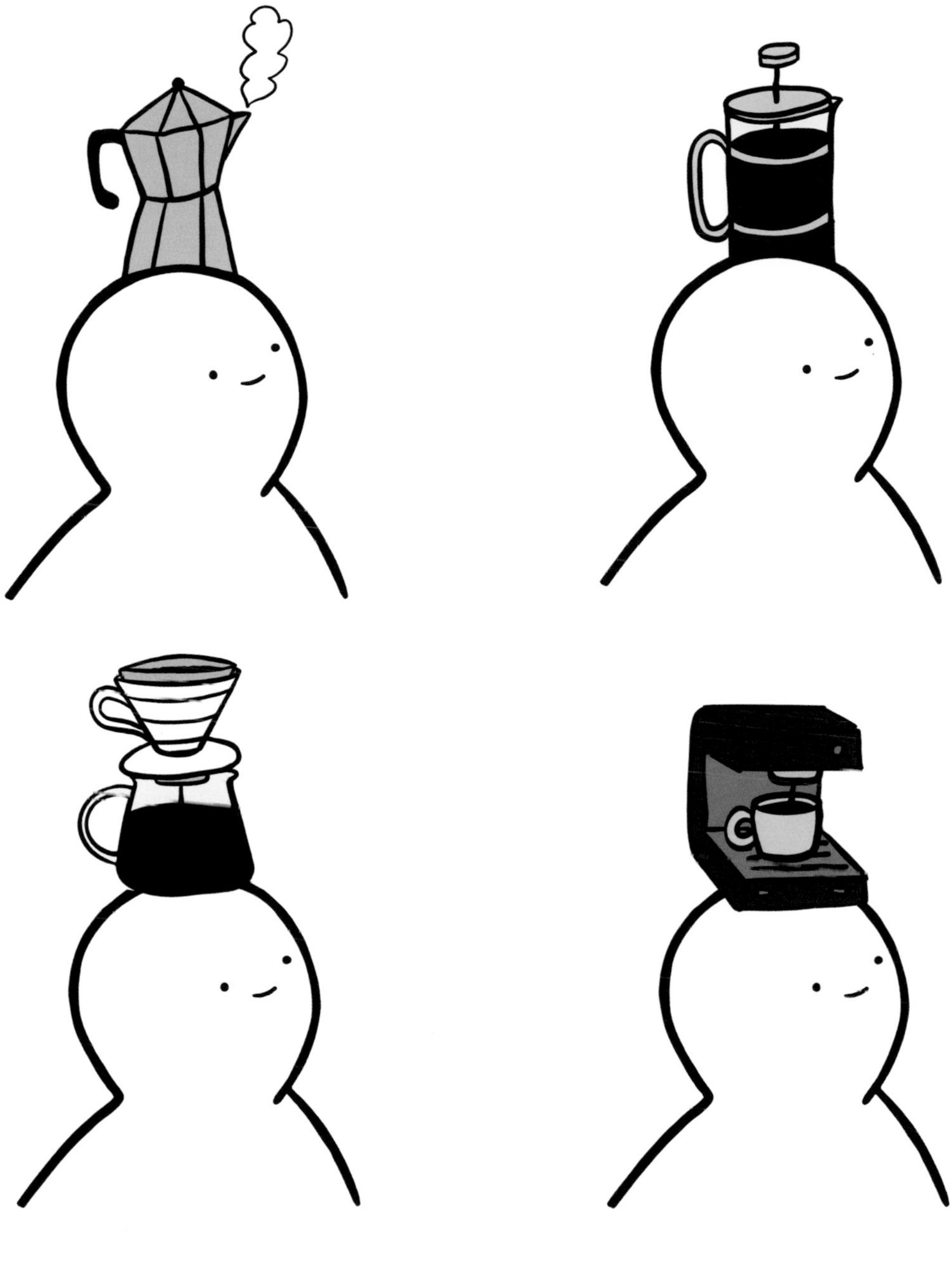

SORRY I DIDN'T HEAR WHAT YOU SAID AT LUNCH, I WAS ALREADY THINKING ABOUT DINNER.

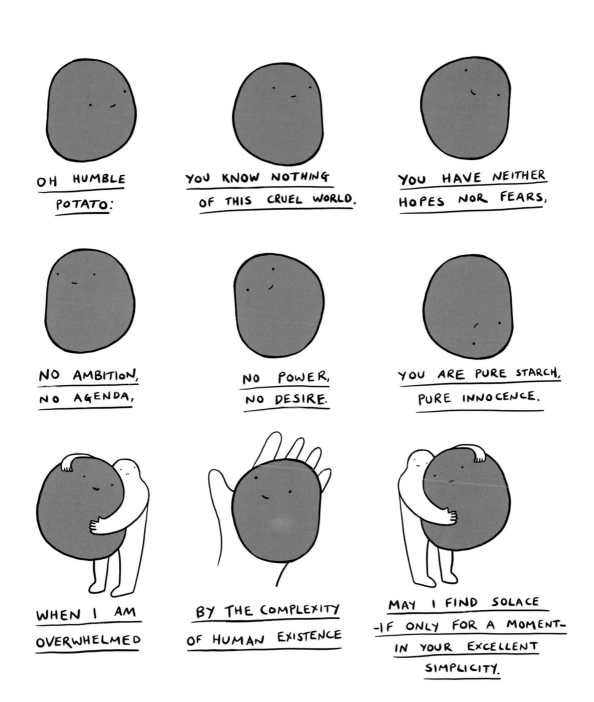

OH HUMBLE POTATO:

YOU KNOW NOTHING OF THIS CRUEL WORLD.

YOU HAVE NEITHER HOPES NOR FEARS,

NO AMBITION, NO AGENDA,

NO POWER, NO DESIRE.

YOU ARE PURE STARCH, PURE INNOCENCE.

WHEN I AM OVERWHELMED

BY THE COMPLEXITY OF HUMAN EXISTENCE

MAY I FIND SOLACE -IF ONLY FOR A MOMENT- IN YOUR EXCELLENT SIMPLICITY.

THE FOUR TEMPERATURES OF HOT BEVERAGES:

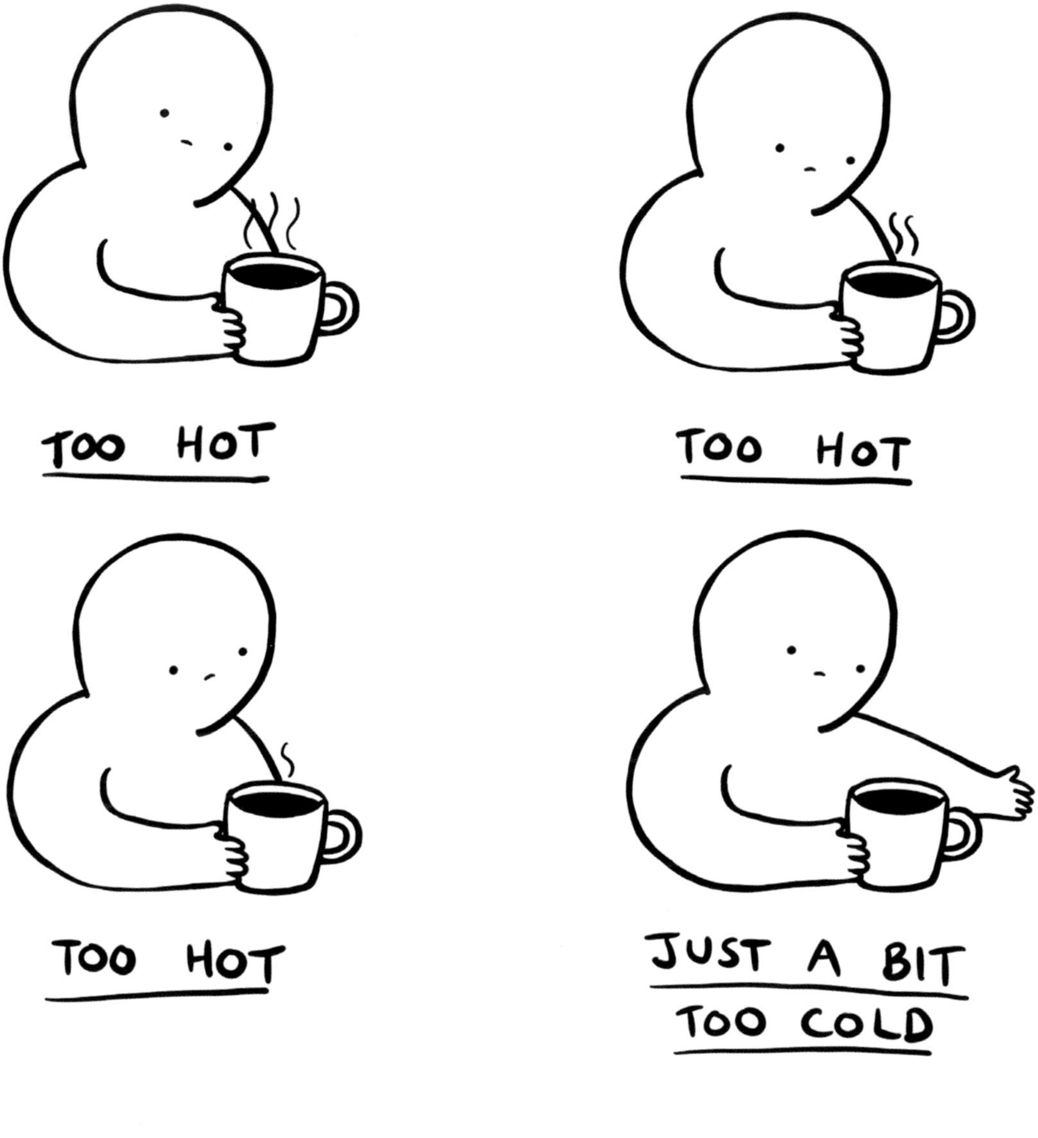
TOO HOT
TOO HOT
TOO HOT
JUST A BIT TOO COLD

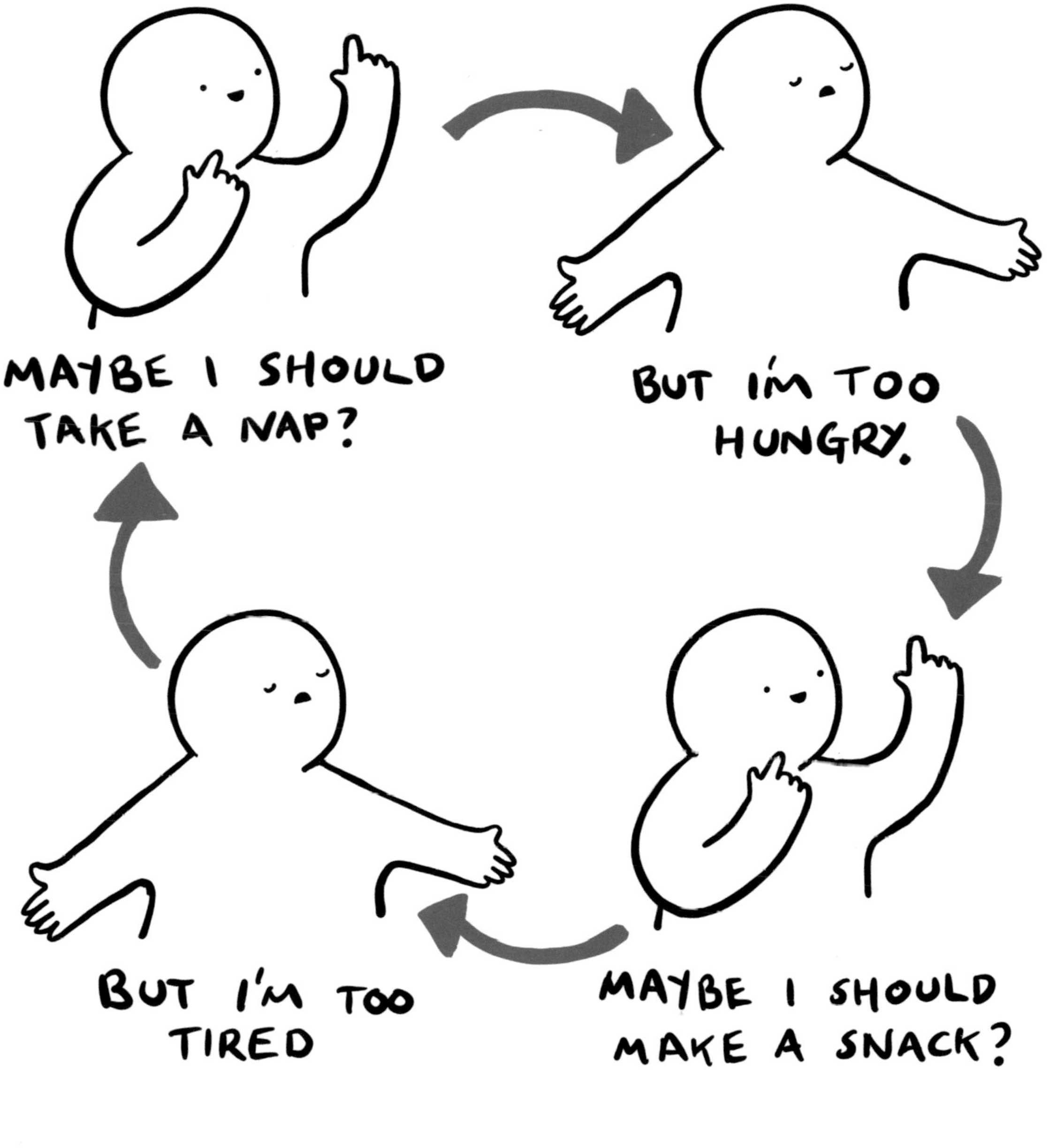
MAYBE I SHOULD TAKE A NAP?
BUT I'M TOO HUNGRY.
MAYBE I SHOULD MAKE A SNACK?
BUT I'M TOO TIRED

I WANT TO BE LIKE COFFEE:

STRONG BUT NOT BITTER,
FULL OF ENERGY BUT NOT ANNOYING,
HOT BUT NOT INTIMIDATING,
BELOVED.

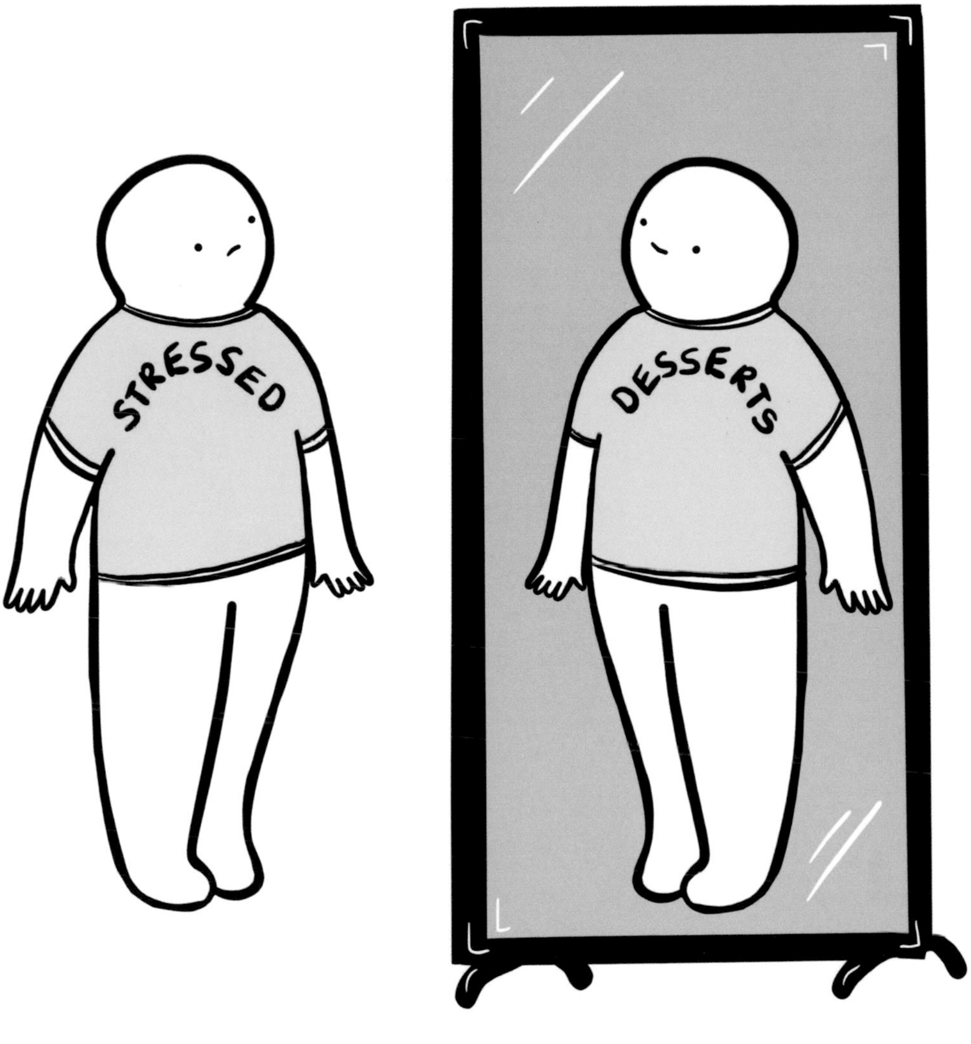
STRESSED
DESSERTS

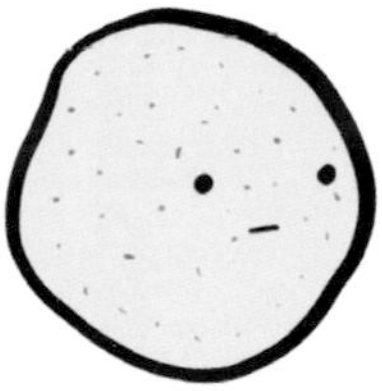

WHAT IF I'M NOT A TOUGH COOKIE?

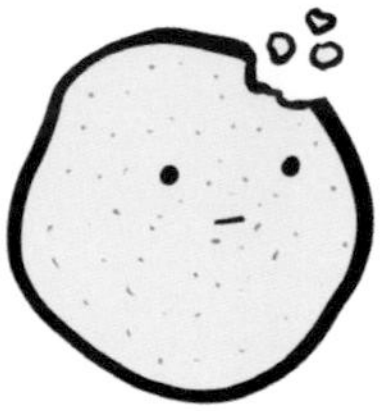

WHAT IF I'M A COOKIE THAT HAS BEEN KNOWN TO CRUMBLE UNDER PRESSURE?

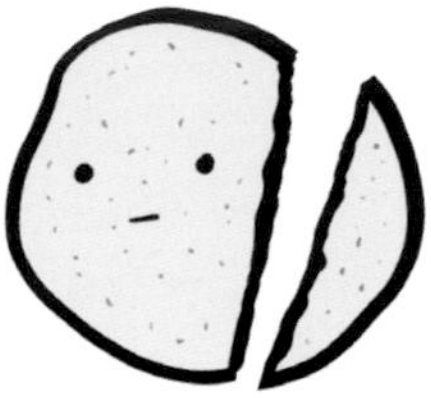

A COOKIE THAT HAS BEEN KNOWN TO SNAP?

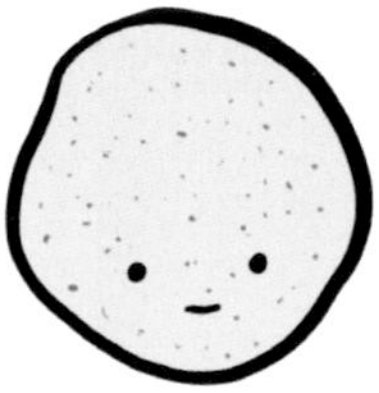

WHAT IF I'M A SUPER SWEET, WARM AND SLIGHTLY FRAGILE COOKIE?

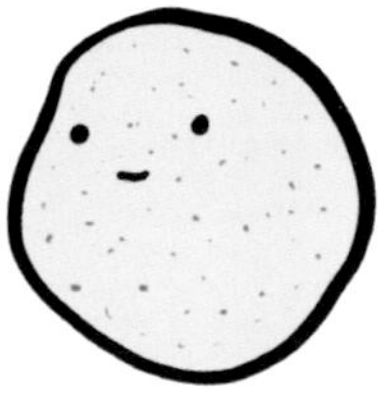

WHAT IF, DESPITE MY CRUNCHY EXTERIOR, I'M A SOFT, GOOEY COOKIE IN THE MIDDLE?

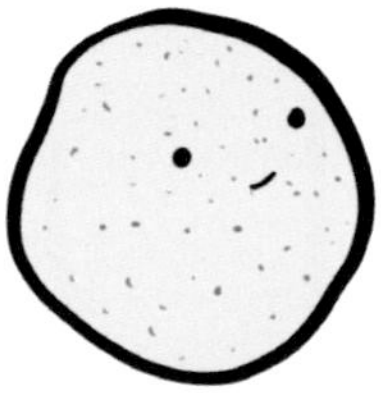

UPON REFLECTION, I SOUND LIKE AN ABSOLUTELY PERFECT COOKIE.

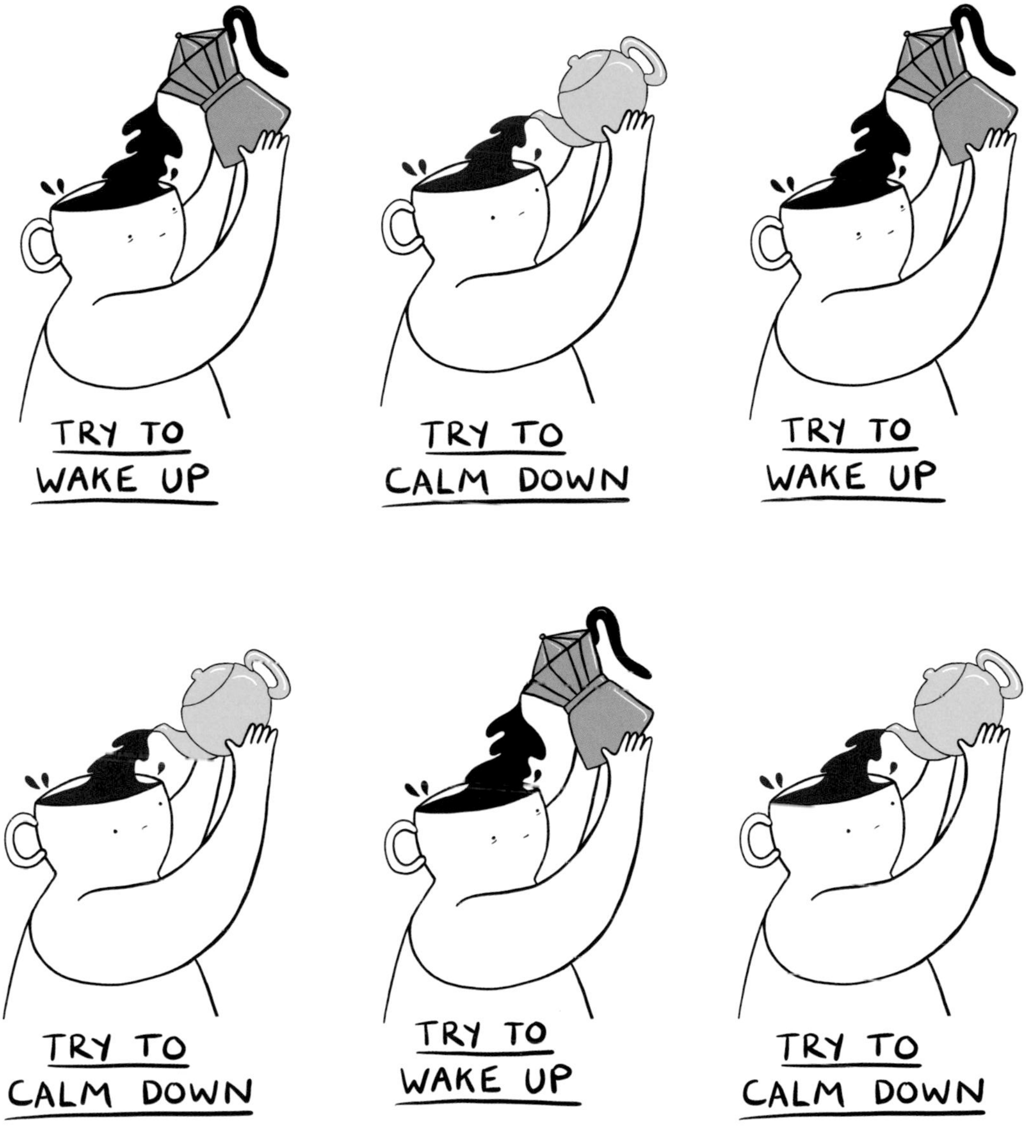
TRY TO WAKE UP
TRY TO CALM DOWN
TRY TO WAKE UP
TRY TO CALM DOWN
TRY TO WAKE UP
TRY TO CALM DOWN

SIGNS YOU MIGHT BE
ENTERING YOUR TURNIP ERA:

YOU'RE WEIRD, SWEET, RECLUSIVE
AND BETTER WITH BUTTER.

WHEN ONE DOOR CLOSES...

SLAM!

ANOTHER DOOR OPENS.

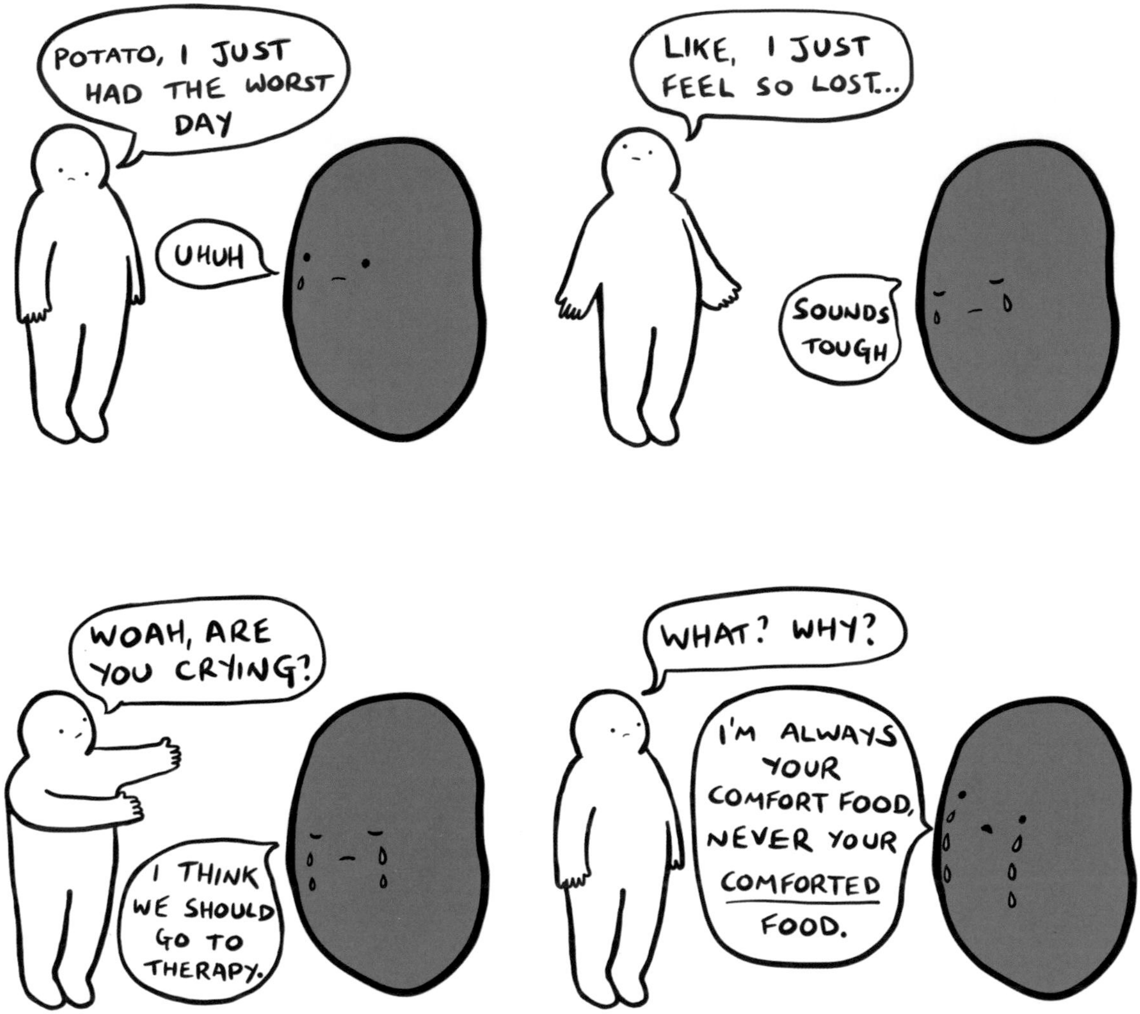
POTATO, I JUST HAD THE WORST DAY
UHUH
LIKE, I JUST FEEL SO LOST...
SOUNDS TOUGH
WOAH, ARE YOU CRYING?
I THINK WE SHOULD GO TO THERAPY.
WHAT? WHY?
I'M ALWAYS YOUR COMFORT FOOD, NEVER YOUR COMFORTED FOOD.

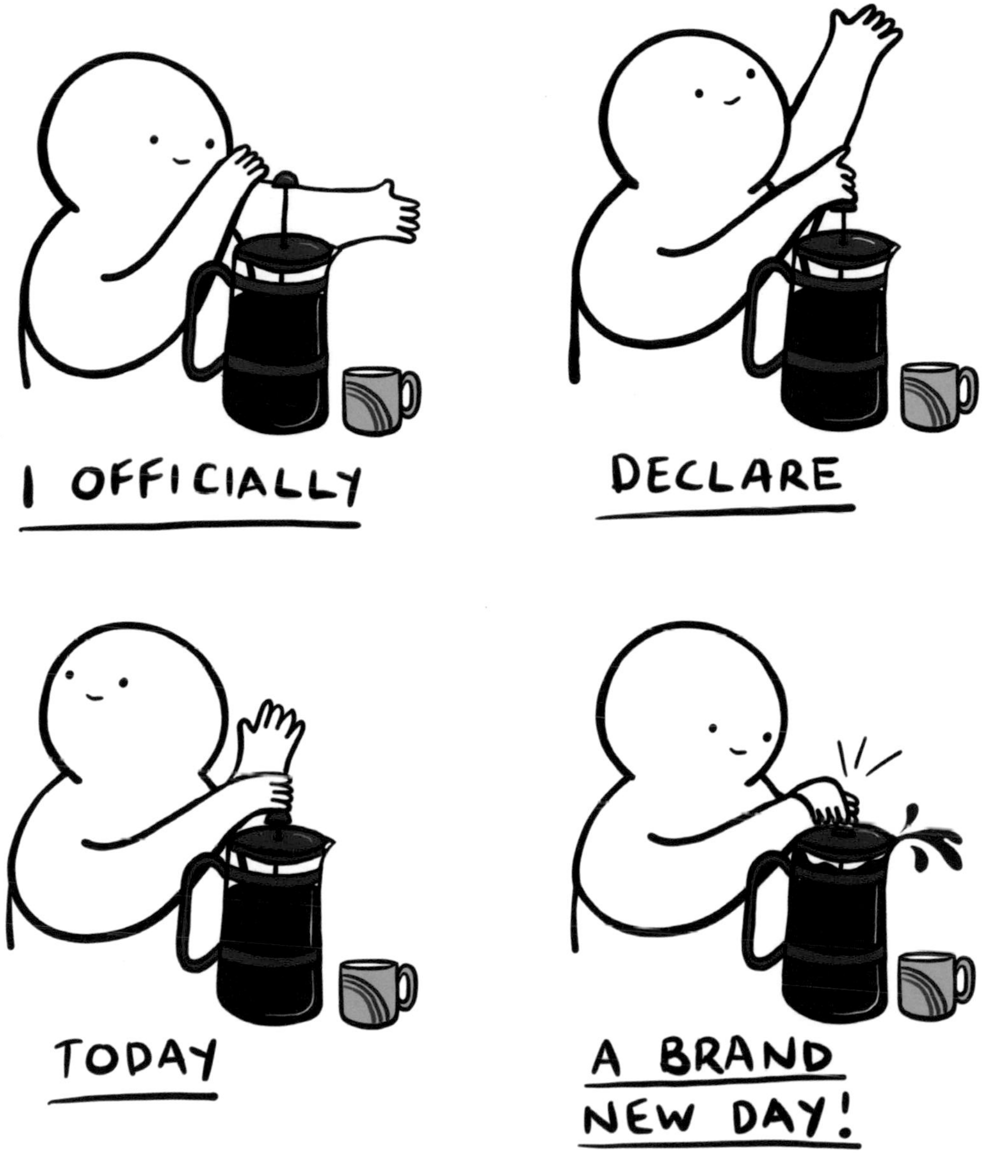
I OFFICIALLY
DECLARE
TODAY
A BRAND NEW DAY!

JUST MIGHT WORK

OK, TIME TO GET TO WORK

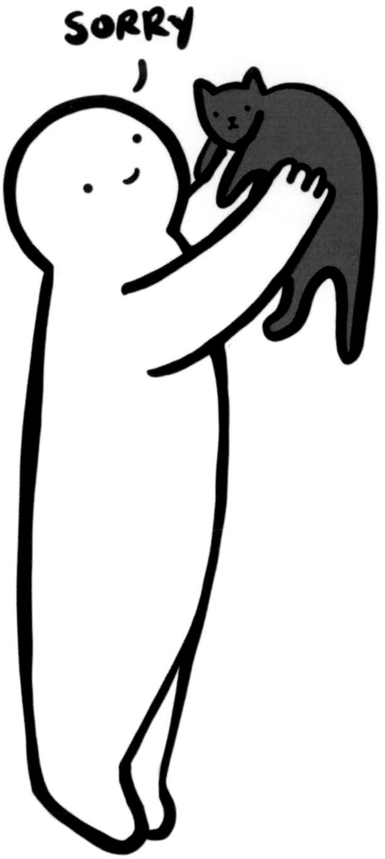
SORRY

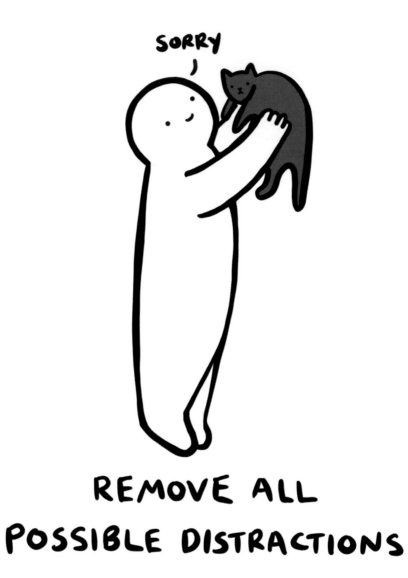

REMOVE ALL
POSSIBLE DISTRACTIONS

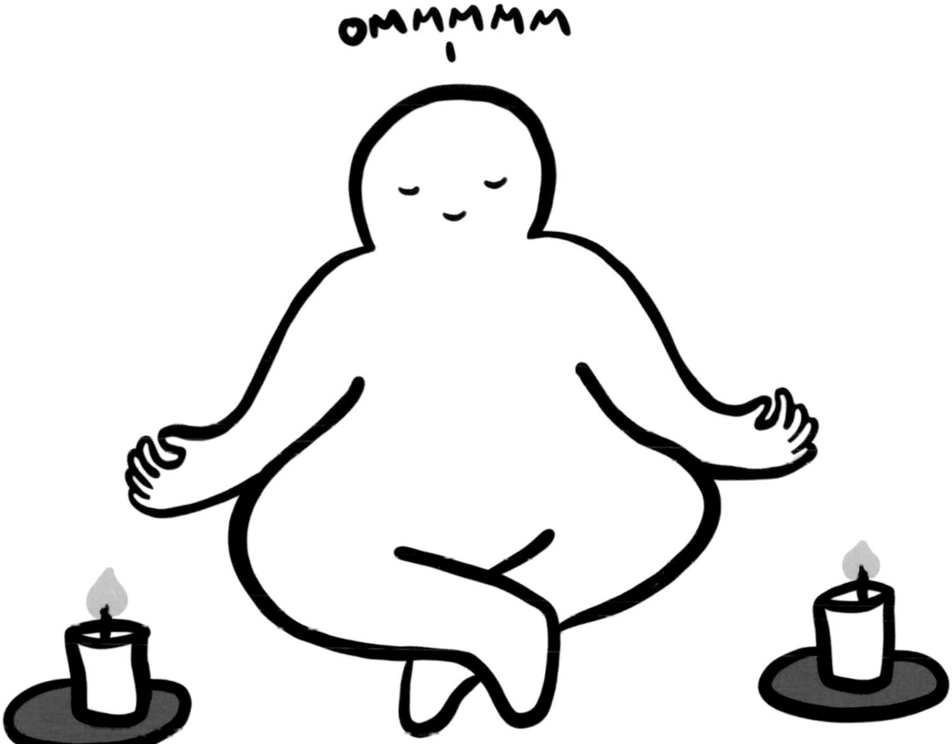
OMMMMM

GET INTO THE RIGHT HEADSPACE

FIND THE PERFECT
PLAYLIST

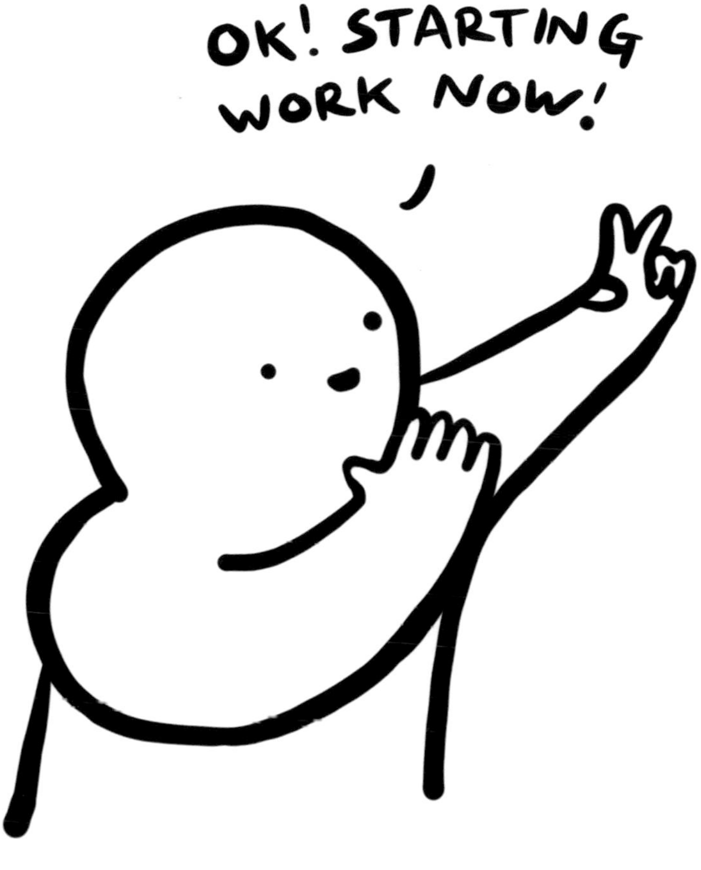
OK! STARTING WORK NOW!

SPREAD THE WORD

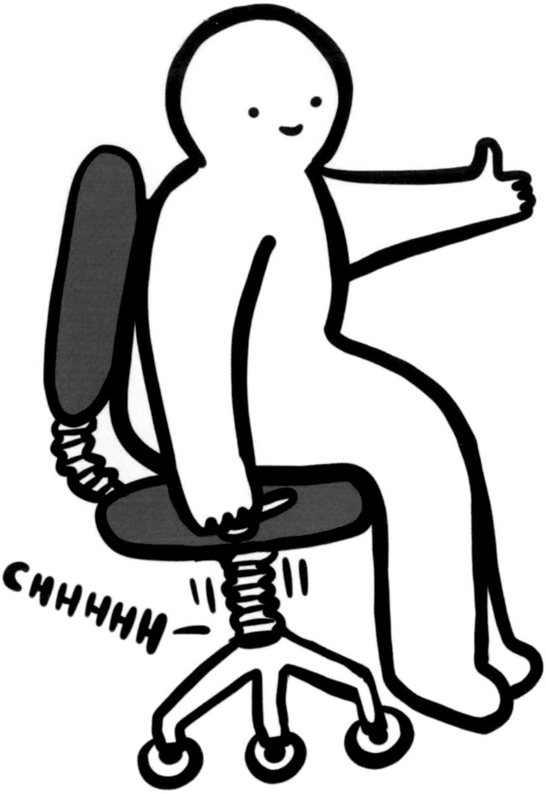
CHHHHHH—

FINESSE WORKSTATION ERGONOMICS

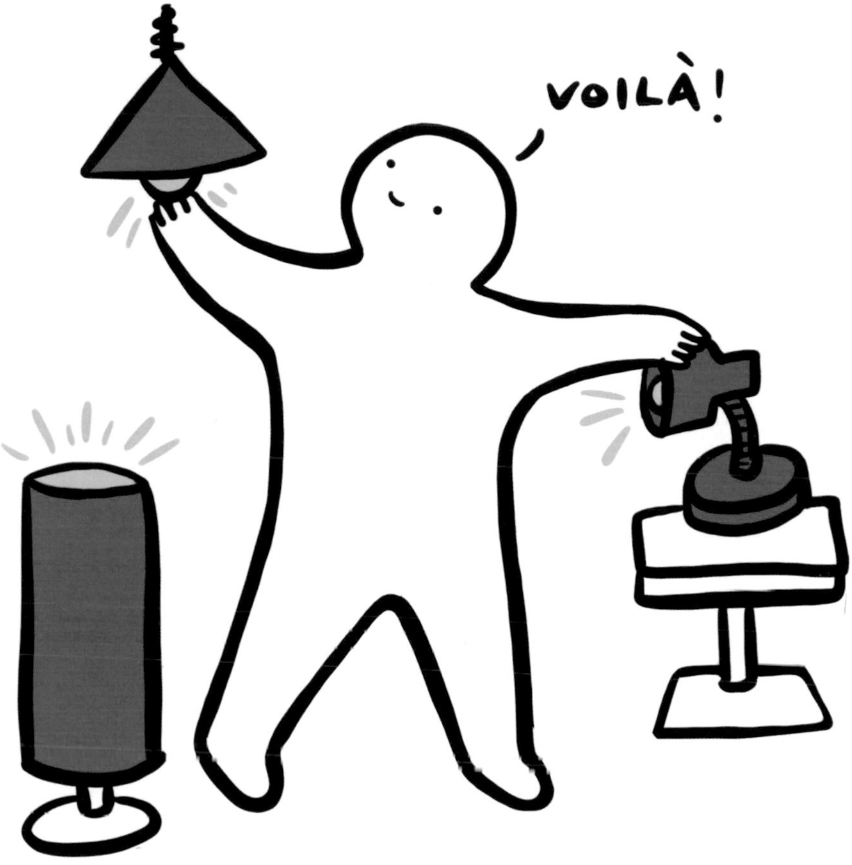
VOILÀ!

ADJUST LIGHTING

TIDY DESK=
TIDY MIND

AAAAAND I THINK THAT'S
ME DONE FOR THE DAY

RESTING PANIC FACE

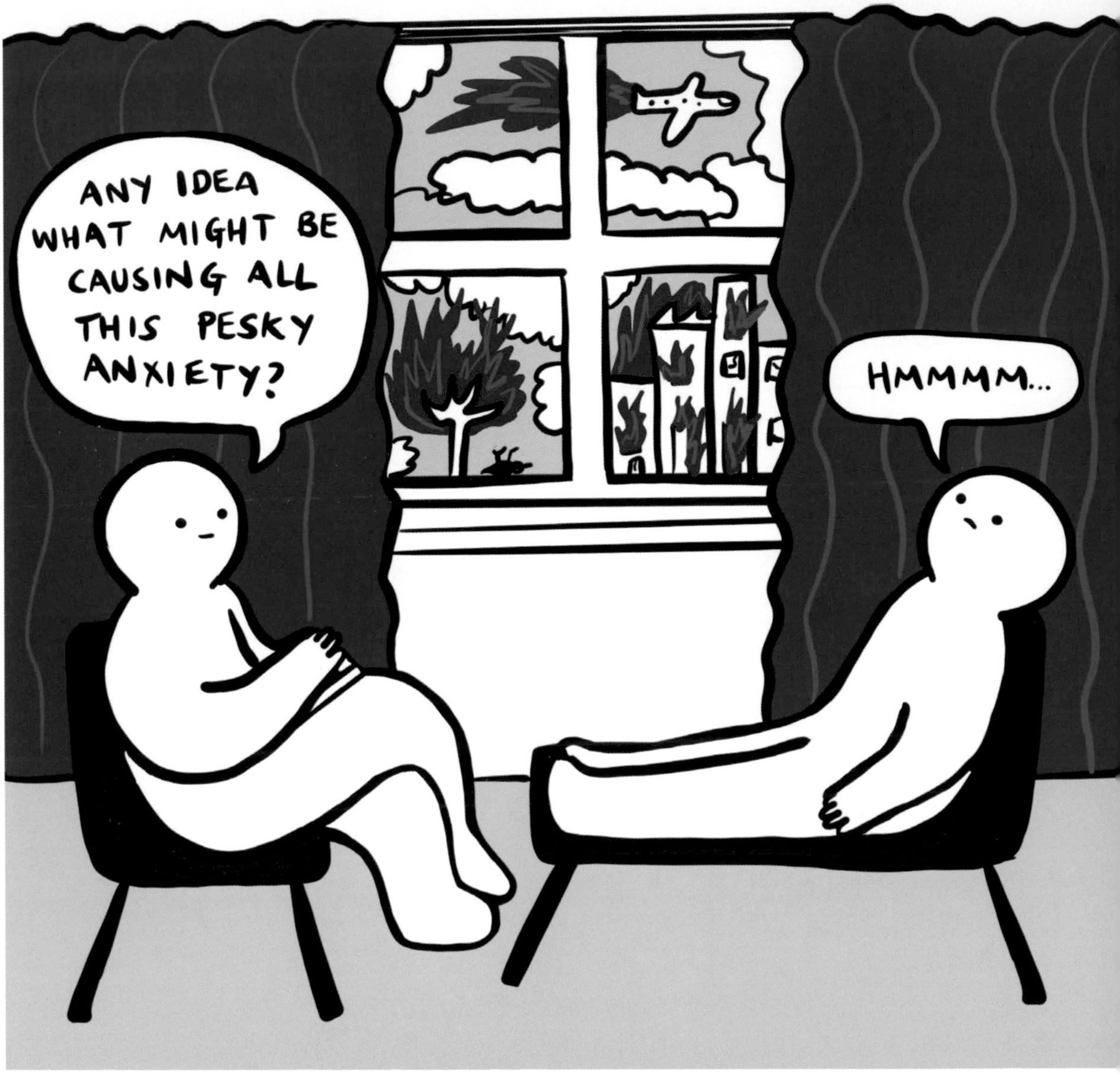
ANY IDEA WHAT MIGHT BE CAUSING ALL THIS PESKY ANXIETY?
HMMMM...

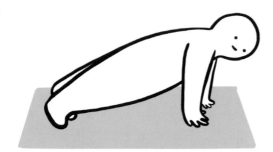

TRYING

TO BE BETTER

IS MAKING

ME FEEL WORSE.

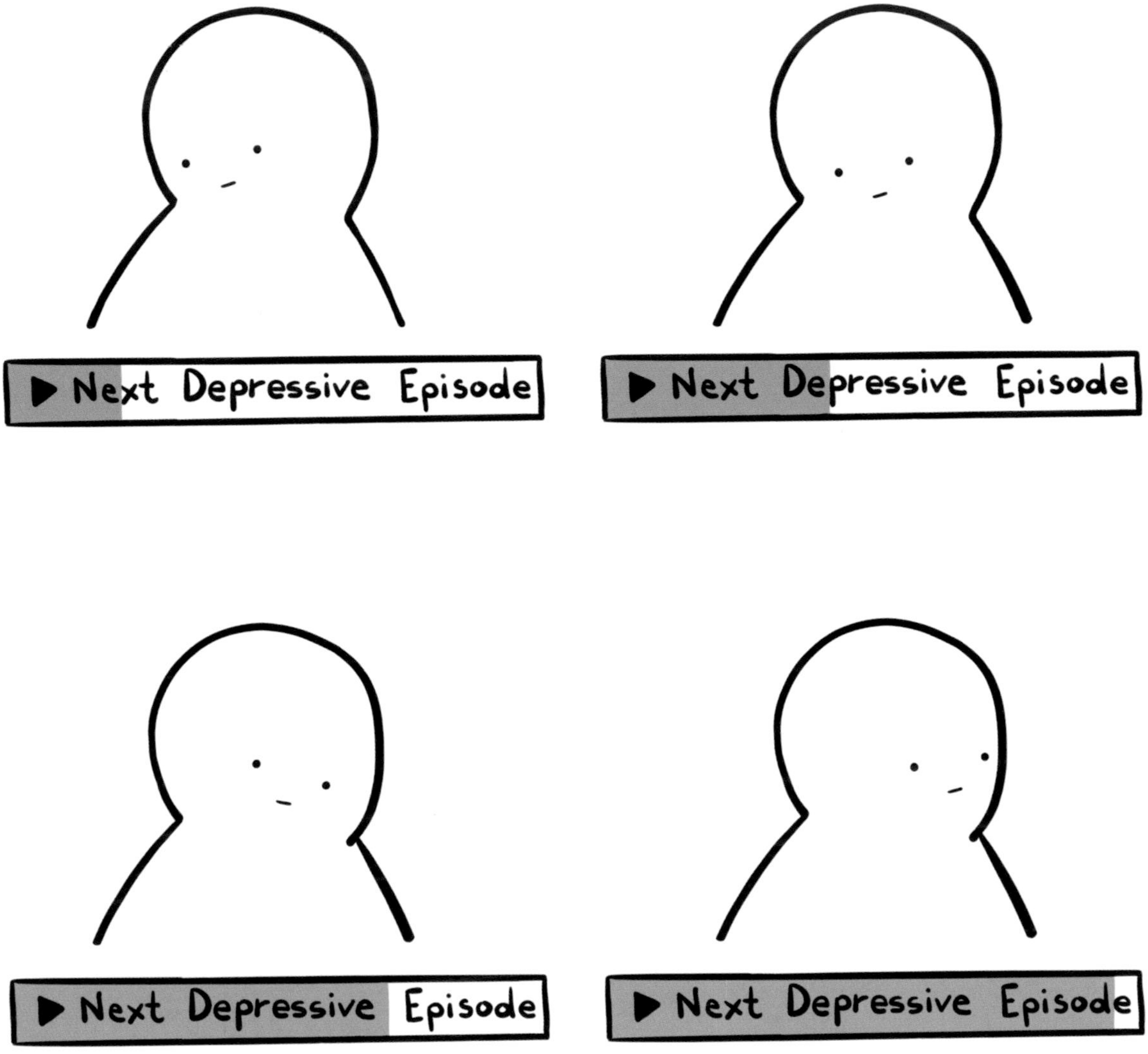
Next Depressive Episode
Next Depressive Episode
Next Depressive Episode
Next Depressive Episode

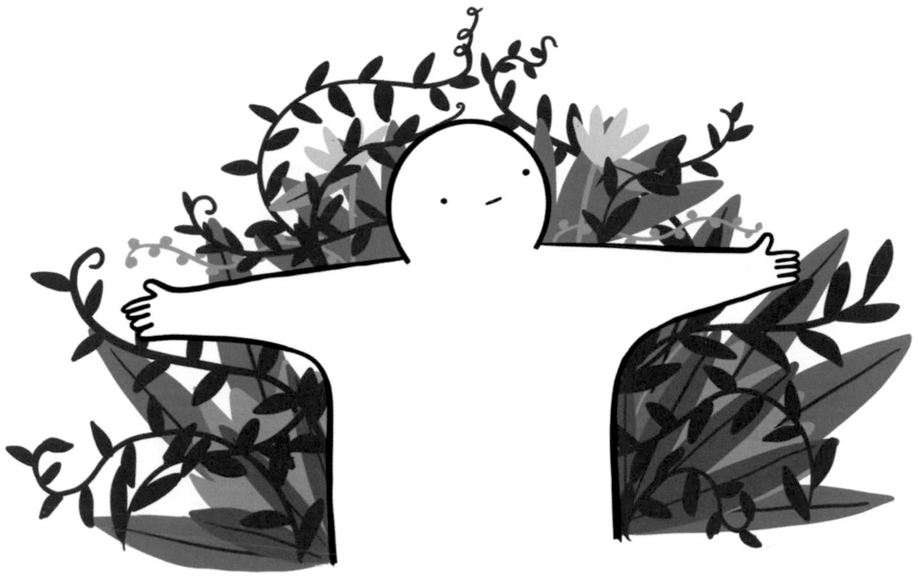

IT'S A JUNGLE OUT THERE

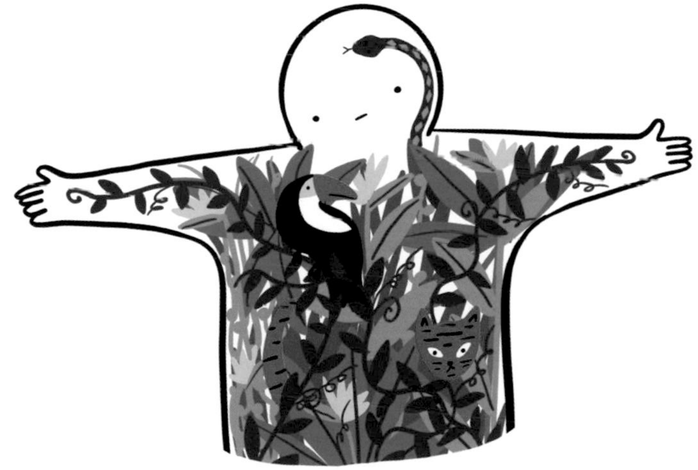

AND IT'S A JUNGLE IN HERE, TOO

ME, TRYING TO FORGIVE MYSELF:

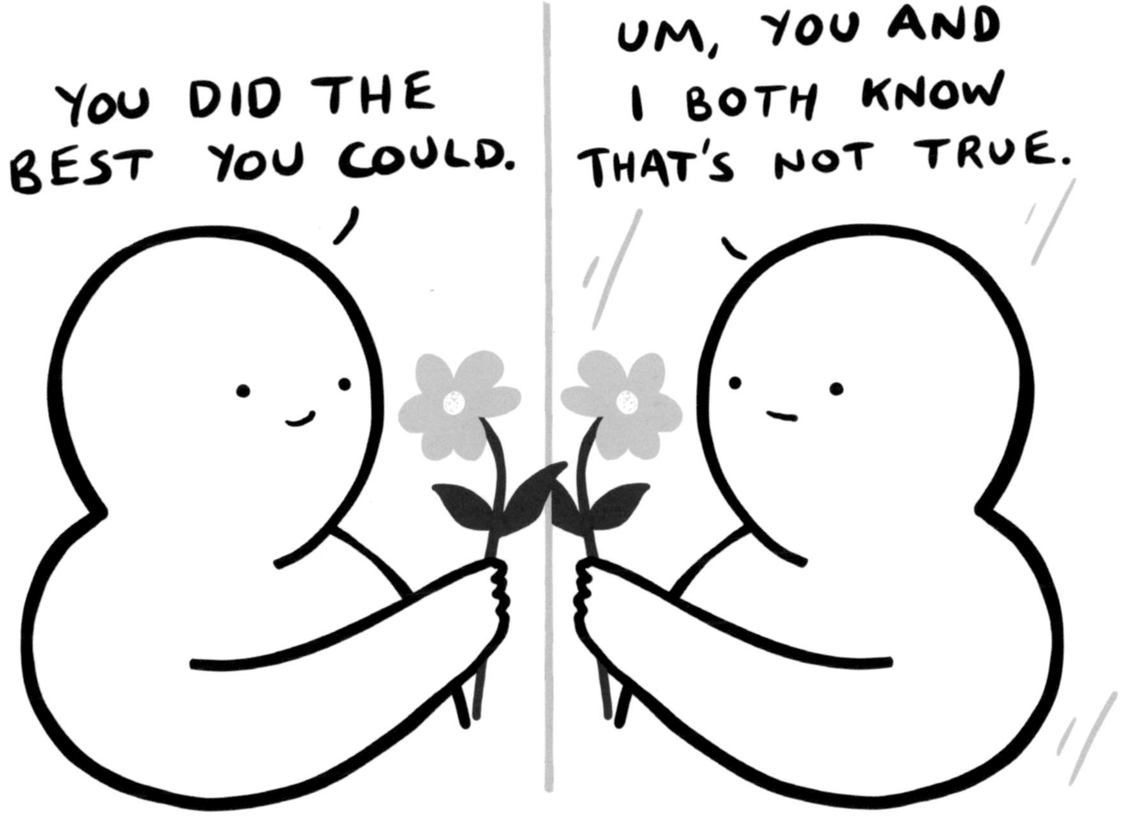

YOU DID THE BEST YOU COULD.
UM, YOU AND I BOTH KNOW THAT'S NOT TRUE.

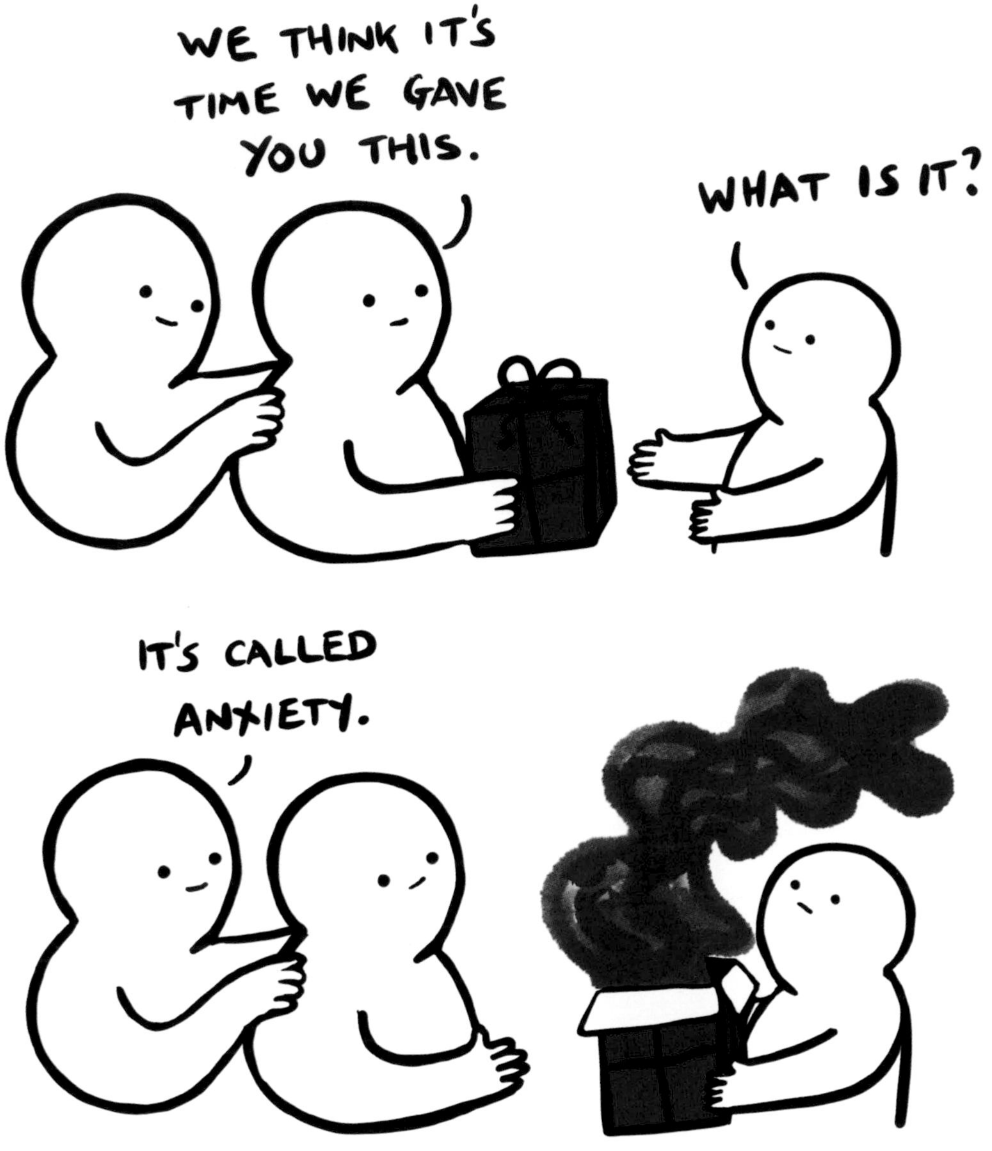
WE THINK IT'S TIME WE GAVE YOU THIS.
WHAT IS IT?
IT'S CALLED ANXIETY.

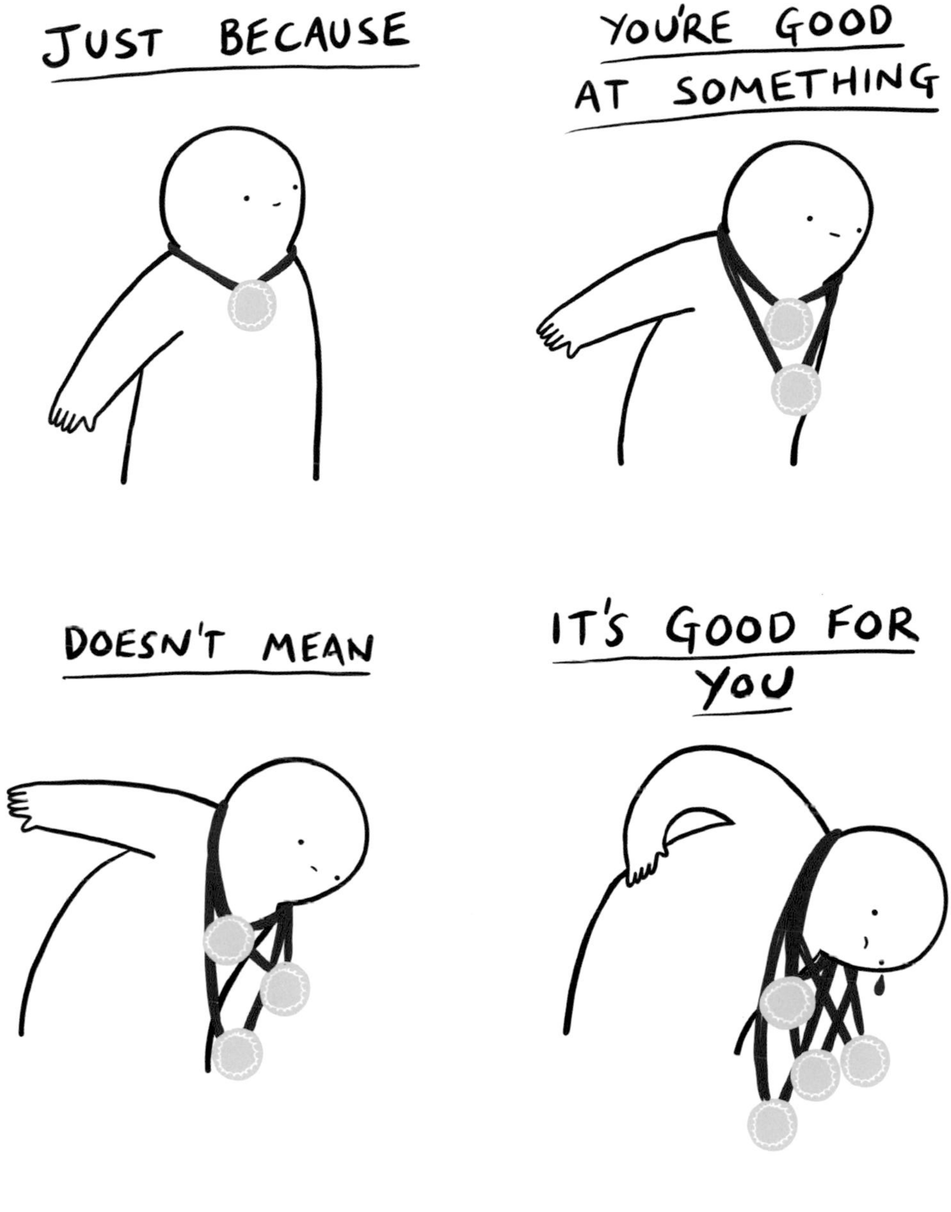
JUST BECAUSE
YOU'RE GOOD AT SOMETHING
DOESN'T MEAN
IT'S GOOD FOR YOU

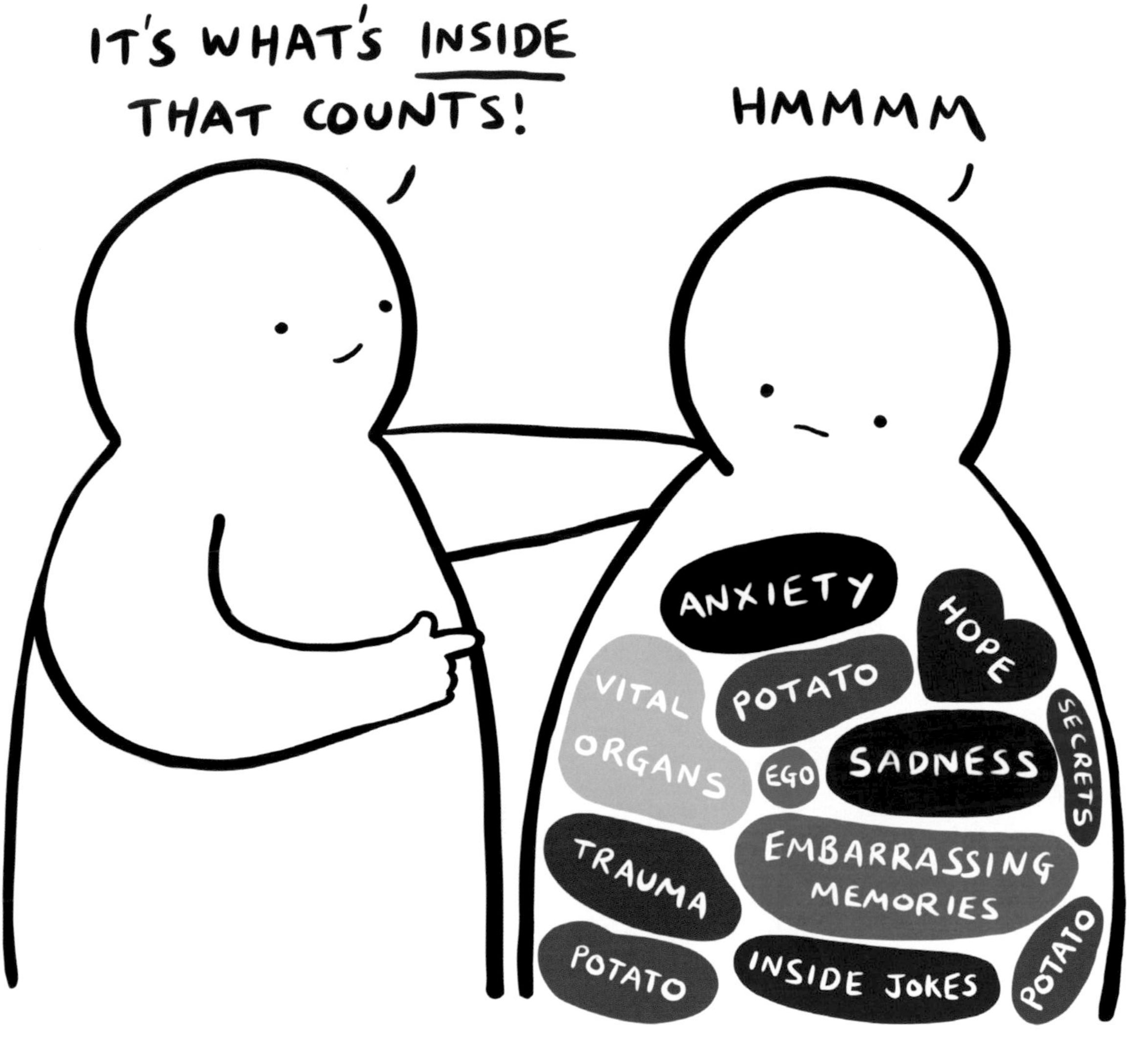
IT'S WHAT'S INSIDE THAT COUNTS!
HMMMM
ANXIETY
HOPE
VITAL ORGANS
POTATO
SECRETS
EGO
SADNESS
TRAUMA
EMBARRASSING MEMORIES
POTATO
INSIDE JOKES
POTATO

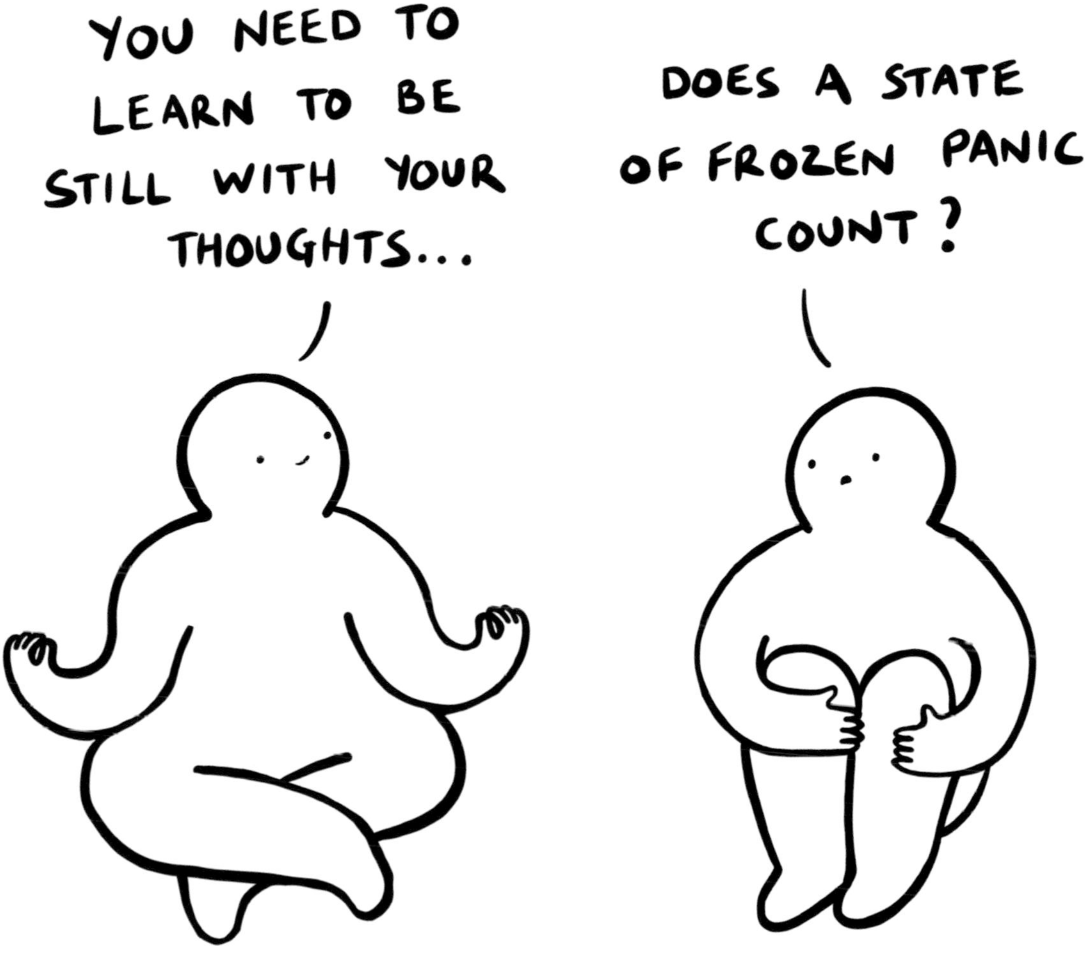
YOU NEED TO LEARN TO BE STILL WITH YOUR THOUGHTS...
DOES A STATE OF FROZEN PANIC COUNT?

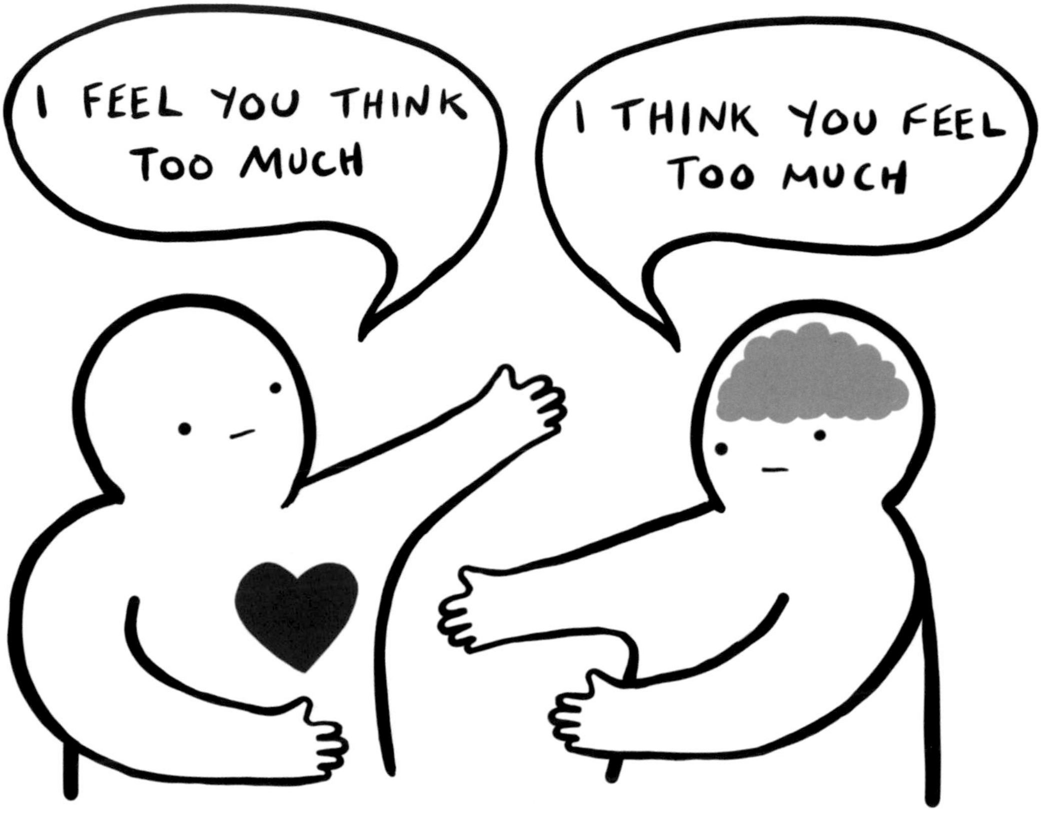
I FEEL YOU THINK TOO MUCH
I THINK YOU FEEL TOO MUCH

IT'S ALL
FALLING
APART

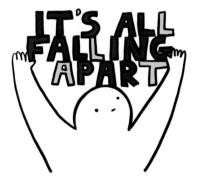

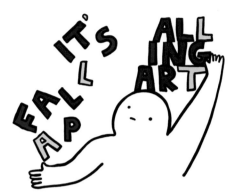

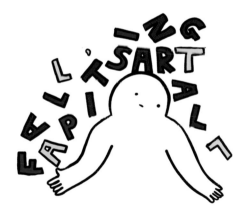

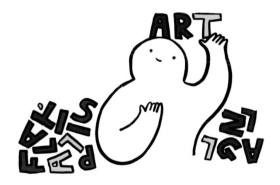

GOOD MORNING SUN!

GOOD MORNING TREES!

GOOD MORNING
NEBULOUS CLOUD OF
CRIPPLING UNCERTAINTY!

GOOD MORNING FLOWERS!

GET UP AND GO

STRAIGHT BACK TO BED

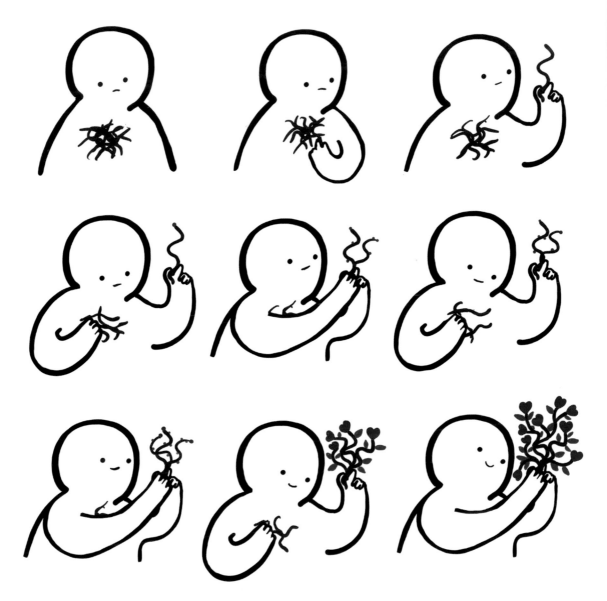

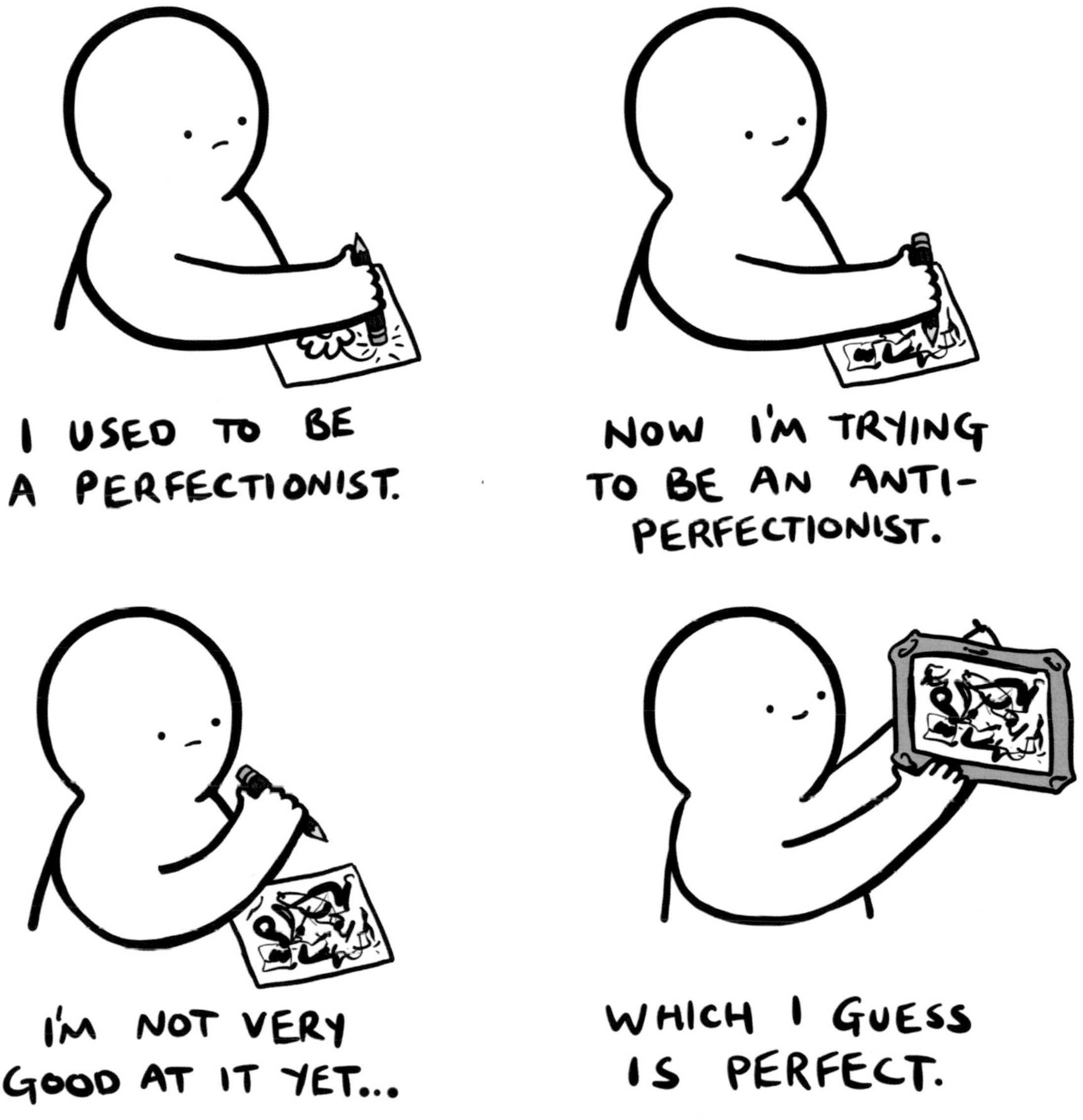
I USED TO BE A PERFECTIONIST.
NOW I'M TRYING TO BE AN ANTI-PERFECTIONIST.
I'M NOT VERY GOOD AT IT YET...
WHICH I GUESS IS PERFECT.

SOMETIMES I CARRY MY SADNESS

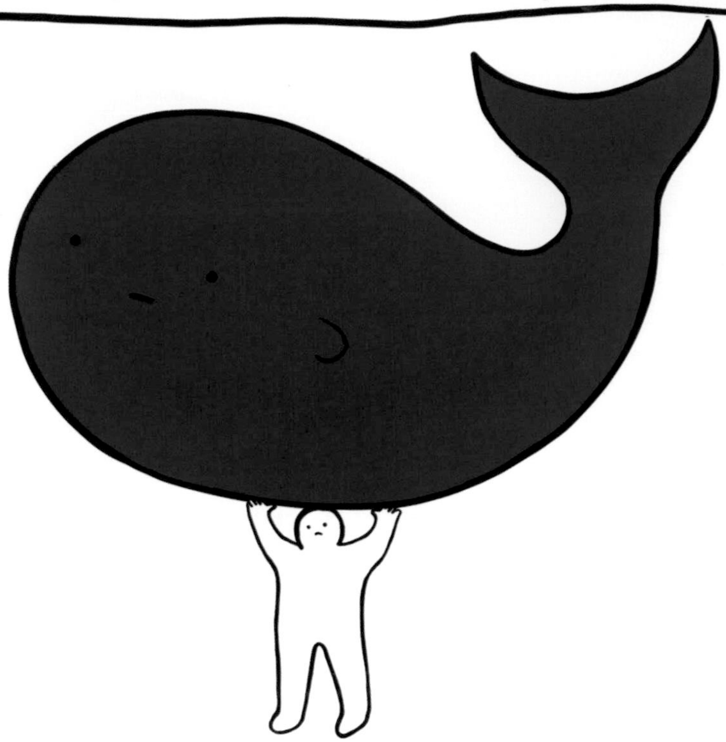

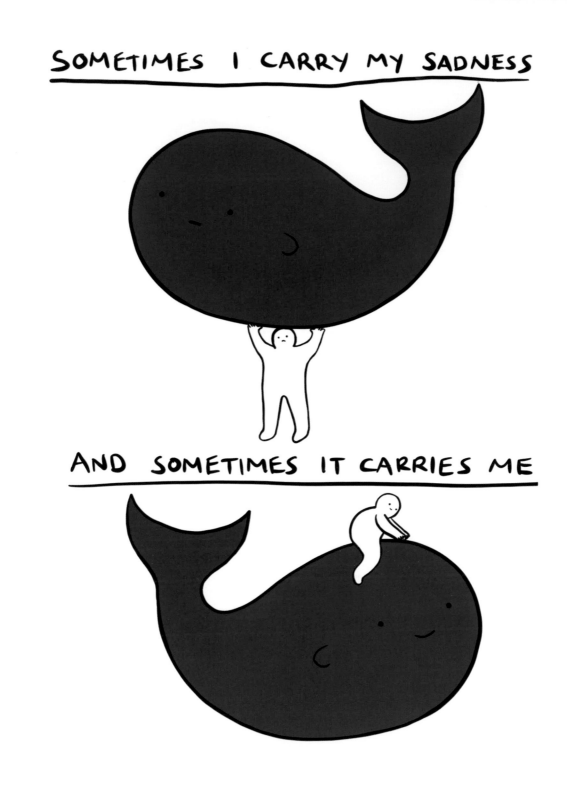

AND SOMETIMES IT CARRIES ME

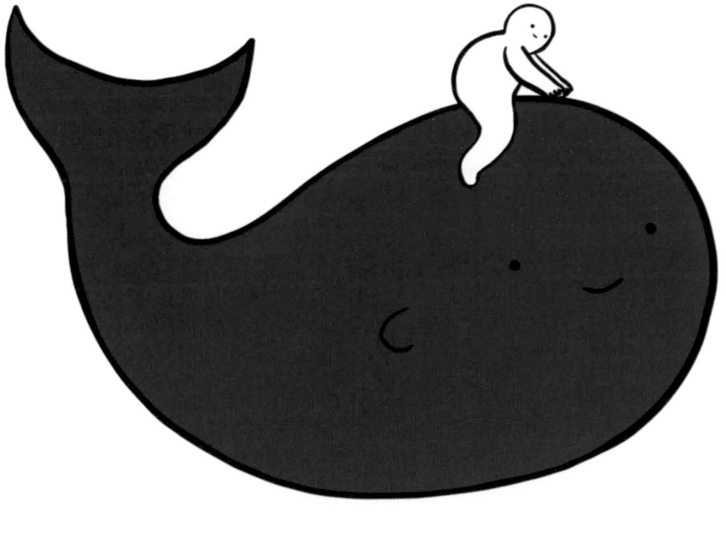

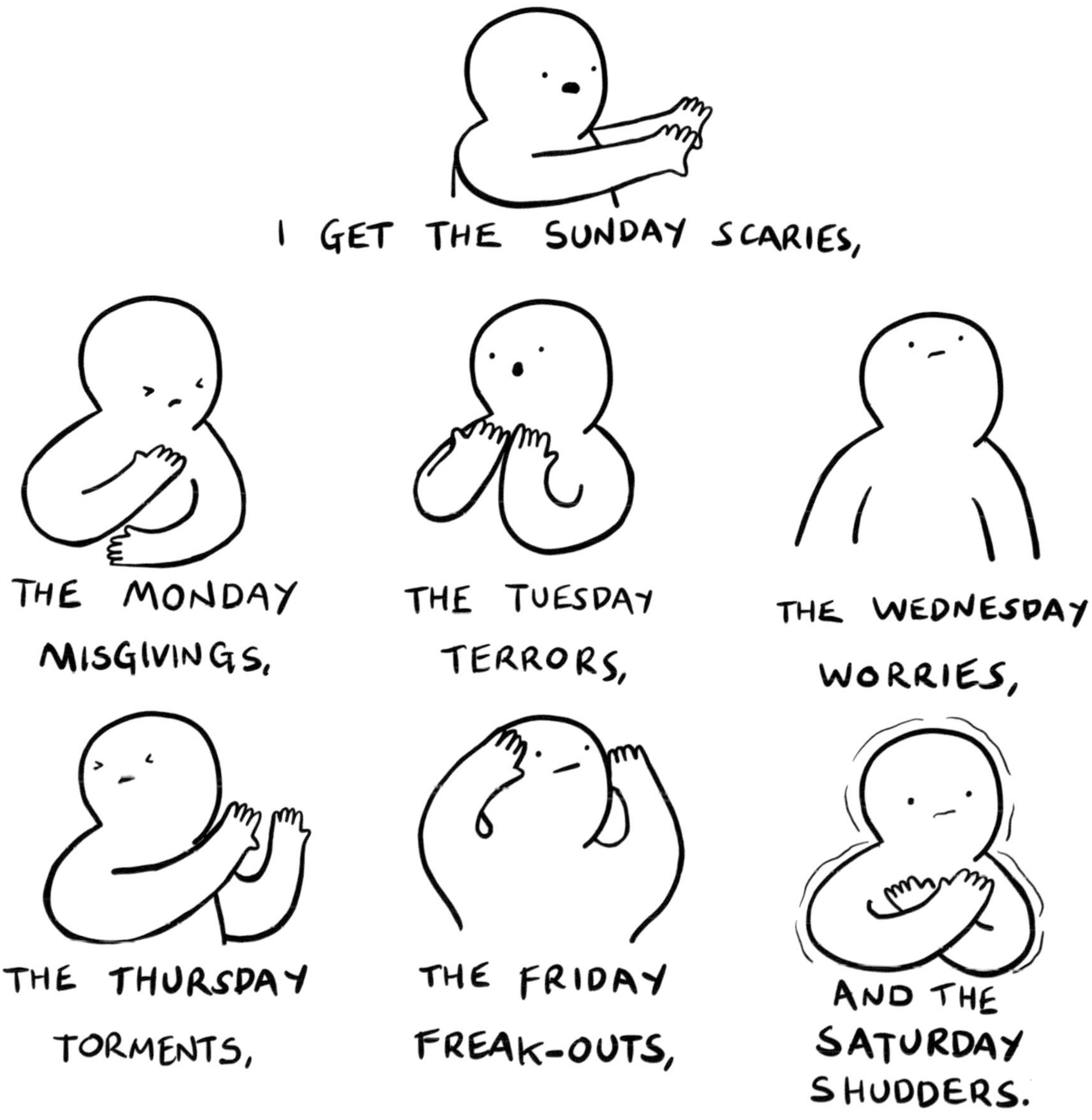
I GET THE SUNDAY SCARIES,
THE MONDAY MISGIVINGS,
THE TUESDAY TERRORS,
THE WEDNESDAY WORRIES,
THE THURSDAY TORMENTS,
THE FRIDAY FREAK-OUTS,
AND THE SATURDAY SHUDDERS.

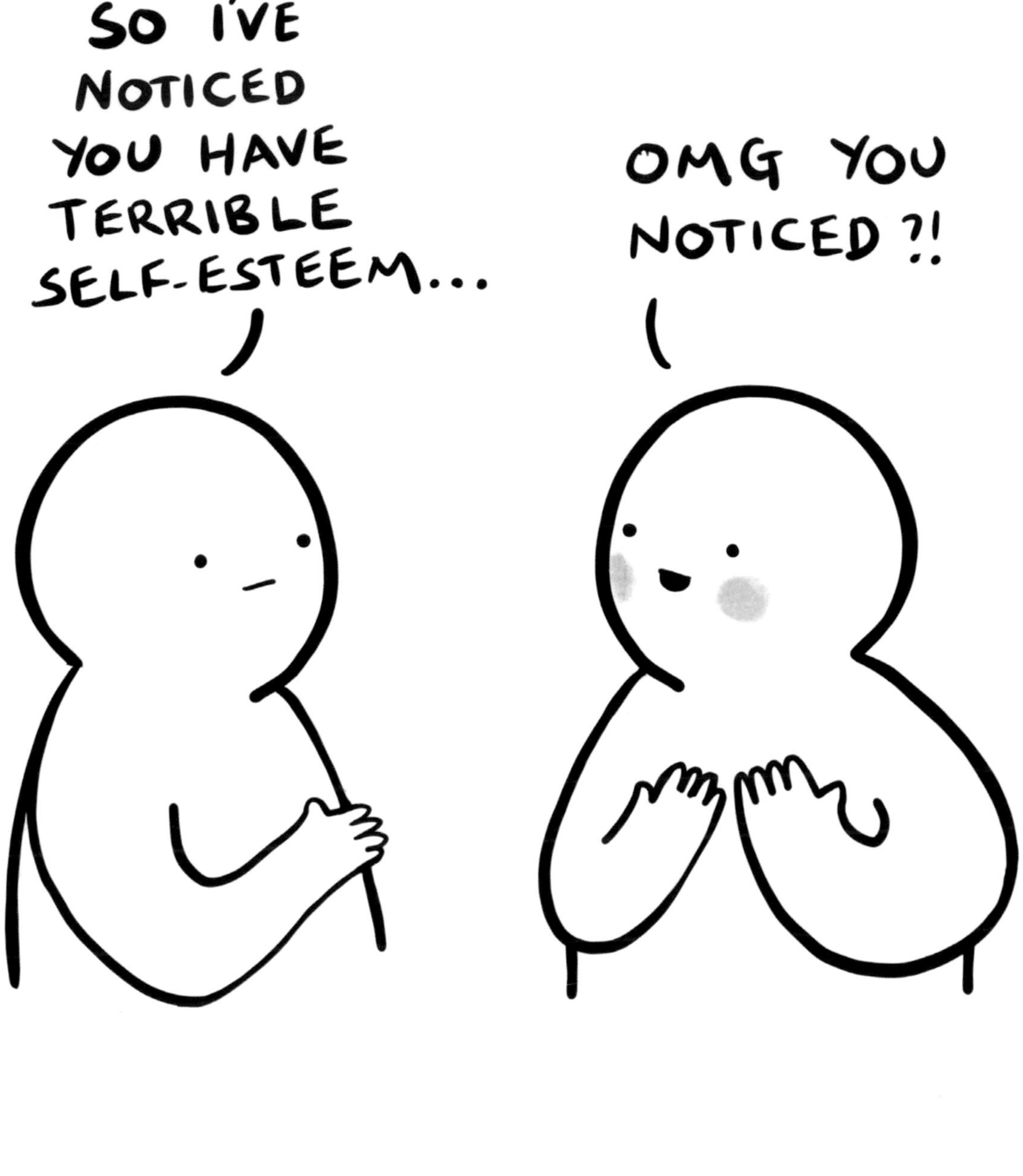
SO I'VE NOTICED YOU HAVE TERRIBLE SELF-ESTEEM...
OMG YOU NOTICED?!

ONE IS PEACEFUL
TWO IS COMPANY
THREE'S A CROWD
FOUR IS FULL-BLOWN SOCIAL ANXIETY

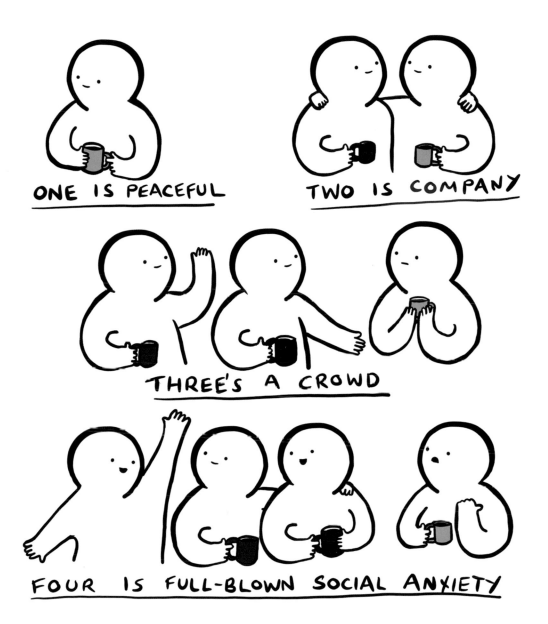

NONTOXIC POSITIVITY

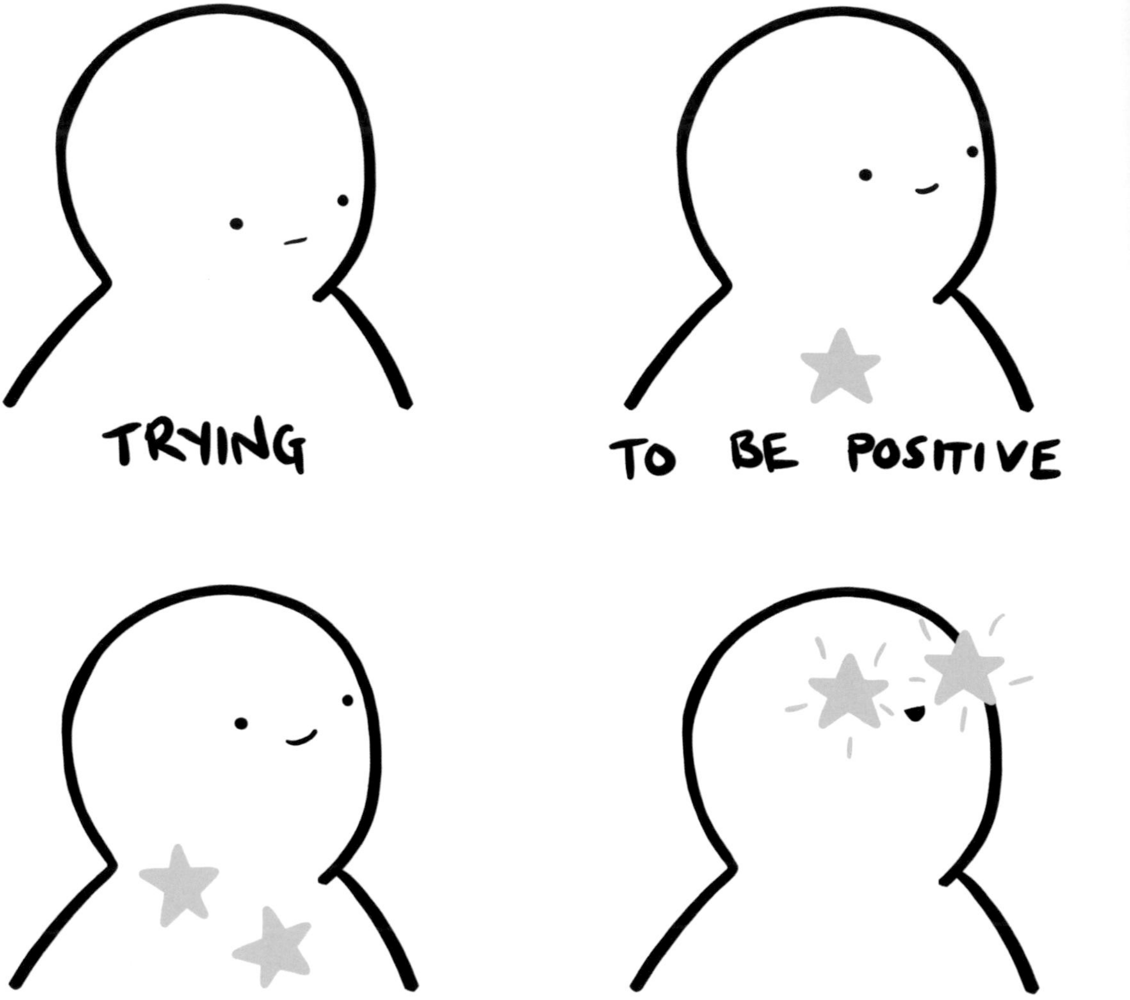
TRYING
TO BE POSITIVE
WITHOUT BEING
POSITIVELY DELUSIONAL.

FULL OF HOPE

AND POTATO

DON'T JUST LOOK
ON THE BRIGHT SIDE

AND IGNORE THE
DARK SIDE.

SOMETIMES
ACKNOWLEDGING
THE DARK SIDE

MAKES THE
BRIGHT SIDE
EVEN BRIGHTER.

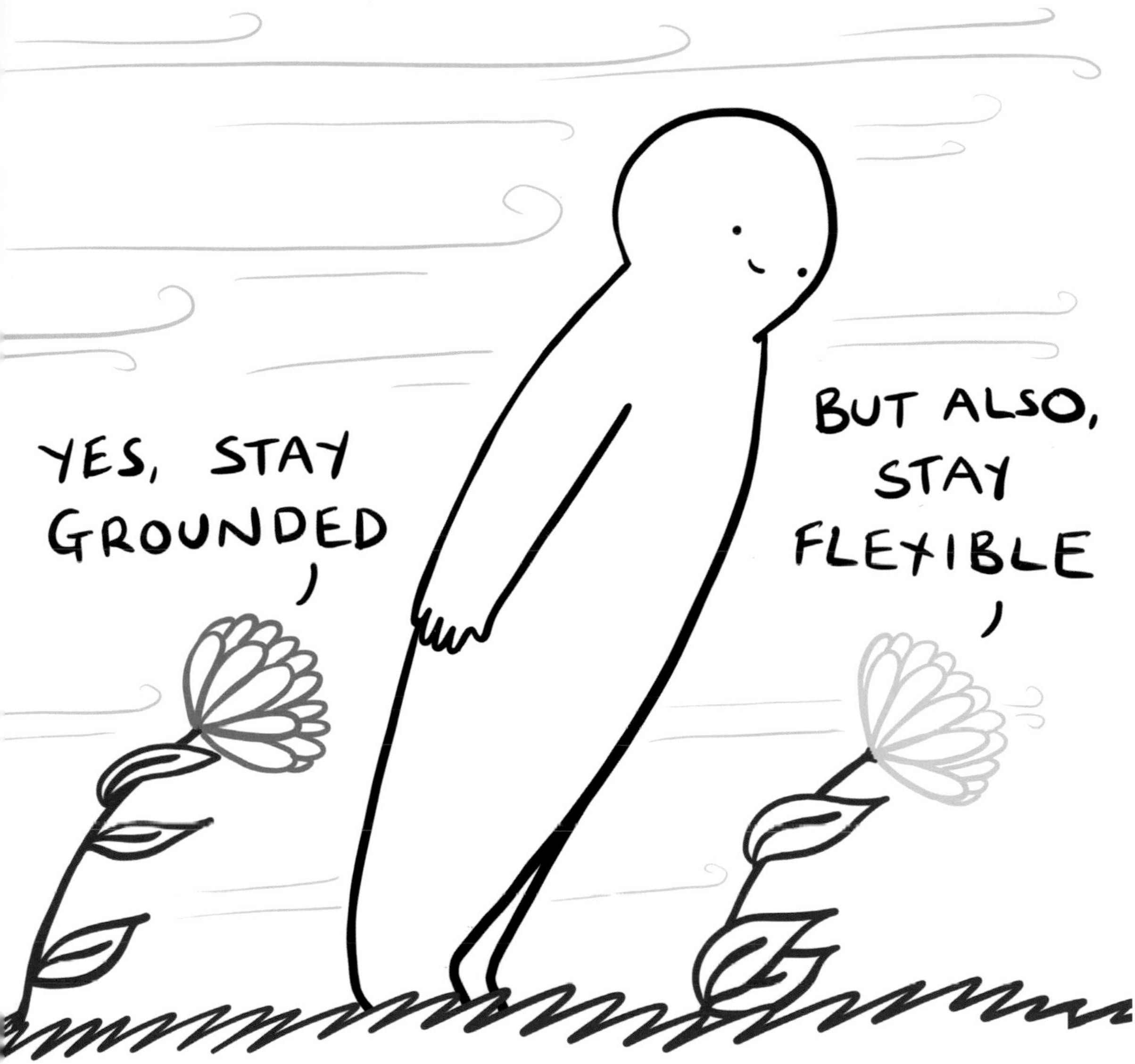
YES, STAY GROUNDED
BUT ALSO, STAY FLEXIBLE

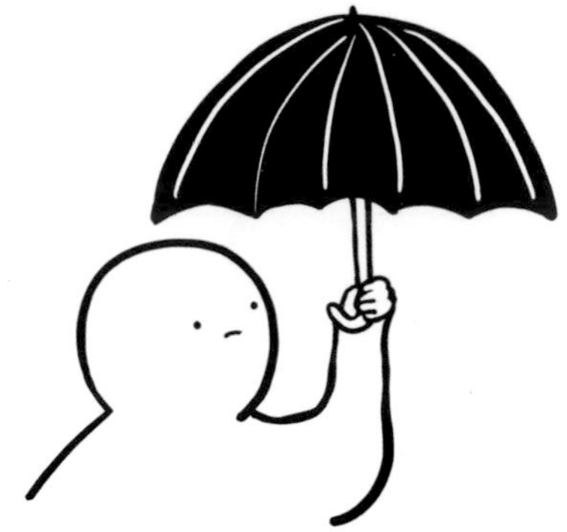

PLAN FOR THE WORST,

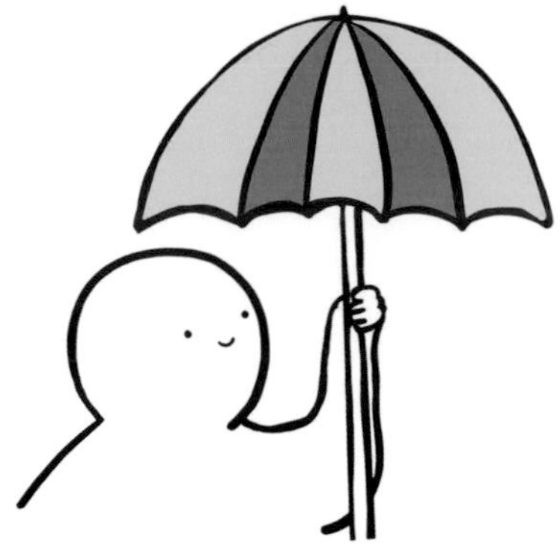

HOPE FOR THE BEST,

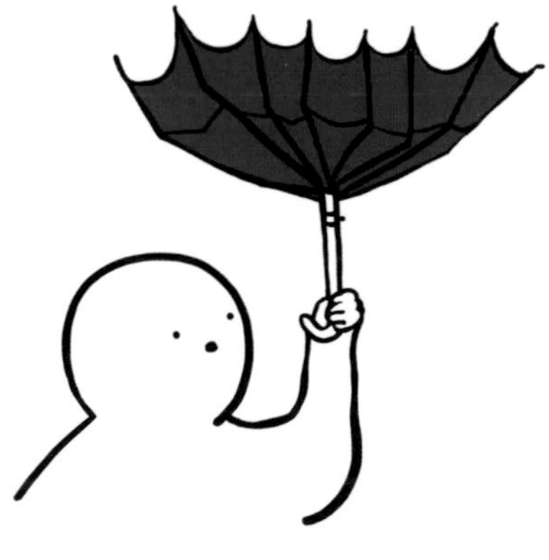

EXPECT THE UNEXPECTED,

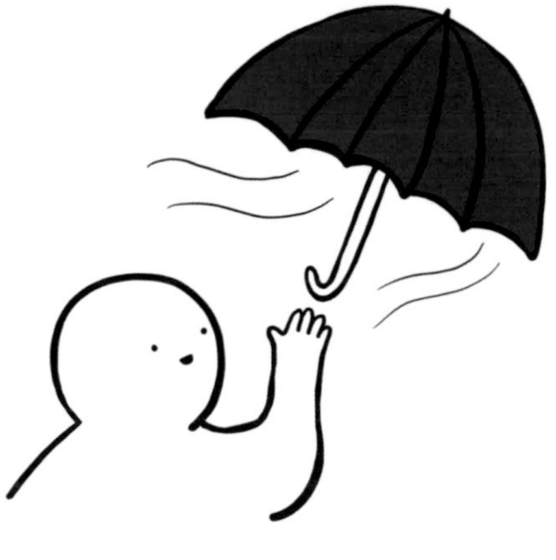

LET GO OF THE REST.

LOVE WILL FIND A WAY

BUT IT MIGHT TAKE A
PRETTY CIRCUITOUS ROUTE

IF AT FIRST

YOU DON'T SUCCEED,

TRY, TRY

NOT TO SPIRAL INTO THE KIND OF SELF-LOATHING YOU'VE BEEN CONDITIONED TO FEEL BY A SYSTEM THAT PROMOTES UNATTAINABLE GOALS AND THEN CONVERTS YOUR RESULTING INSECURITIES INTO PROFIT.

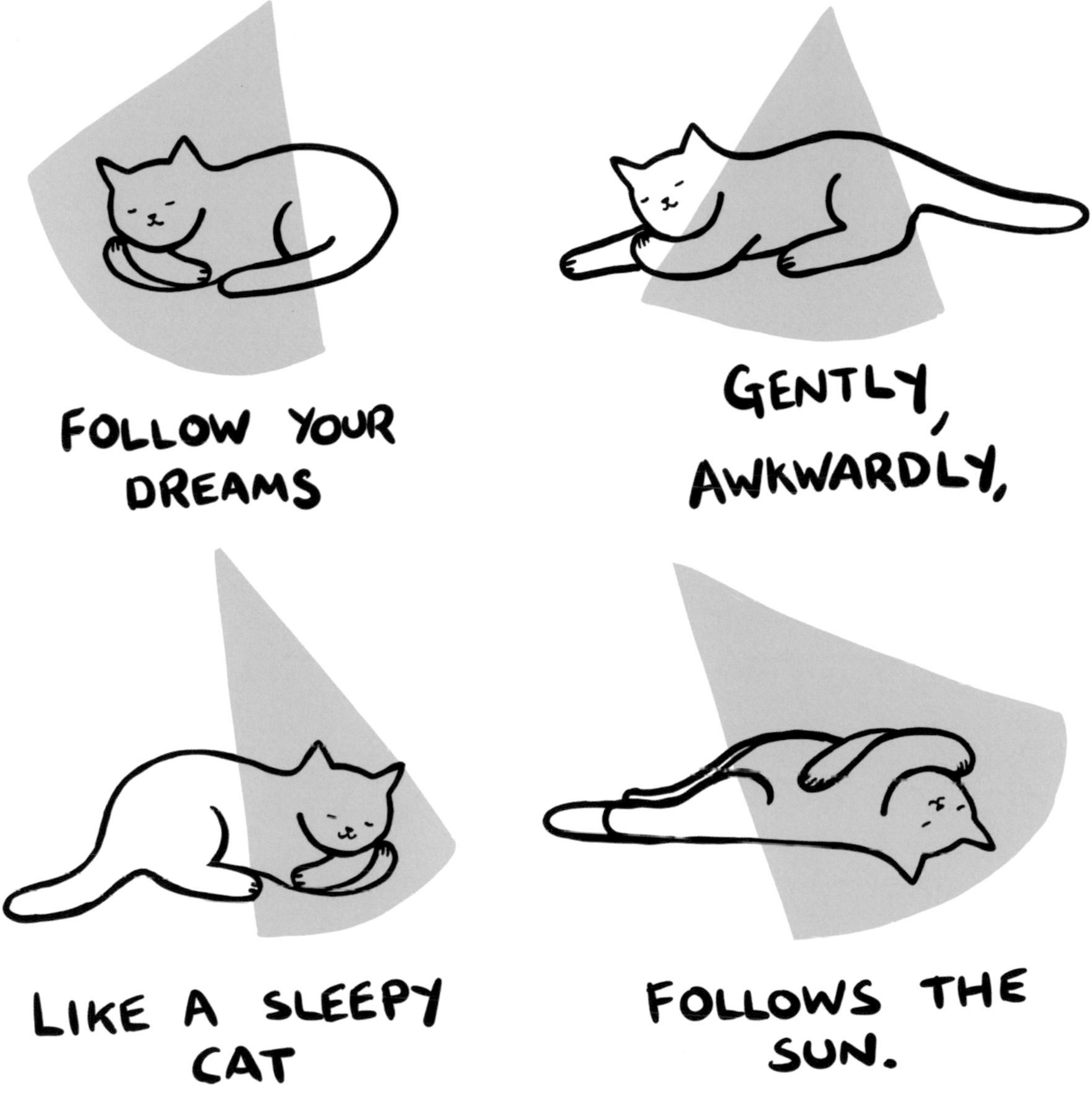
FOLLOW YOUR DREAMS
GENTLY, AWKWARDLY,
LIKE A SLEEPY CAT
FOLLOWS THE SUN.

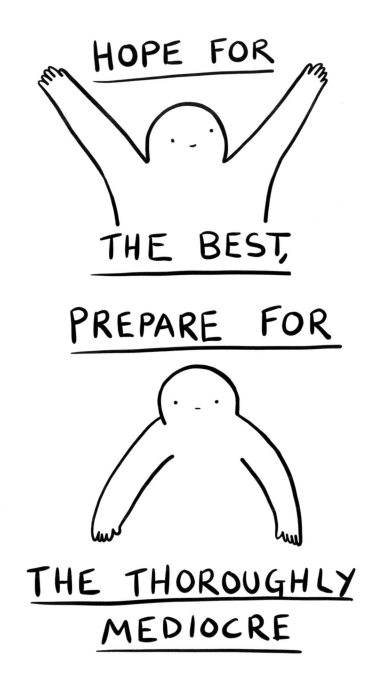

HOPE FOR

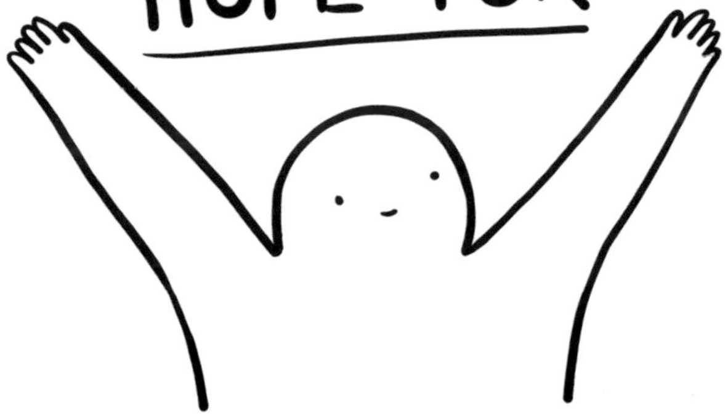

THE BEST,

PREPARE FOR

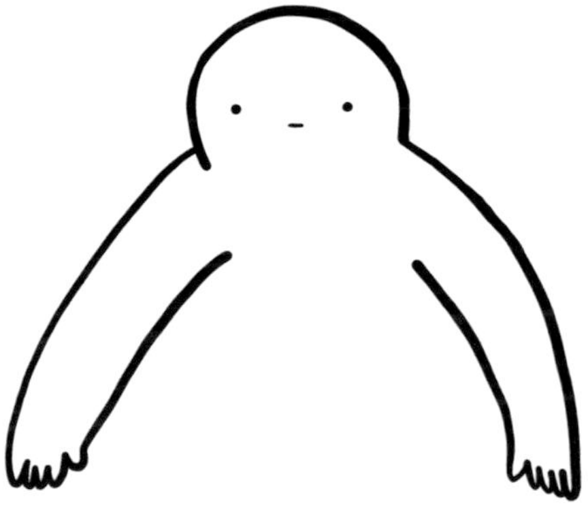

THE THOROUGHLY MEDIOCRE

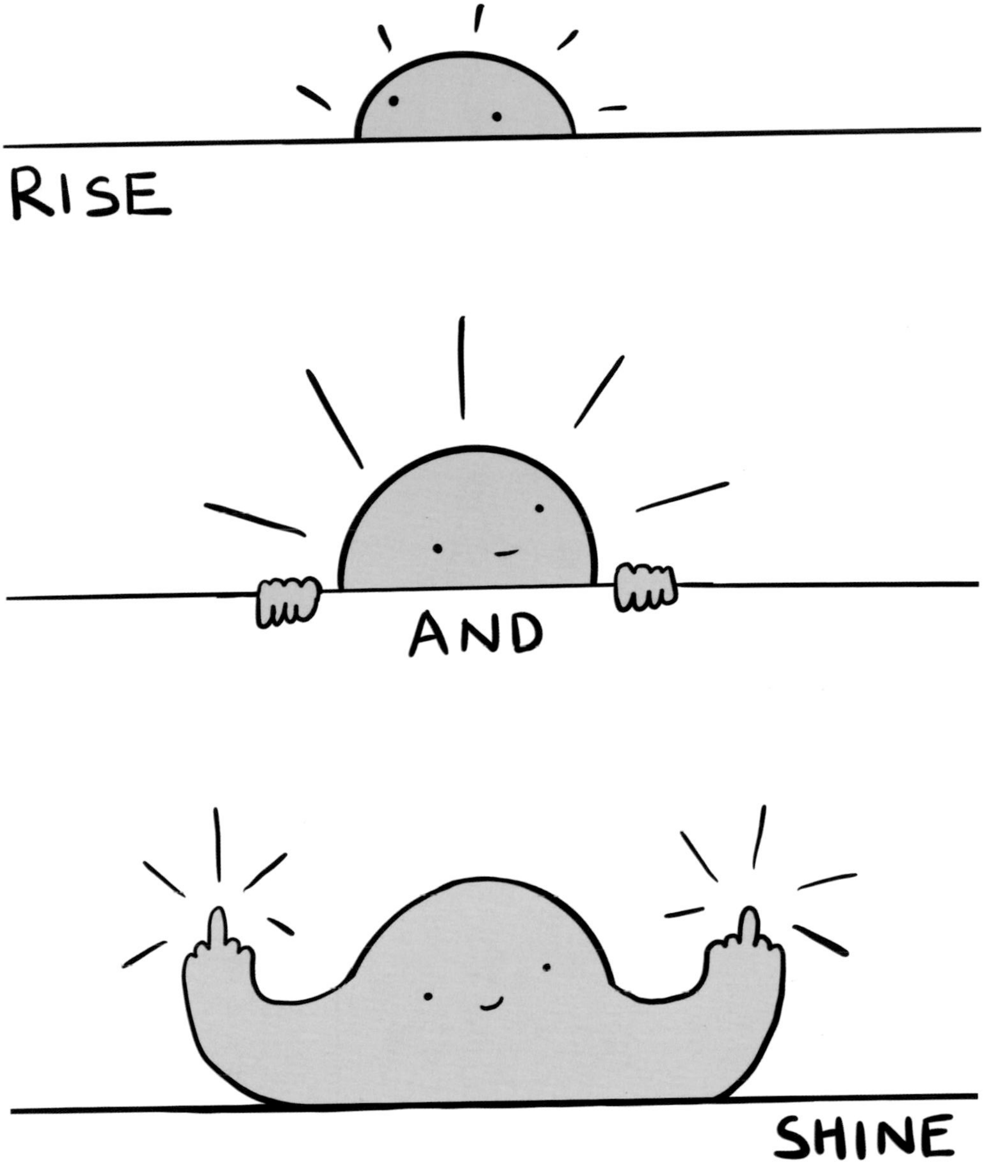
RISE
AND
SHINE

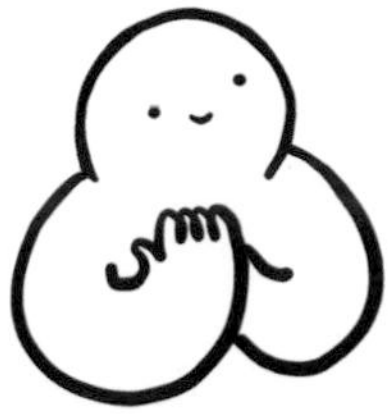

YOU DESERVE HAPPINESS

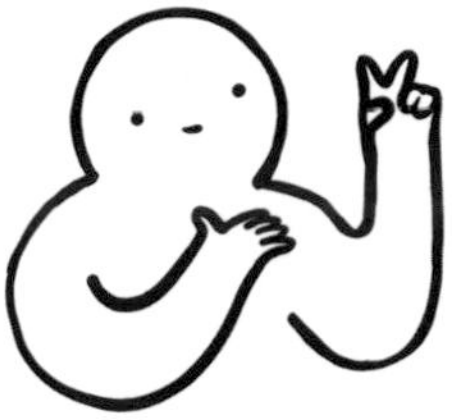

YOU DESERVE PEACE

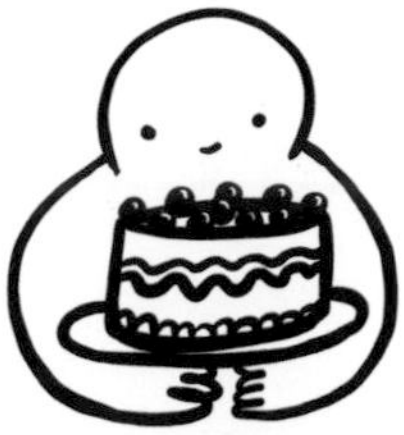

YOU DESERVE CAKE

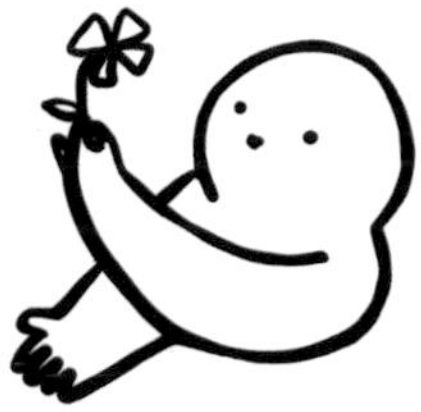

YOU DESERVE LUCK

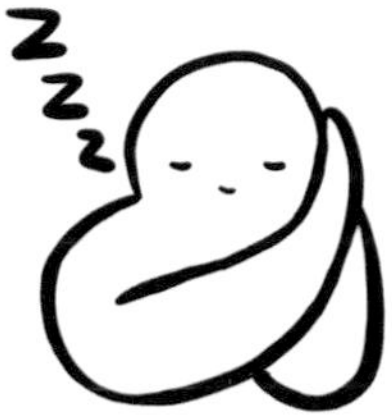

YOU DESERVE REST

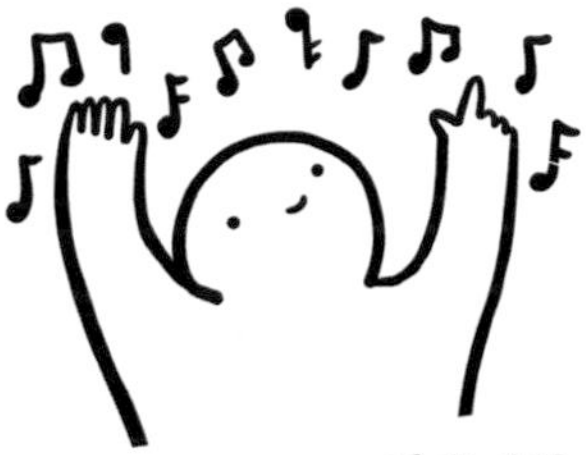

YOU DESERVE YOUR FAVOURITE SONG TO COME ON IN THE SUPERMARKET

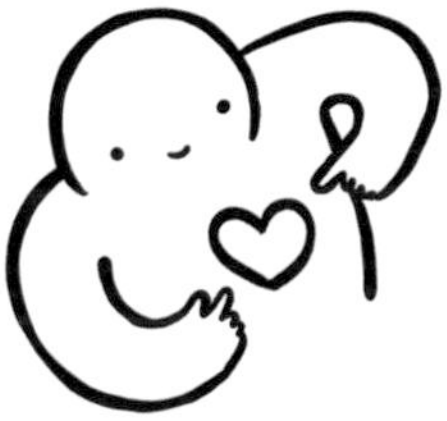

YOU DESERVE LOVE

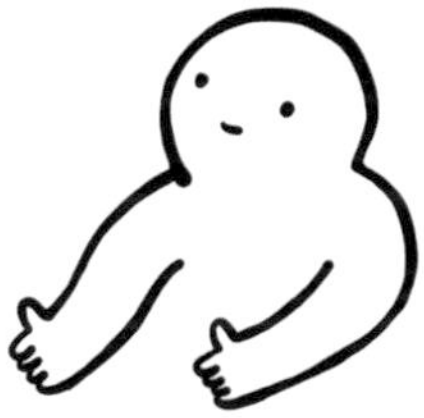

YOU DESERVE RESPECT

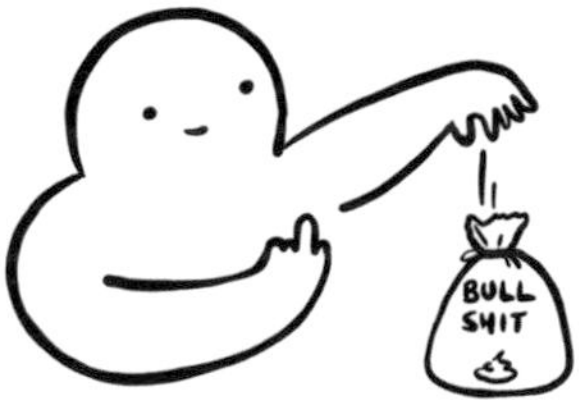
BULL SHIT

YOU DESERVE A LIFE FREE OF BULLSHIT

IF YOU CAN'T

BE KIND TO
YOURSELF TODAY,

TRY AT LEAST

TO BE CIVIL.

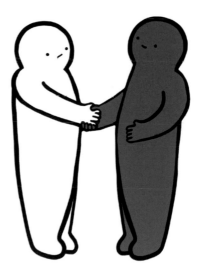

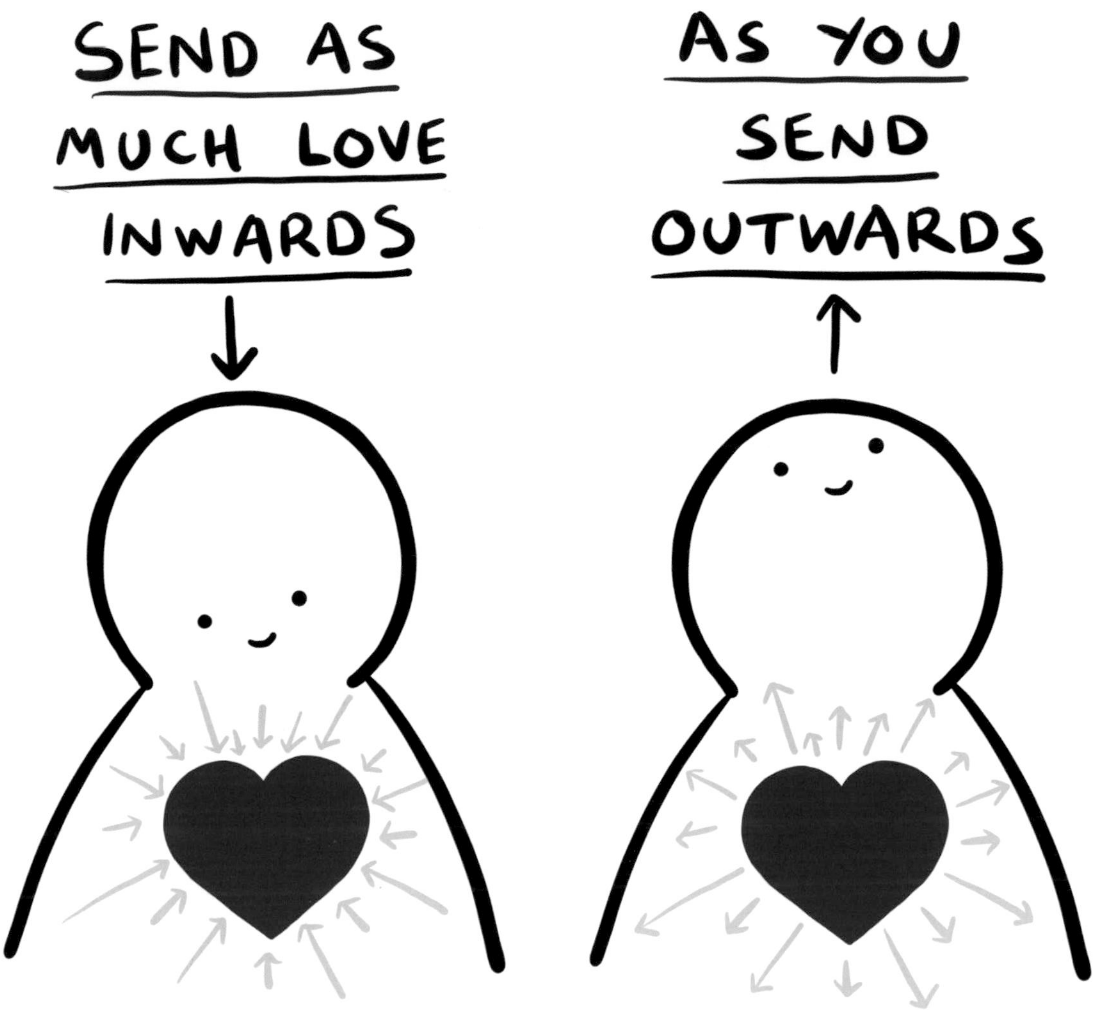
SEND AS MUCH LOVE INWARDS
AS YOU SEND OUTWARDS

BE

THUMBS UP!

KIND

" PAT " PAT "

TO YOUR

HIGH FIVE

MIND

HUG

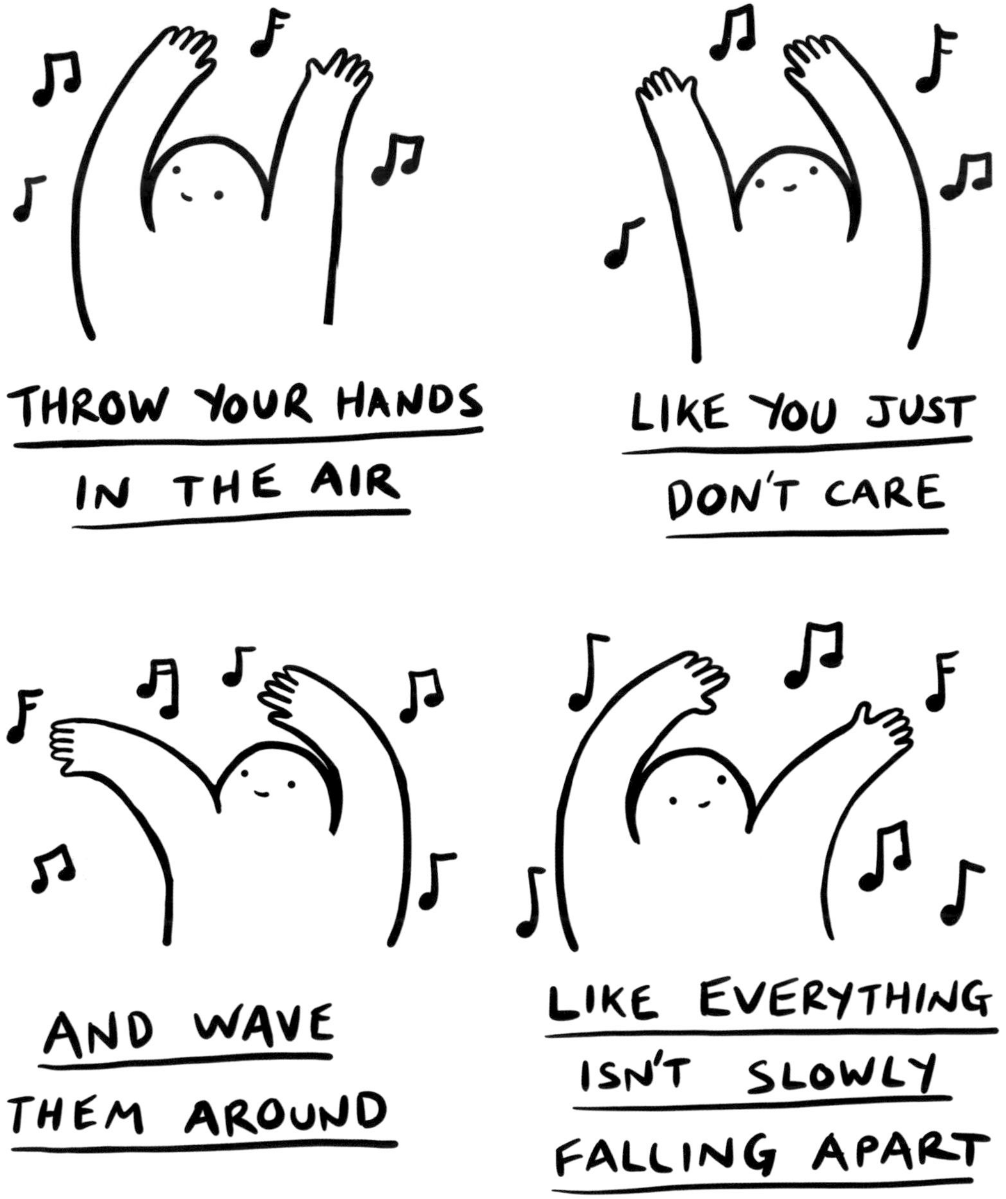
THROW YOUR HANDS IN THE AIR
LIKE YOU JUST DON'T CARE
AND WAVE THEM AROUND
LIKE EVERYTHING ISN'T SLOWLY FALLING APART

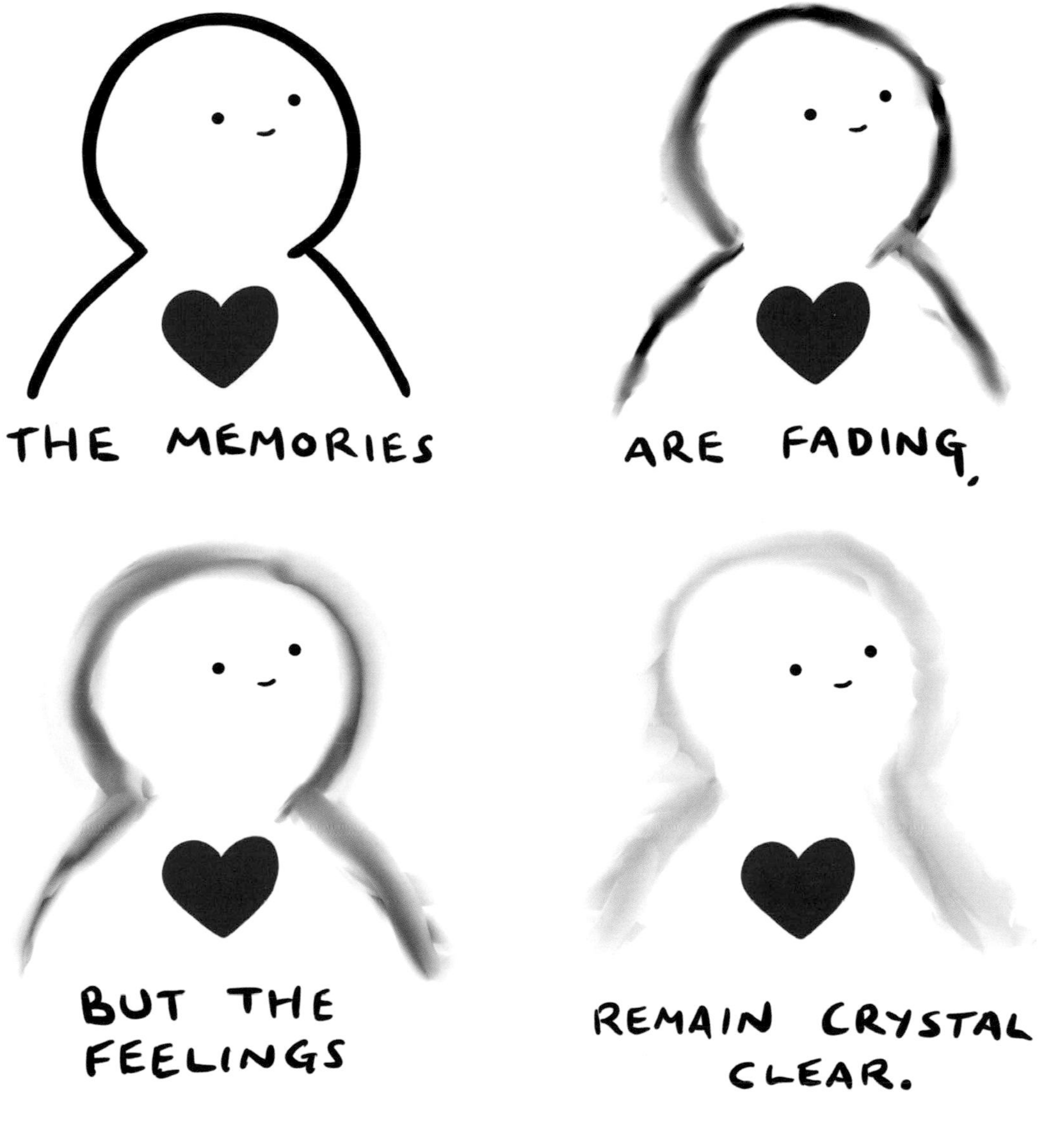
THE MEMORIES
ARE FADING,
BUT THE FEELINGS
REMAIN CRYSTAL CLEAR.

THRIVING

ALSO
THRIVING

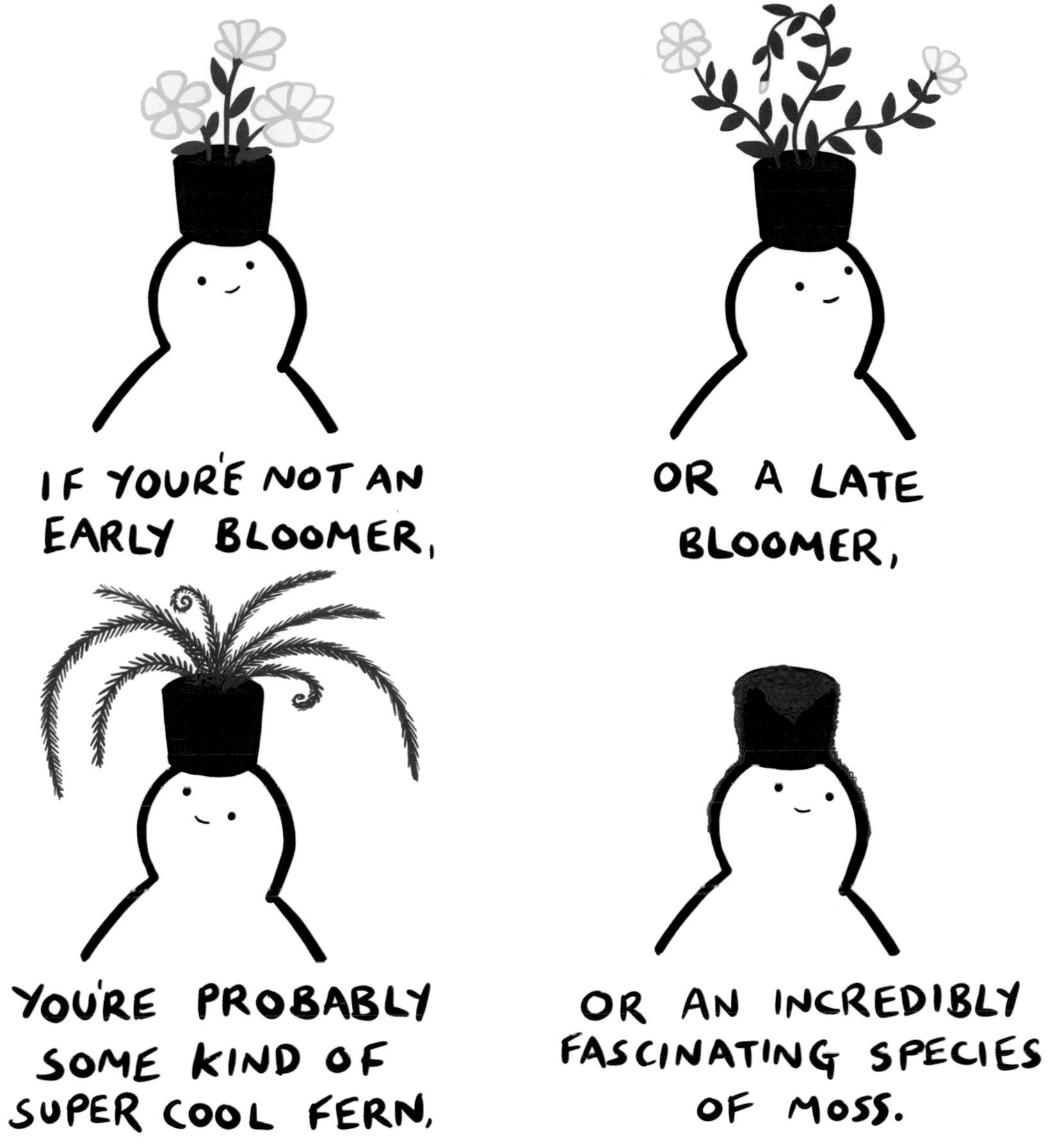
IF YOU'RE NOT AN EARLY BLOOMER,
OR A LATE BLOOMER,
YOU'RE PROBABLY SOME KIND OF SUPER COOL FERN,
OR AN INCREDIBLY FASCINATING SPECIES OF MOSS.

NOT EVERYTHING'S
GOING TO BE OK.

SOME THINGS ARE
GOING TO BE
PRETTY BAD.

AND SOME THINGS
ARE GOING TO BE
REALLY, REALLY
GOOD.

I THINK I'M OK
WITH NOT EVERYTHING
BEING JUST OK.

EVERYONE GROWS IN
DIFFERENT DIRECTIONS

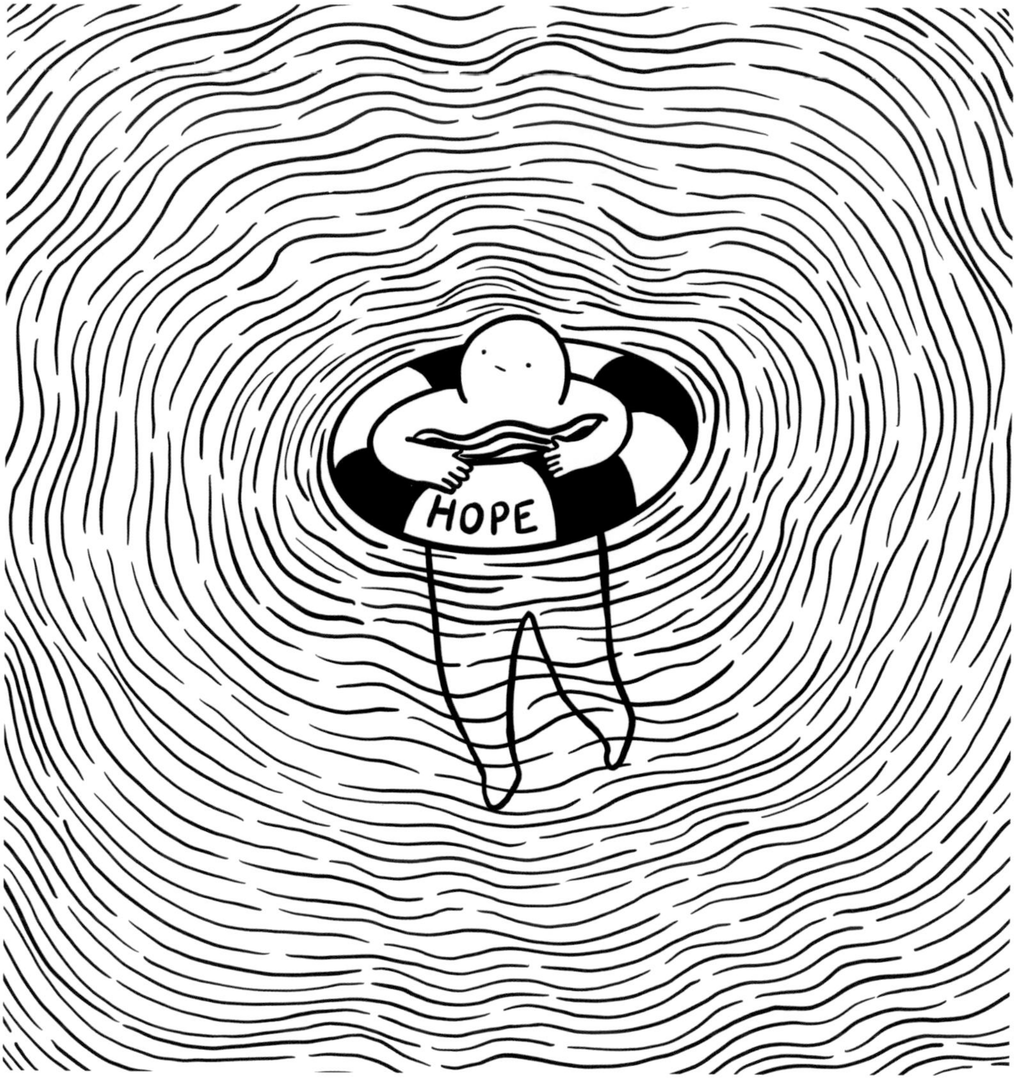
HOPE

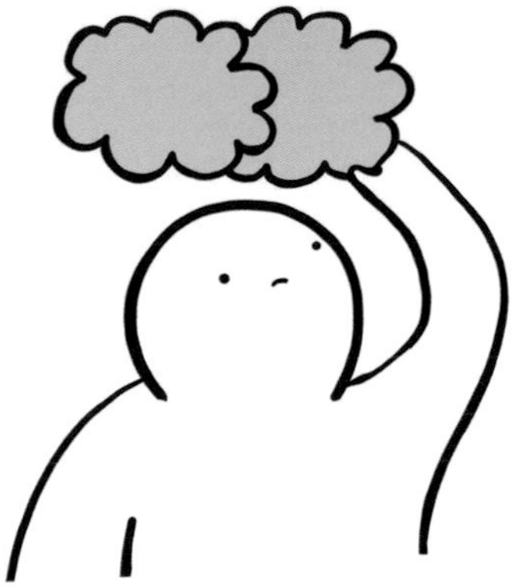

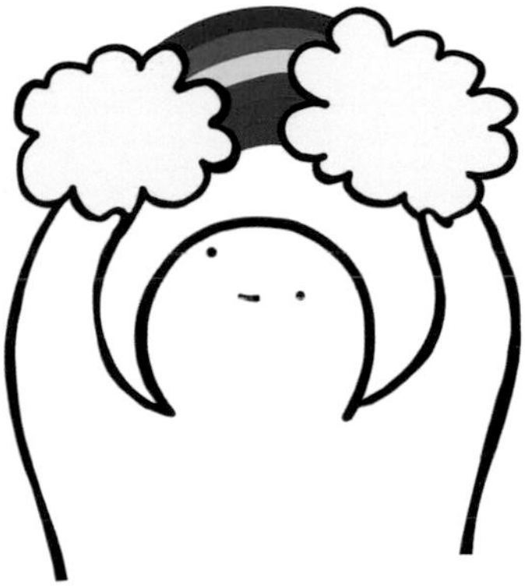

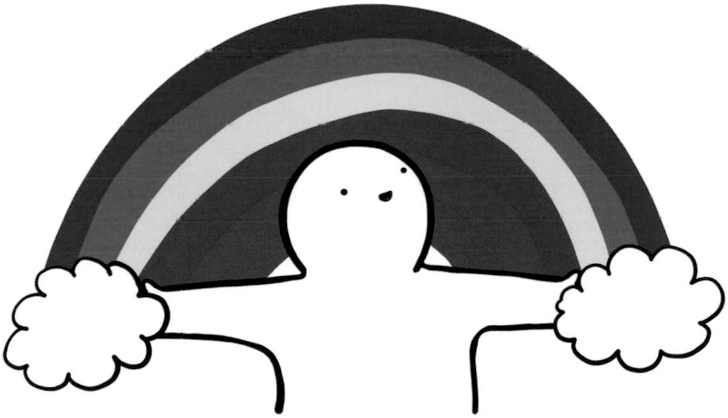

ACKNOWLEDGMENTS

THANK YOU FOR READING THIS BOOK. FOR WHAT IT'S WORTH, I DO ACTUALLY THINK YOU'RE DOING REALLY WELL, GIVEN THE CIRCUMSTANCES.

A MASSIVE THANKS TO MY INCREDIBLE SUPPORTERS ON PATREON, MY BRILLIANT FOLLOWERS ON INSTAGRAM, THE EXCELLENT LUCAS AND THE TEAM AT ANDREWS MCMEEL, AND THE WONDERFUL KATE AT PRESENT PERFECT FOR MAKING THIS BOOK POSSIBLE.

AND A HUGE SHOUT-OUT TO CHARLOTTE, DESIREE, MARIS PIPER, RUSSET BURBANK, AND THE REST OF THE FAM (YOU KNOW WHO YOU ARE) FOR SUPPORTING ME ON THIS JOURNEY.

WORRY LINES:
YOU'RE DOING REALLY WELL
GIVEN THE CIRCUMSTANCES

Andrews McMeel Publishing
a division of Andrews McMeel Universal
1130 Walnut Street, Kansas City, Missouri 64106

www.andrewsmcmeel.com

24 25 26 27 28 SDB 10 9 8 7 6 5 4 3 2 1

ISBN: 978-1-5248-9028-5

Library of Congress Control Number: 2023950087

@worry_ _ lines
www.worrylines.net

Editor: Lucas Wetzel
Art Director: Diane Marsh
Production Editor: Brianna Westervelt
Production Manager: Chadd Keim

ATTENTION: SCHOOLS AND BUSINESSES
Andrews McMeel books are available at quantity discounts with bulk purchase for educational, business, or sales promotional use. For information, please e-mail the Andrews McMeel Publishing Special Sales Department: sales@amuniversal.com.